Accounting Standards: true or false?

Are International Accounting Standards closing the 'expectation gap' between what accounts are believed to represent and what they actually do represent? Or widening it still further?

This book argues that 'fair value accounting' is a good label for stifling criticism; but it is highly misleading.

- It is more difficult to distinguish between actual transactions and hypothetical values.
- Stewardship reporting on the *safekeeping* of resources is compromised without any improvement in performance reporting on their *efficient use*.
- Gains are liable to be reported even though the business has deteriorated.
- The inbuilt bias towards 'short termism' prevents rational comparison either between firms or with alternative forms of investment.

Tracing a fundamental flaw in the conventional academic wisdom back to the nineteenth century, this book proposes an alternative conceptual framework. Effective corporate governance *is* achievable, not by expensive and counterproductive regulations like the US Sarbanes-Oxley Act, but by an enhanced accounting information system that exposes corporate management to the full rigour of market forces.

This thought-provoking piece of analysis challenges the current direction of accounting standards and proposes an alternative. Its novel perspective on financial reporting provides a framework for debating some of the key contemporary issues facing the accountancy profession. Readable and accessible to a wide audience, it will be of interest to all accountants – students, academics, and practitioners.

Dr. Anthony Rayman is a chartered accountant and former university lecturer. His articles have been published in the *Journal of Accounting Research* (USA), *Accounting and Business Research*, *Accountancy*, and the *Financial Times*. His book *Economics Through the Looking-Glass* has been described in *The Business Economist* as 'masterful and convincing . . . compulsory reading for all younger economists'.

Accounting Standards: true or false?

R.A. Rayman

Routledge
Taylor & Francis Group

LONDON AND NEW YORK

First published 2006
by Routledge
2 Park Square, Milton Park, Abingdon, Oxon OX14 4RN

Simultaneously published in the USA and Canada
by Routledge
270 Madison Ave, New York, NY 10016

Routledge is an imprint of the Taylor & Francis Group

© 2006 R.A. Rayman

Typeset in Perpetua and Bell Gothic by
Keystroke, Jacaranda Lodge, Wolverhampton
Printed and bound in Great Britain by
MPG Books Ltd, Bodmin, Cornwall

British Library Cataloguing in Publication Data
A catalogue record for this book is available from the British Library

Library of Congress Cataloging in Publication Data
A catalog record for this book has been requested

ISBN 0–415–37780–3 (hbk)
ISBN 0–415–37781–1 (pbk)

To Jackie and Bryan

Contents

CONTENTS

Foreword

Global financial reporting is currently undergoing its greatest change in 25 years. Close to 100 countries world-wide, including the entire European Union, now require the use of International Financial Reporting Standards by at least all listed companies. This means that the world is on the threshold of having only two major financial reporting regimes: US Generally Accepted Accounting Principles and International Financial Reporting Standards, a statement that would have been considered astonishing even a decade ago, yet today seems not only obvious, but normal.

At the same time, accounting standards – and the financial reports that result from their application – have changed significantly. The sheer complexity of many modern types of transaction makes them extremely difficult for even the most experienced company directors to understand. Complexity is also an aspect of the modern financial report presented to shareholders. In order to ensure that these reports contain all the required information they have become huge documents, to the extent that even experts have difficulty understanding them.

This imposes on standard-setters an even greater responsibility to develop accounting standards that translate into financial reports that are truly relevant to the needs of shareholders and are readily understandable by them. In short, business complexity should not be an excuse to sacrifice relevance, understandability and truth and fairness in financial reporting. However, the standard-setters seem to have chosen a path of imposing on companies additional and ever more complex reporting requirements that can be understood only by experts, and which lead ultimately to voluminous, highly technical corporate financial reports that are becoming less and less understandable by the ordinary shareholder. More importantly, though, this raises fundamental questions about the accounting system itself and whether it results in true and fair reporting that meets fully the information and stewardship needs of shareholders.

This is the challenge taken up by Anthony Rayman in this book. The author starts with the premise that conventional wisdom is that any shortcomings in modern financial reporting should be blamed, not on the system itself, but on its practical implementation. The theme of the book is that the opposite is true and that the principal difficulties in using accounting data are the result, not of deficiencies in the practical application of accounting concepts, but of fundamental deficiencies in the concepts themselves. In other words, the main obstacle to progress in financial reporting is the belief on the part of standard-setters and regulators that there is nothing wrong with the financial reporting system that cannot be cured simply by 'improving' the accounting standards by which it is implemented.

However, in challenging this conventional wisdom head on, the author faces the formidable task of dealing with vested intellectual interests. As he acknowledges, too much research has been devoted to the development of accounting standards; and too many reputations have been too deeply committed. Nevertheless, he unpicks modern financial reporting theory and practice in a systematic and masterly way. He examines the writings of many of the prominent economists and accounting academics, from Adam Smith, Fisher and Keynes to Hicks, Kay and Mayer; from Canning, Edwards & Bell and Chambers to Solomons, Tweedie and Whittington. He exposes what he describes as the fatal flaw in the notion of economic income and discusses the theoretical blind alley of modern conceptual frameworks for financial reporting. He debates what he terms the present value fallacy and describes the shortcomings of modern investment theory.

However, what is particularly commendable about this book is that it not only provides criticism, it offers solutions as well. The author's search for truth in accounting ends with a discussion of what he terms 'the vital distinction between funds and value' and the articulation of his system that involves the segregation of funds and value. This system is well illustrated in numerous tables throughout the book, and in detail in an appendix.

This is a book for all thinking accountants – be they academics, students, practitioners, finance directors, investors, standard-setters or regulators – and I commend it to all. It is unlikely that anyone will agree with everything in the book, but that's what makes it so appealing: it pushes the boundaries of conventional accounting wisdom so hard that it demands a response from those who share Dr Rayman's desire to find truth in accounting.

Dr Allister Wilson*

August 2005

* Allister Wilson is the Senior Technical Partner and Head of International Financial Reporting in the UK firm of Ernst & Young LLP. However, the views expressed here are his own.

Introduction

Of all the schemes for parting investors from their capital, few have attracted more criticism – or amusement – than an enterprise promoted at about the time of the South Sea Bubble *'for carrying on an undertaking of great advantage, but nobody to know what it is'*.

It is number 17 on the list of 'Bubble-Companies' declared illegal by order of the Lords Justices assembled in Privy Council on 12 July 1720. Number 36 is 'for a wheel for perpetual motion'; number 76 is 'for extracting silver from lead' (Mackay, 1841: 60–63).

The childlike gullibility of investors in those far-off days seldom fails to raise a complacent smile – particularly from those whose savings and pensions are invested in the equity share capital of public companies *'for earning a rate of return of great advantage, but nobody to know what it is'*.

That may sound far-fetched. After all, in today's more enlightened times, investors now have protection. Public companies have to file accounts; and it is a requirement of English law that they shall present a 'true and fair view'.

> The balance sheet shall give a true and fair view of the state of affairs of the company as at the end of the financial year; and the profit and loss account shall give a true and fair view of the profit or loss of the company for the financial year.
>
> (Companies Act 1985: section 228(2))

Similar legal requirements exist in other countries. In the United States, for example, the Sarbanes-Oxley Act 2002 requires a company's principal officers to sign a declaration that 'the financial statements, and other financial information included in the report, fairly present in all material respects the financial condition and results of operations' (section 302).

To guarantee the highest possible standards of financial reporting, accounting standards bodies have been established in many parts of the world. The most influential are the Accounting Standards Board in the UK (ASB), the Financial Accounting Standards Board in the USA (FASB), and, in response to pressure for the harmonization of global standards, the International Accounting Standards Board (IASB). From 1 January 2005, companies whose securities are traded on a regulated market of any Member State of the

European Union are required to prepare accounts in conformity with International Financial Reporting Standards (*IFRSs*).*

The intention behind the standard-setting process is admirable; and it is expressed by the major bodies in terms that are almost identical.

> Financial reporting is not an end in itself but is intended to provide information that is useful in making business and economic decisions – for making reasoned choices among alternative uses of scarce resources in the conduct of business and economic activities.
>
> (FASB, 1978: 5)

> The object of financial statements is to provide information about the reporting entity's financial performance and financial position that is useful to a wide range of users for assessing the stewardship of the entity's management and for making economic decisions.
>
> (ASB, 2005: 24)

> The objective of financial statements is to provide information about the financial position, performance and changes in financial position of an entity that is useful to a wide range of users in making economic decisions.
>
> (IASB, 2005: 36)

The term 'financial reporting' refers to '*general purpose external financial reporting by business enterprises*' (FASB, 1978: 14) as opposed to internal management accounting.

A 'true and fair view' (or 'fair presentation') is at the very top of the list of priorities. 'The concept of a true and fair view lies at the heart of financial reporting. . . . It is the ultimate test for financial statements and, as such, has a powerful, direct effect on accounting practice' (ASB, 2005: 20; cf. IASB, 2005: 42).

One of the stated objectives is 'to provide information about the reporting entity's financial performance' which includes 'the return it obtains on the resources it controls' (ASB, 2005: 24 and 27). 'A successful investor or creditor receives not only a return *of* investment but also a return *on* that investment' (FASB, 1978: 18). In the words of one of the most distinguished writers in the history of accounting: 'the rate of return' is '*the most important matter that the accountant has to deal with in a year's reports*' (Canning, 1929: 259).

Although there are various other measures of activity and profitability, they are normally used to build up a picture of an entity's overall performance: 'the return it obtains on the resources it controls'. Because of its role as a means of comparison between different firms and between alternative forms of investment, 'the rate of return' on investment plays a vital role in the efficient functioning of a free-market economy.

---

* The Accounting Standards Board (ASB) and the Auditing Practices Board (APB) are operating bodies of the Financial Reporting Council (FRC) which is the UK's independent regulator for corporate reporting and governance.

COMPETITION AND THE 'INVISIBLE HAND'

Adam Smith is much maligned, particularly by those who have never read a word of his writings. His abhorrence of selfishness is perfectly clear.

> To feel much for others, and little for ourselves, . . . to restrain our selfish, and to indulge our benevolent, affections, constitutes the perfection of human nature; and can alone produce among mankind that harmony of sentiments and passions in which consists their whole grace and propriety.
>
> (1759: 27)

Unfortunately, not everyone lives up to these ideals. Smith's well-known recipe for 'accelerating the progress of the society towards real wealth and greatness', *in spite of* individual greed and self-interest, is the 'invisible hand' of free competition.

> It is only for the sake of profit that any man employs a capital in the support of industry. . . . He intends only his own gain, and he is in this, as in many other cases, led by an invisible hand to promote an end which was no part of his intention. . . . By pursuing his own interest he frequently promotes that of the society more effectually than when he really intends to promote it.
>
> (1776: vol. 1, 421)

As long as competition is genuine, the only way for a firm to attract customers is by offering them a 'better deal' than its competitors in terms of price and quality; and the only way to attract employees is by offering them a 'better deal' in terms of remuneration and career prospects. It is the existence of competing firms that provides customers and employees with an alternative and protects them from exploitation.

Competition alone is not enough. The other essential is relevant information. Buyers and sellers cannot take advantage of market opportunities, unless they are aware of them. Above all, they cannot make rational choices, unless they know exactly what it is that they are buying and selling. They do not normally buy and sell packages without knowing their contents. It would be highly unusual to find an item advertised for sale as '*a product of great advantage, but nobody to know what it is*'.

But there is a weak link in the free-market system; and it is identified by Adam Smith himself.

> The directors of [public limited] companies, . . . being the managers rather of other people's money than of their own, it cannot well be expected, that they should watch over it with the same anxious vigilance with which the partners in a private copartnery frequently watch over their own. . . . Negligence and profusion, therefore, must always prevail, more or less, in the management of the affairs of such a company.
>
> (1776, vol. 2, 233)

3

The 'invisible hand' cannot operate, unless the 'managers of other people's money' are forced to attract investors by offering them a better rate of return than they can get elsewhere. But that type of competition cannot be effective unless relevant information is available about the returns 'wrapped up' in the various alternative investment 'packages'.

When it comes to a 'true and fair view', therefore, Canning is not exaggerating: 'the rate of return' is, indeed, *the most important matter that the accountant has to deal with in a year's reports*.

THE 'KALDOR CRITERION'

In a free-market economy, the accounting system has to be judged by free-market principles.

> The main purpose of accounting is to exhibit, for the proprietors of the business, the actual results in terms as nearly comparable as can be to the expected results; in terms, in other words, which make it possible for the proprietors to judge whether the business is a 'success' and fulfils those expectations in the light of which they invested their capital, and which they alone are ultimately capable of deciding.
>
> (Kaldor, 1955: 67, 68)

Suppose that, during a firm's life, its managers plan to earn 20 per cent per annum on the investors' capital. Everything goes exactly according to plan: 20 per cent per annum is actually earned and delivered to investors. What should the accounts report as a 'true and fair view' of the return on capital?

According to the 'Kaldor criterion', the answer is perfectly straightforward.

> If 20 per cent per annum is the rate of return that is planned, and
> if 20 per cent per annum is the rate of return that is actually delivered,
> then 20 per cent per annum is the rate of return that should be reported.

Otherwise 'a gross misstatement is made about *the most important matter that the accountant has to deal with in a year's reports*' (Canning, 1929: 259).

In these circumstances, the reporting of anything other than 20 per cent per annum raises serious questions of ethics.

If the standard setters sincerely believe that 'the concept of a true and fair view . . . is the ultimate test for financial statements' (ASB, 2005: 20), then the first priority must be to make sure that the 'Kaldor criterion' is fulfilled.

4

ECONOMY WITH THE TRUTH?

It often happens, however, that the rate of return derived from the accounts turns out to be significantly different from the rate of return actually earned. This is reflected in accounting terminology. The return based on figures published as 'true and fair' in the accounts is described as the 'accounting return' in order to distinguish it from the return actually earned which is described as the 'true yield' (Solomon, 1971: 165) or the 'true rate of return' (Kay, 1976: 459).

Possible causes of the discrepancy between what is actually earned and what is reported in the accounts are:

1 technical accounting problems (like the depreciation of fixed assets, the valuation of stocks and work-in-progress, and the treatment of expenditure on research and development);
2 practical difficulties (like risk, uncertainty, and changing prices); and
3 human failings (like dishonesty, negligence, or simple error).

Accounting standards are therefore designed to take care of these problems. But to leave the impression that their solution will be sufficient to 'provide information about the reporting entity's financial performance' that is useful 'for making economic decisions' which includes 'the return it obtains on the resources it controls' (ASB, 2005: 24 and 27) comes dangerously close to economy with the truth.

Accounting standards bodies are well aware that the accounting return is influenced by the volume of activity. In periods of above-average activity, the 'accounting return' can be significantly higher than the 'true return'; in periods of below-average activity, it can be significantly lower. Even if all the other problems are solved, a firm's accounts will present a 'true and fair view' of 'the return it obtains on the resources it controls' only on the assumption that each accounting period is a replica of every other. The trouble with this 'hidden' assumption is that, in normal circumstances, it is *known* to be false.

As a general rule, therefore, accounts do *not* obey the 'Kaldor criterion'. Even if there are no assets other than cash, even if everything goes according to plan, even if there are no price changes of any kind, and even if the accounts are prepared with utmost competence and unimpeachable integrity, they are still liable to be seriously misleading. This is something that the accounting standards bodies neglect to mention.

Over the years, several high-profile cases have underlined the necessity for standards to curb the dishonesty, negligence, or plain incompetence of *individuals*. They should not be used as a cover-up to distract attention from the real culprit – the *system* itself.

5

THE NATURE OF THE ACCOUNTING SYSTEM

The conventional system of accounting has survived for over five hundred years, because it is a perfect instrument for the essential task of recording transactions and keeping track of resources. The monetary figures used to represent resources are traditionally based on their 'historical cost' of acquisition. These historical figures provide 'backward-looking symbols of volume' which are ideal for *stewardship* reporting on the 'safekeeping' of resources, but less than ideal for *performance* reporting on their 'efficient use'.

A great deal of research has therefore been devoted to replacing the 'backward-looking symbols of volume' with 'forward-looking measures of value'. Over the past thirty-odd years, in the quest for 'relevance', various alternatives have been the subject of exposure drafts, (provisional) standards, and statements of principle. They include current purchasing power equivalent, current replacement cost, and deprival value (also known as 'value to the owner' or 'value to the business'). 'Fair value', which is the subject of current controversy, is simply the latest in a fairly long line.

The accuracy or relevance of the method of valuation is, however, beside the point. The use of 'value change' as a measure of economic performance is based on a fallacy exposed over a century ago. The fallacy probably owes its survival to a misunderstanding of the work of Hicks (1939). Correction of the error points towards an alternative conceptual framework based on the work of Fisher (1906).

The consequences likely to emerge, when standard setters insist on forcing the conventional accounting system into a role for which it is not suited, have been apparent for many years.

> It is difficult to extract sunbeams (measures of return on capital) from cucumbers (conventional stewardship accounts), however cleverly you slice them. . . . The danger is that [they] will ruin the cucumbers and still leave us all in the dark.
>
> (*Accountancy Age*, 11 June 1976)

That is precisely what seems to have happened where professional standards have fallen below the level expected in Britain. Recent financial scandals involving Enron, WorldCom, and Parmalat cannot, however, be regarded solely as an issue of audit failure; they may be evidence of systemic failure involving management fraud, corporate governance failure, and regulatory failure. Nevertheless, they are a warning of the danger of neglecting the vital forensic skills necessary for effective auditing (often misguidedly dismissed as 'bean counting') without any improvement in the quality of performance reporting.

'Fair value accounting' is a label that may make matters worse. Even if every item in the accounts is stated at its fair value – defined as the amount for which it 'could be exchanged . . . between knowledgeable, willing parties in an arm's length transaction' (IASB, 2005: 1672) – the validity of the accounting return remains dependent on the assumption of an unchanging volume of activity, an assumption that is normally false.

6

THE ECONOMIC CONSEQUENCES

Reliable information on the return on capital invested in different areas of economic activity is crucial to the efficient allocation of the economy's capital resources.

So long as the information in published accounts is liable to be misleading, investors and others are liable to be misled. They have no rational basis for informed comparisons either between different firms or with other forms of investment.

> A company may be on course for a planned return on capital of 15 per cent per annum; but, if the bulk of its activity is concentrated in the early years, its first-year accounts may report a return of, say, 20 per cent. Another company (whose directors resist the temptation of going for quick returns) may be on course for a planned return of 25 per cent per annum; but its first-year accounts may report a return of only 10 per cent. It makes no sense to judge a marathon on the results of the first 50 yards.
>
> (*Financial Times*, 12 December 2002)

The public perception of business success or failure is largely determined by what appears in the accounts; and this produces an inevitable incentive to 'short-termism'. A company director whose career depends on what appears in the annual report may become more preoccupied with the company's next set of accounts than with its long-term economic health. It is difficult to imagine a more serious example of conflict of interest.

The dangers are obvious. Resources are not diverted away from inefficient firms towards more efficient firms, and activities that would contribute more to the whole economy are neglected in favour of those that contribute less. If business corporations fail to make the best use of their resources, it is not just the shareholders who are affected; the whole economy is worse off.

There is also a macro-economic dimension. The tendency to overstate the reported return on capital during periods of above-average activity and to understate it during periods of below-average activity generates undue optimism when the economy is overheating and undue pessimism when it is stagnating. By reinforcing cyclical fluctuations in this way, conventional accounts can have a destabilizing effect on the economy as a whole.

Effective management is vital for economic prosperity. But, apart from spectacular success or spectacular failure, it is often difficult to distinguish between good management and bad. 'The main damage from the present system does not stem from the few companies . . . where things go spectacularly wrong. The real worry concerns the many companies where, unspectacularly, things merely go less than right' (*The Economist*, 29 August 1970: 9). In spite of three decades of development in accounting standards, it remains true today.

7

BACK TO BASICS

Canning's criticism of accounting development may be three-quarters of a century old, but it still applies.

> The work of the accountant and the writings on accounting, until very recently, proceeded by a sort of patchwork and tinkering. To be sure, the patching was often shrewdly planned and executed, but it was patchwork nevertheless in the sense that there was little going back to fundamentals for a fresh start.
>
> (1929: 9)

'Patchwork and tinkering' is a fair description of the work of the standard-setting bodies over the past thirty years as they have grappled with a system of accounting which has become unsuitable for the purpose of performance reporting. The object of this book is to follow Canning's advice by 'going back to fundamentals for a fresh start'.

When a product is bought and sold in the market, information is required, not on what the package is worth – that is for the buyers and sellers to decide for themselves – but simply on what the package contains. (Trading standards authorities regulate the description of the contents, not their value.) If the product in question is some form of financial investment, 'what the package contains' is the return on capital that managers obtain on behalf of investors. Perhaps the accounting standards authorities should act like their trading standards counterparts?

In the majority of cases (including bank and building society deposits, national savings, government securities, local authority and industrial loans, etc.) there *is* a description of what the investment package contains: information on the return on capital is provided as a matter of routine. All these investments have different lengths of life and are subject to different degrees of risk. The advertised rate of return does not tell investors what the investment is worth. It is, however, a piece of information which is necessary to enable them to work out the value for themselves. Rational decisions, whether to buy, hold, or sell, can then be made by individuals in accordance with their subjective valuations and in the light of any alternative opportunities available to them.

The object of this book is to develop a system of accounting that, in spite of the uncertainty and complexity of the real world, is able to make the 'managers of other people's money' publicly accountable for the rate of return they are planning to achieve.

Times have changed since the speculative 'bubbles' of the 1720s. Many more people have their savings and pensions invested, either directly or indirectly, in the equity capital of public companies. It is no longer acceptable that the accounts of these companies should disclose little more than that they are enterprises *'for earning a return of great advantage, but nobody to know what it is'*.

PLAN OF THE BOOK

In any type of economy, from free-enterprise capitalism to state-controlled socialism, 'truth in accounting' is essential for the efficient use of its capital resources. The argument put forward in this book is that the conventional system of accounting has a major flaw that has to be corrected. Instead of being based on undisclosed assumptions known to be false, accounting information needs to be based on disclosed assumptions believed to be true.

A method of reforming the accounting system to accommodate this change is outlined in Part V. The segregation of records of fact from estimates of value enables stewardship reporting on the *safekeeping* of resources to be independent of performance reporting on their *efficient* use. The division of responsibility between the auditor and management can then be redefined in a way that offers a real prospect of achieving the object of public accountability. The publication and continuous monitoring of the planned investment rate is designed to bring business management within the control of market forces and to bring comparability to business investment.

Before embarking on the question of accounting reform, however, it is necessary to explore the reasons why the present system, instead of revealing the truth about business performance, is liable to cover it up. There is, of course, no deliberate intention to deceive. The fundamental problem is that good intentions are thwarted by mistaken theory. Part II exposes basic flaws in the concept of income and in the theory of value. Part III describes the theoretical blind alley in which accounting standards bodies are now trapped as an inevitable result.

The main obstacle to progress in accounting reform is the reluctance to admit that there is anything wrong with the system. 'The principal difficulties in using accounting data are the result, not of fundamental deficiencies in accounting concepts, but in the practical application of these concepts' (Kay and Mayer, 1986: 206). Part IV goes 'back to basics' in order to remove this obstacle by showing that the fault lies, not in the practical implementation of the system, but in the system itself.

In order to keep cross-references to a minimum and to dispense with footnotes entirely, tables and quotations are repeated throughout the text whenever they are required. The object is to make each chapter as self-contained as possible - without the distraction of constant reference backwards and forwards. Apologies are therefore offered to those readers who may be irritated by the repetition. Technical issues, related but not essential to the argument, are dealt with in the Appendices. Extracts from UK standards and statements extant at 30 April 2005 are taken from the collections published by the Accounting Standards Board (2005) and the Auditing Practices Board (2005). Similarly, extracts from international standards and statements extant at 1 January 2005 are taken from the collection published by the International Accounting Standards Board (2005). Although individual standards and statements are not always specified in the text, they are identified in the Index.

The first step in the argument is to identify the flaws in the present system. How is it that sincere devotion to the cause of a 'true and fair view' of business performance can, in spite of the best intentions, lead to the publication of financial statements that can be seriously misleading – not only where the accounting rules are bent, but also where they are strictly observed?

Like many questions in accounting, the answer begins with the procedure for 'counting beans'.

Part I

The noble art of counting beans

Chapter 1

Stewardship reporting: the physical dimension

RECORD KEEPING

To some extent accounting is a prisoner of its historical development. It probably developed from the need, even in the Ancient world, for records (a) of asset holdings and (b) of relations with other parties. It was not until the growth of commerce in the Middle Ages, however, that the system of double-entry bookkeeping evolved. (Pacioli's famous treatise on the system employed in Venice was published in 1494.) Both objectives were realized simultaneously by the 'dual classification' of resources, (a) according to the nature of the resources, and (b) according to the 'equity' in those resources.

Table 1.1 illustrates the application of the double-entry principle to the contents of a garden shed. The left-hand side satisfies the first requirement by classifying the contents of the garden shed 'according to the nature of the resources'. The right-hand side satisfies the second requirement by classifying the contents of the garden shed 'according to the equity in those resources'. This dual classification of resources gives a 'true and fair' view: it shows clearly (a) what is in the shed, and (b) to whom it belongs.

Although it is a comprehensive list of the contents of the garden shed, it is no more than that. This type of record keeping is sometimes dismissed as mere 'bean counting'. It provides no information whatever on the physical condition of the items; nor does it give any indication of their economic value. Nevertheless, it is essential in the operation of most businesses.

It is rather like the cataloguing system used in a library, where books are normally classified (a) by subject and (b) by borrower. Without a catalogue, it would be impossible to 'keep track of the stock'. In order to run a business, it is also necessary to 'keep track

Table 1.1 *List of items in the garden shed at 31 March*

(a) Nature of item	(b) Owner of item
Lawn mower	Self
Hedge-trimmer	Next-door neighbour
Spade	Self
Wheelbarrow	Brother-in-law

of the stock'. The cataloguing system is the 'double-entry' method used for the items in the garden shed. If the Garden Shed is a limited company, the list is same, but some of the labels are different.

The items 'in the business' are called 'assets' (from which future benefits are expected). The 'equities' (or claims on the assets) are subdivided into two main categories: equities belonging to the company's owners (the shareholders) are called 'capital'; and equities belonging to outsiders (the creditors) are called 'liabilities'. These categories are shown in Table 1.2.

To convert the list into a balance sheet, all the assets and all the equities need to be stated in terms of some 'unit of account'. Accounting in terms of physical units (Goldberg, 1965: 42) achieves perfect accuracy in Table 1.3.

Where there are numerous assets of many different types, however, complex physical expressions are not very practical for published accounts. A common denominator is required; and the universal choice for the role of unit of account is money.

This raises what is perhaps the oldest and most difficult accounting problem of all. How are the physical units to be converted into money? The most convenient method is to use the objectively verifiable evidence of an actual transaction. The original ('historical') cost, for which there is usually the documentary evidence of a purchase invoice, is the traditional choice.

Suppose that the original purchase cost of each of the items is known: £120 for the lawn mower, £10 for the spade, £40 for the hedge-trimmer, and £20 for the wheelbarrow. The use of money as the unit of account is illustrated in Table 1.4.

Table 1.2   List of items in the Garden Shed Company Ltd at 31 March

(a) Assets	(b) Equities
Lawn mower } .... {	Capital of shareholders
Spade }	(self)
Hedge-trimmer } .... {	Liabilities to creditors
Wheelbarrow }	(neighbour and brother-in-law)

Table 1.3   ('Physical') balance sheet of the Garden Shed Company Ltd at 31 March

Assets	unit of account	Equities	unit of account
Lawn mower	1 L	Capital:	
Spade	1 S	shareholders	1 L + 1 S
Hedge-trimmer	1 H	Liabilities:	
Wheelbarrow	1 W	creditors	1 H + 1 W
	1L+1S+1H+1W		1L+1S+1H+1W

Table 1.4 ('Monetary') balance sheet of the Garden Shed Company Ltd at 31 March

Assets	£	Equities	£
Lawn mower	120	Capital:	
Spade	10	shareholders	130
Hedge-trimmer	40	Liabilities:	
Wheelbarrow	20	creditors	60
	190		190

Compared with the 'physical' balance sheet, the 'monetary' balance sheet shows a clear gain in mathematical elegance; and it does so without any loss of information. It still gives a complete picture of the items in the shed and to whom they belong. It indicates that, in the Garden Shed (Company), there are garden tools (assets) with a total cost of £190. Of that total, tools costing £130 belong to the owner, and tools costing £60 belong to other parties (the next-door neighbour and the brother-in-law). No information appears to have been lost, but some has been gained: the balance sheet now includes details of cost.

A double-entry system based on historical cost is ideal for the purpose of 'keeping track of a firm's assets' – for 'counting the beans'. It is therefore ideal for the purpose of 'stewardship reporting' in the narrow sense to be discussed in the next few paragraphs.

THE DISTINCTION BETWEEN 'STEWARDSHIP' AND 'PERFORMANCE'

In its *Statement of Principles for Financial Reporting*, the UK Accounting Standards Board makes clear that it 'regards stewardship as being not merely about the safekeeping and proper use of an entity's resources but also about their efficient and profitable use' (2005: 89). This echoes the view of the US Financial Accounting Standards Board on the 'stewardship responsibility [of management] for the use of enterprise resources entrusted to it'.

> Management of an enterprise is periodically accountable to the owners not only for the custody and safekeeping of enterprise resources but also for their efficient and profitable use. . . . Management, owners, and others emphasize enterprise performance or profitability in describing how management has discharged its stewardship accountability.
>
> (1978: 25)

In this book, by contrast, the opposite line is taken. 'Stewardship reporting' on 'the custody and safekeeping of enterprise resources' is clearly distinguished from 'performance reporting' on 'their efficient and profitable use'.

15

On the meaning of 'performance', however, this book takes the same view as the standard-setting bodies. 'The financial performance of an entity comprises the return it obtains on the resources it controls, the components of that return and the characteristics of those components' (ASB, 2005: 27; cf. FASB, 1978: 19).

It is difficult to compare the performance of firms of different sizes with each other or with alternative forms of investment in any other way. This supports the view that 'the rate of return' is *the most important matter that the accountant has to deal with in a year's reports*' (Canning, 1929: 259).

Throughout this book, therefore, a clear distinction is maintained between *stewardship reporting* on the 'safekeeping' of resources and *performance reporting* on their 'efficient use'. The argument developed in Parts I to IV is that information designed for one purpose is frequently inappropriate for the other. The result is a 'hybrid' system of accounting in which records of fact are mixed up with estimates of value. The solution proposed in Part V is a 'segregated' system of accounting in which 'stewardship reporting' is kept strictly separate from 'performance reporting'.

'STEWARDSHIP REPORTING' ON THE 'SAFEKEEPING' OF RESOURCES

Suppose that a syndicate is formed for the purpose of buying £1 lottery tickets. Managers are appointed to collect the money, to buy the tickets, and to choose the numbers. There are 100 members in the syndicate, and each one contributes £10. The syndicate managers are therefore in charge of £1,000 of other people's money.

How can members of the syndicate be sure that (1) the whole of the £1,000 is actually spent on lottery tickets, and (2) the whole of any prize money is paid in to the syndicate? One answer is the installation of a system of 'internal control' for the detection of fraud or error together with the appointment of an independent auditor to report on the system. An effective system normally requires division of responsibility – with a clear separation between those who handle the assets and those who keep the records.

No audit procedure can prevent mistakes or misappropriation, but, by making it as difficult as possible to escape detection, it can operate as a powerful deterrent.

Without any audit procedures, there is no way of telling whether syndicate managers are (1) using all the contributions to buy tickets and (2) paying in the whole of any prize money. An effective system of 'internal control' would probably include procedures to be carried out by people who are independent of the managers:

1 compilation of a record (before the draw) of the 1,000 sets of numbers;
2 inspection without notice to verify the holding of cash or tickets totalling £1,000;
3 calculation (after the draw) of prize money (by checking the record of numbers against a published list of winning numbers).

Table 1.5 *Balance sheet of the syndicate on the day before the draw*

Assets	£	Equities	£
Lottery tickets	1,000	Capital:	
		members	1,000
	1,000		1,000

Table 1.6 *Balance sheet of the syndicate on the day after the draw*

Assets	£	Equities	£
Cash	150	Capital:	
		members	1,000
		less: Loss	(850)
	150		150

It is normal practice for the auditor to test the system and to verify the accounts. The balance sheet, on the day before the draw, is shown in Table 1.5.

If the auditors are satisfied with the operation of the system of internal control, they are entitled to report that the balance sheet fulfils the requirements of section 228(2) of the Companies Act 1985 by giving 'a true and fair view of the state of affairs' of the syndicate. The balance sheet simply indicates the possession of 1,000 lottery tickets costing £1 each. It is no business of the auditors to comment on the system of picking numbers, nor is a 'clean' (unqualified) audit report a comment either way on the likelihood of the tickets being winners or losers.

Suppose that the syndicate is not very successful: tickets which cost £1,000 win only £150 in prize money. The balance sheet in Table 1.6, on the day after the 'prize draw', is very different from the balance sheet on the day before.

It is quite possible that members of the syndicate would be critical of the performance of the managers and would question their ability to pick numbers. It is less likely that they would blame the auditors. Both balance sheets are perfectly accurate. The 'truth and fairness' of the view is not open to question.

But, suppose the syndicate is a business firm?

THE GAME OF BUSINESS AND THE MYTH OF THE ENTREPRENEUR

Business, too, is a lottery. It is certainly a game of skill, but it is also a game of chance. All business assets are, to an extent, lottery tickets. Some are winners; some are losers.

The risks and the rewards vary enormously. Sometimes they are negligible; sometimes they are overwhelming. Some managers have the skill or good fortune to pick winners; others are less skilful or not quite so lucky.

Ever since the Industrial Revolution, the advance of technology has meant the concentration of capital and the growth of large business organizations. Instead of managing their own capital, it is common for investors to pool their resources by becoming shareholders in corporations run by professional managers. The inevitable result is the divorce of ownership from control as shareholders in limited companies hand over valuable economic resources to be managed on their behalf by professional directors. A vast amount of business and commerce in the developed world is conducted by public limited liability companies.

In the game of business, many company directors are not entrepreneurs whose own money is at stake; they are professional players who are paid a salary (plus other benefits) to gamble with other people's chips. Sometimes they win; sometimes they lose. Occasionally, the losses are spectacular. A company's balance sheet published at the end of its financial year may show a list of assets — lottery tickets in the game of business — costing hundreds of millions of pounds. That list may have been accurately verified by a firm of auditors as a 'true and fair view' of the company's financial position. Nevertheless, it is entirely possible that within a short time the company can collapse as it becomes clear that the assets have turned out to be almost worthless.

Shareholders who discover that their savings have been lost are entitled to feel aggrieved. Their complaints are likely to be taken up by press, radio, and television.

And the target of their criticism?

Those who were hired for their reputation for picking winners and who only managed to pick losers? Not always! The real weight of media criticism often falls on the company's auditors in particular and on the accountancy profession in general.

That is rather odd.

The members of a lottery syndicate would put the blame on those whose job it is to pick the numbers. Why is it that the shareholders in a 'business syndicate' reserve their fury for those whose job it is to inspect the books?

The answer lies in the way that business accounting has developed.

Chapter 2

Business accounting

As the trend towards the divorce of ownership from control gathered pace following the Industrial Revolution, a legal obligation was imposed upon those entrusted with the management of valuable resources to render an account of their stewardship to the owners of those resources. The primary object was the detection and prevention of fraud and error. Financial accounting therefore developed as a branch of applied law rather than as a branch of applied economics.

Recognition that no industrialized economy, whether capitalist or socialist, can manage without a financial 'cataloguing system' (for 'counting the beans') transcends all political boundaries.

> One can scarcely conceive of *capitalism* without double-entry book-keeping.
>   (Sombart, 1902: 9, emphasis supplied)

> Book-keeping and control – these are the chief things necessary for the smooth and correct functioning of the first phase of *communist* society.
>   (Lenin, 1917: 237, emphasis supplied)

The traditional audit function involves tracing the flow of resources from acquisition to disposal. For 'stewardship reporting' (in the narrow sense indicated in the previous chapter) on the honest use of resources, financial accounts are therefore ideal.

Suppose a company is set up with £10,000 cash as its initial capital. The whole of the £10,000 cash is used to purchase four widgets. Like that of the garden shed in the previous chapter, the company's balance sheet in Table 2.1 can be drawn up in physical terms. '4

Table 2.1 *Balance sheet of the company*

Assets		Equities	
Widgets	4 W	Shareholders' capital	£10,000
	4 W		£10,000

Table 2.2 *Balance sheet of the company*

Assets	£	Equities	£
Widgets	10,000	Shareholders' capital	10,000
	10,000		10,000

Widgets' is an accurate description of the assets held by the company. It is a view which is perfectly 'true and fair'. Where there is a varied assortment of different types of asset, however, a physical description is both clumsy and impractical.

Complex physical expressions are avoided in Table 2.2 by the use of a monetary symbol as a common denominator.

What the second balance sheet gains over the first in mathematical elegance, however, it loses in economic relevance. '£10,000' is merely a symbol which indicates the existence of four widgets. The relationship does not apply in reverse. '4 Widgets' does not indicate the existence of £10,000 either in cash or in value. Conventional accounting figures are therefore symbols, not of value, but of quantity. They are, in Hicksian terminology, 'backward-looking measures of volume' rather than 'forward-looking measures of value' (1973: 157).

But there is no harm in that: the system is ideal for 'counting beans'.

The traditional audit function of tracing the flow of resources from acquisition to disposal does not require an assessment of the *value* of a firm's assets; it requires no more than the verification of their *existence*. For this essential but limited purpose, measures of quantity are quite sufficient; there is no need for measures of value. 'Backward-looking measures of volume' are ideal.

The exact interpretation of the 'backward-looking measures of volume' – and thus the precise meaning of the conventional accounting figures – depends on the 'accounting code' for 'attaching' monetary symbols to assets.

THE 'ACCOUNTING CODE'

The conventional form of 'code' is based on the flow of funds (or purchase potential) between the firm and other parties as a result of exchange transactions. The term 'funds' is used to denote 'current non-specific claims' (see Appendix D) and therefore covers the flow of cash or credit. Inputs into the production process are recorded at cost price (the funds outflow) when they are purchased. Outputs are recorded at selling price (the funds inflow) when they are eventually sold. This provides a simple and convenient code, the key to which is the objectively verifiable evidence of the legal claims arising out of the process of exchange.

Suppose that the four widgets are each sold for £3,600 in cash. But it takes two years to sell them. In Table 2.3, a profit and loss account has been drawn up for the two-year

Table 2.3 *Profit and loss account for the two years*

	£
Sales revenue [4 widgets @ £3,600 each]	14,400
less: Cost of sales	(10,000)
Accounting profit	4,400

period in order to calculate the *change* in the shareholders' equity during the period. It shows an increase or accounting profit of £4,400.

At the end of the two-year period, the balance sheet in Table 2.4 shows that the only asset is a cash balance of £14,400. The increase of £4,400 over the capital contribution of £10,000 belongs to the shareholders.

All these figures are based on objectively verifiable exchange transactions or funds flows. £10,000 cash was paid out on the purchase of widgets; £14,400 cash was received on their sale. The cash increase is £4,400 over two years. If the company is liquidated and the cash proceeds are distributed to the shareholders, the return on capital is the equivalent of 20 per cent per annum over two years. (£10,000 deposited in a bank for two years would have had to earn interest of 20 per cent per annum during that time in order to have accumulated to £14,400.)

Provided that it is acceptable to wait until all the assets have been sold, the 'accounting code' presents few problems. But that might mean waiting until the end of a firm's life before preparing any accounts. The necessity for up-to-date information dictates the production of accounting reports at regular intervals. Section 227 of the Companies Act 1985 reflects traditional business practice by imposing upon the directors of limited companies a duty to prepare annual accounts for each financial year. The life of the company is therefore arbitrarily divided into 'accounting periods' of no more than a year.

This creates the necessity of devising an 'accounting code' for assets that are still in the process of conversion at the end of the accounting period. The purchase of inputs and the sale of output give rise to exchange transactions with the 'outside world'. As input goes through the 'internal' process of conversion into output, however, no 'external' transactions are directly involved. Accounting symbols for the assets 'in

Table 2.4 *Balance sheet of the company at the end of the second year*

Assets	£	Equities	£
Cash	14,400	Shareholders' capital	10,000
		Retained profit	4,400
	14,400		14,400

21

progress' have to be constructed without the aid of the market evidence of *current* transactions.

The conventional procedure is to apportion funds flows, which have occurred as a result of *previous* transactions, between 'capital' and 'revenue'. Flows deemed to relate to the current period are classified as 'revenue'; flows deemed to relate to subsequent periods are classified as 'capital'.

The transaction by which an asset is acquired, for example, is recorded by reference to the funds outflow on its acquisition – its historical cost. When the asset is used, the cost of the used portion is charged as an 'expense' in the profit and loss account (and classified as 'revenue'). The cost of any unused remainder is carried forward as an 'asset' in the balance sheet (and classified as 'capital').

As no external market evidence is available in respect of internal operations, the procedure for determining which costs should be regarded as 'used up' and which costs should be regarded as 'left over' is governed by a set of rules known as 'accounting principles'.

Because of the diversity of business situations, some discretion is allowed in making the distinction between 'capital' and 'revenue'. The price of this flexibility is a multiplicity of 'codes'. The cost of stock-in-trade, for example, may be calculated on the 'first in, first out' (fifo), 'last in, first out' (lifo), or 'average cost' basis. The cost of fixed assets may be 'depreciated' by a variety of methods over different estimated life spans. Overhead costs (including research and development expenditure) may be added to inventories or written off as expenses. This does not alter the nature of the 'accounting code'. It simply makes it more complicated.

Sometimes the code is very simple and involves the mere 'attachment' of historical cost when an asset is acquired. Suppose the first widget is purchased for £2,200, the second for £2,400, the third for £2,600, and the fourth for £2,800. If all four widgets are held at the balance sheet date, they may be shown in the balance sheet at a figure of £10,000. '£10,000' is an indication neither of their value in use nor of their value in exchange. It is an indication simply of their existence. All that is required to interpret the figures is a 'key' to the 'accounting code' – in this case, the use of invoice cost.

Sometimes the code is rather more complicated and involves the 'apportionment' of historical cost between 'capital' and 'revenue' when an asset is used.

Suppose that three of the four widgets are sold at the very end of the first year. Table 2.5 illustrates how the historical cost of £10,000 can be apportioned between capital and revenue by various different codes. The 'cost of sales' according to the 'first in, first out' code, for example, is calculated on the assumption that the three widgets sold are the first three purchased, and that the one widget in stock is the last one purchased.

The three different codes give rise to the three different versions of the year's accounts presented in Table 2.6.

Each of the three versions discloses an equally 'true and fair view' of the disposal of three widgets and the holding of one widget *to anyone who knows which code is being used*. None of the versions gives a reliable indication of the value of the widgets that have been

Table 2.5 *The application of different 'accounting codes'*

	Revenue (flow of resources) expense in profit & loss account 'Cost of sales'	Capital (stock of resources) asset in balance sheet 'Stock in trade'
'First in, first out' code	[£2,200 + £2,400 + £2,600 =] £7,200	£2,800
'Average cost' code	[£2,500 + £2,500 + £2,500 =] £7,500	£2,500
'Last in, first out' code	[£2,400 + £2,600 + £2,800 =] £7,800	£2,200

Table 2.6 *Balance sheets at the end of Year 1 (in terms of historical cost)*

	Fifo £	Average £	Lifo £
Assets			
Stock in trade	2,800	2,500	2,200
Cash	10,800	10,800	10,800
Total assets	13,600	13,300	13,000
Equities	£	£	£
Capital	10,000	10,000	10,000
Profit*			
Revenue from sales	10,800	10,800	10,800
less: Cost of sales	7,200	7,500	7,800
Profit	3,600	3,300	3,000
Total equities	13,600	13,300	13,000
Return on capital $\dfrac{\text{Profit}}{\text{Capital}}$	$\dfrac{3,600}{10,000} = 36\%$	$\dfrac{3,300}{10,000} = 33\%$	$\dfrac{3,000}{10,000} = 30\%$

* Note: Details of the flows of revenue and expense would normally be shown in a separate profit and loss account. Only the balance of retained profit would appear in the balance sheet.

sold or of the widget that is still held. The accounting figures are alternative descriptions of the physical flow and stock of resources.

Although there are considerable differences between the three versions, they all tell the same story. The reason for the differences is that they tell the story in different languages. Each version provides an equally accurate description of the sale of three widgets during the year and the holding of one widget plus £10,800 cash at the end of the year. The first version says so in 'fifo' code; the second version says so in 'average cost' code; and the third version says so in 'lifo' code.

23

Table 2.7 *Balance sheet at the end of Year 1 (in 'real' terms)*

Stock of resources	
Stock in trade	1W
Cash	£10,800
Total assets	£10,800 + 1W
Equities in resources	
Capital [£10,000 - £10,000 + 4W]	4W
Flow of resources:	
Revenue from sales	£10,800
less: Cost of sales	– 3W
Change in volume of resources	£10,800 – 3W
Total equities	£10,800 + 1W

In spite of the differences in the monetary figures, there is only one correct interpretation of the 'accounting code'. The meaning of the 'backward-looking measures of volume' cannot be accurately conveyed unless they are translated into 'real' terms – as in Table 2.7.

Whatever the choice of 'accounting code', this is 'bean counting' *par excellence*: it gives a perfectly accurate picture of the *number* of beans. No view could be 'truer or fairer'.

THE PHYSICAL DIMENSION – RESOURCE ACCOUNTING

Conventional accounts are therefore 'resource accounts' designed for the physical dimension of stewardship reporting (in the narrow sense indicated in the previous chapter). The profit and loss account describes the *flow* of resources involved in operations *during the accounting period*. The balance sheet describes the *stock* of resources and the equities in those resources *at the balance sheet date*.

The accounting profit, as reported in the conventional historical accounts, ranges from £3,000 to £3,600 and the balance sheet value ranges from £13,000 to £13,600, depending on which method of stock valuation (or 'code') is chosen.

The only difference between the various conventional alternatives is that the 'accounting codes' – the languages in which the physical description is expressed – are different. The description itself is the same.

The figure of accounting profit, like every other conventional accounting figure, is a 'backward-looking measure of volume' rather than a 'forward-looking measure of value'. In this case, the physical flow which it symbolizes (by the figures £3,000, £3,300, or £3,600) is the 'inflow' of £10,800 cash in return for an 'outflow' of three widgets.

It is not a question of whether accounting profit is a good measure of business performance or a bad measure of business performance. The point is that it is not a measure of performance at all.

The point is emphasized in one of the best remembered of the old *Recommendations on Accounting Principles*.

> It has long been accepted in accounting practice that a balance sheet . . . is an historical record and not a statement of current worth. Stated briefly its function is to show in monetary terms the capital, reserves and liabilities of a business at the date as at which it is prepared and the manner in which the total moneys representing them have been distributed over the several types of assets. Similarly a profit and loss account is an historical record.
>
> (ICAEW, 1952: para. 1).

These historical documents are, however, perfect instruments for resource accounting and reporting on stewardship. As long as they are familiar with the particular 'accounting code' in use, the auditors can report whether or not the balance sheet meets the requirement of the Companies Act 1985, section 228(2) by giving a 'true and fair view' of what assets the company owns, even though they may not have the slightest idea of what those assets are worth. Such knowledge is, however, unnecessary. For this purpose, an accurate count of the *number* of 'beans' is sufficient; their value is irrelevant.

Simply by verifying the existence of the assets at the balance sheet date and by testing a representative sample of the transactions undertaken during the accounting period, the auditors are able to satisfy themselves whether or not the assets have been properly used on the company's business. Whether or not they have been wisely used is an entirely different matter. It is, of course, a matter of particular concern to investors – and consequently to auditors. For that purpose, however, it is necessary to venture beyond the physical dimension of the conventional accounts into the dimension of value.

It is failure to appreciate that the conventional system of accounting is not an adequate vehicle for this journey that is responsible for many of the centuries-old problems that still beset the accountancy profession.

Chapter 3

Performance reporting: the value dimension

The transplantation of conventional accounting figures from the physical dimension of stewardship reporting into the value dimension of performance reporting imposes upon the conventional system of accounting a strain which it is not designed to bear. 'Backward-looking measures of volume' have to be misinterpreted as 'forward-looking measures of value'. The procedure for 'attaching' monetary figures to assets ceases to be merely the choice of a symbol of volume; it becomes an act of valuation. The choice of 'code', which for stewardship purposes is of no consequence, then assumes an importance which is critical.

In the illustration in the previous chapter, the choice of method of stock valuation is responsible for three different versions of the accounting return on capital ranging from 30 per cent to 36 per cent. Yet all three of them fail by the 'Kaldor criterion'. If the company is wound up at the end of Year 2 and the cash balance of £14,400 is distributed to the shareholders, the rate of return on the £10,000 invested is the equivalent of 20 per cent per annum over the two-year period. It is true that any overstatement in the accounts of Year 1 will be 'corrected' by a corresponding understatement in the accounts of Year 2. But one of the reasons why accounts are published annually is so that decisions can be made on the basis of up-to-date information. 'Corrections' in the accounts of Year 2 are of little use to those who have already been misled by the accounts of Year 1. 'Two wrongs do not make a right, even in accounting' (MacNeal, 1939: 284).

It is the widespread misuse of accounting profit as an index of business performance by critics and defenders alike which invites complaints against the accountancy profession. It is alleged, for example, that accounting reports are arbitrary because they reflect the choice of accounting 'codes' (or 'principles') rather than the performance of the enterprise; that they are liable to retrospective adjustment because the validity of the asset 'valuations' depends on the outcome of future events; and that they are drawn up in terms of a monetary unit of measurement which is unstable because its purchasing power is liable to change. Such criticism is, however, misdirected. It applies to the conventional 'resource accounts', not in their proper role as reports on 'stewardship', but to their miscasting as reports on 'performance'.

What is worse, this type of criticism amounts to a defence of the conventional system of accounting in the inappropriate role of performance reporting. For the object of criticism is not the system itself but the way in which it is applied. The blame is either placed on those responsible for its implementation (who are criticized for employing arbitrary, non-standard, or 'creative' techniques); or else it is placed on the difficulty of the conditions (of business uncertainty and economic instability) with which they have to contend.

The implication that there is nothing wrong with the system itself suits critics of the profession who are keen to expose the evils of 'creative accounting'. It also suits supporters who have a vested interest as suppliers of improved accounting standards. But it begs the most important question of all: is a system of accounting designed for stewardship reporting on the 'safekeeping' of resources appropriate for the role of performance reporting on their 'efficient use'?

To answer this question, it is instructive to travel back for a few centuries to the world of mediaeval Venice, where accounting has its traditional origins. 'Typical of Venetian accounting are the venture or voyage accounts . . . [which] were closed into Profit and Loss after each affair was completely finished. . . . The Venetians . . . often postponed casting a balance for several years' (Roover, 1956: 156, 157).

MEDIAEVAL 'VENTURE' ACCOUNTING

The advantages of venture accounting can be demonstrated by means of a simple comparison between two rival firms. Each firm has been set up with £1 million in cash from investors. In both cases, the whole £1 million is to be spent on inputs for the manufacture of the first batch of product. The entire cash proceeds of the sale of the first batch are then to be spent on inputs for the manufacture of the second batch. This process – of spending the whole of the proceeds of the previous batch on purchasing inputs for the next batch – is to be repeated for a total of six batches.

There is, however, a significant difference between the business plans of the two firms. In the expectation of quick and easy returns, the managers of Short-Term Exploitation Plc plan to manufacture and sell 'Lo-Vals' with an added value of only 10 per cent on cost. But the highest sales volumes are expected in the early years: three batches during the first year, two batches during the second year, and the final batch during the third year. By contrast, the managers of Long-Run Development Plc adopt a long-term strategy. They plan to manufacture and sell 'Hi-Vals' with an added value of 20 per cent on cost. But the highest sales volumes are not expected until the later years: one batch during the first year, two batches during the second year, and the last three batches during the third year. At the end of the third year, both companies are to be wound up and the whole of the cash is to be distributed to the investors.

It is assumed that the two firms are subject to exactly the same degree of risk, that there are no price changes throughout the economy, and that everything goes according to plan. The operations (both expected and actual) of the two firms are shown in Table 3.1. For the sake of simplicity, the cost of renting or leasing premises and equipment is

Table 3.1 *Expected and actual operations of two firms*

	Short-Term Exploitation Plc			Long-Run Development Plc		
Batch	Cash purchase of inputs		Cash sales of Lo-Vals	Cash purchase of inputs		Cash sales of Hi-Vals
	£		£	£		£
First	1,000,000		1,100,000	1,000,000	Year 1	1,200,000
Second	1,100,000	Year 1	1,210,000	1,200,000	Year 2	1,440,000
Third	1,210,000		1,331,000	1,440,000		1,728,000
Fourth	1,331,000	Year 2	1,464,100	1,728,000		2,073,600
Fifth	1,464,100		1,610,510	2,073,600	Year 3	2,488,320
Sixth	1,610,510	Year 3	1,771,561	2,488,320		2,985,984
Total	7,715,610		8,487,171	9,929,920		11,915,904

included in the cash purchase of inputs so that neither firm holds any assets other than cash.

The characteristic feature of 'venture' accounts is that they are not drawn up until after the voyage has been completed, all the assets have been 'realized' by being converted into cash, and the capital is about to be returned to investors. The 'beans', so to speak, are available to be counted.

The venture accounts for the whole (six-batch) 'voyage' of each firm are therefore fairly straightforward. They can be drawn up in accordance with the advice (which has proved invaluable for countless generations of students about to sit their final exams) given by Luca Pacioli: 'For all the cash which you find properly belongs to you, debit Cash and credit your Capital. Include amounts earned at different times in the past, bequeathed to you by deceased relatives, or given to you by some prince' (1494: 105).

The figures presented in Table 3.2 are derived from Table 3.1. For the sake of brevity, details of the profit (normally presented in a separate profit and loss account) are shown on the balance sheets in Table 3.2. Short-Term Exploitation's 'cost of sales' in Table 3.2 is the £7,715,610 total of cash purchases of inputs in Table 3.1; and its 'revenue from sales' in Table 3.2 is the £8,487,171 total of cash sales of Lo-Vals in Table 3.1. Similarly, Long-Run Development's 'cost of sales' in Table 3.2 is the £9,929,920 total of cash purchases of inputs in Table 3.1; and its 'revenue from sales' in Table 3.2 is the £11,915,904 total of cash sales of Hi-Vals in Table 3.1.

The mediaeval venture accounts in Table 3.2 appear to fit perfectly into the FASB's 'Conceptual Framework'.

Investors, lenders, suppliers, and employees . . . invest cash, goods, or services in an enterprise and expect to obtain sufficient . . . in return to make the investment

Table 3.2 Mediaeval 'Venture' accounts for the whole (six-batch) 'voyage'

Balance sheet at the end of voyage†	Short-Term Exploitation Plc	Long-Run Development Plc
Equities	£	£
Capital (at the beginning of the voyage)	1,000,000	1,000,000
Revenue from sales *	8,487,171 (All six	11,915,904 (All six
Less: Cost of sales *	(7,715,610) batches)	(9,929,920) batches)
Profit (for the voyage)	771,561	1,985,984
Total equities	1,771,561	2,985,984
Assets	£	£
Cash	1,771,561	2,985,984
Total assets	1,771,561	2,985,984
Accountant's rate of profit (ARP)		
Accounting Return = $\dfrac{\text{Profit}}{\text{Capital}}$	$\dfrac{£771,561}{£1,000,000} = 77.2\%$	$\dfrac{£1,985,984}{£1,000,000} = 198.6\%$

* These details would normally appear in a separate profit and loss account.
† Immediately prior to the final distribution to investors.

worthwhile. . . . A successful investor or creditor receives not only a return *of* investment but also a return *on* that investment.

(FASB, 1978: 11 and 18)

Since both 'voyages' are over, the return shown in the venture accounts is a question of fact. At the end of three years, investors in Short-Term Exploitation receive a return of £771,561 over and above their original capital of £1,000,000. Expressed as a rate of return on capital invested, it is equal to 77.2 per cent over the three-year period. The *accounting return* derived from the information in the accounts is often referred to as the ROCE – the return on capital employed. In the case of the venture accounts in Table 3.2, it is perfectly accurate. Similarly, the rate of return to investors in Long-Run Development is 198.6 per cent over the three years.

In order to compare the return on investments of different types or of different duration (or with the cost of borrowing), it is normal practice to express the rate of return in the form of an 'average' annual percentage rate (APR). For Short-Term Exploitation Plc, the annual average is $(\sqrt[3]{1.771561} - 1 =) \, 0.21$, or 21 per cent per annum. For Long-Run Development Plc, the annual average is $(\sqrt[3]{2.985984} - 1 =) \, 0.44$, or 44 per cent per annum. Table 3.3 demonstrates that these 'averages' are equal to the

29

Table 3.3 *The rate of return expected and realised*

	Short-Term Exploitation Plc		Long-Run Development Plc	
		£		£
Beginning of Year 1	Contribution	1,000,000	Contribution	1,000,000
End of Year 1	Return @ 21%	210,000	Return @ 44%	440,000
	Balance	1,210,000	Balance	1,440,000
End of Year 2	Return @ 21%	254,100	Return @ 44%	633,600
	Balance	1,464,100	Balance	2,073,600
End of Year 3	Return @ 21%	307,461	Return @ 44%	912,384
	Balance	1,771,561	Balance	2,985,984
	Distribution	-1,771,561	Distribution	-2,985,984
	Balance	0	Balance	0

annual rate that the same amount invested in a bank or building society would have to earn in order to produce the same result.

Kaldor's view of the purpose of accounting in the role of performance reporting has already been quoted in the Introduction; but it is worth repeating.

> The main purpose of accounting is to exhibit, for the proprietors of the business, the actual results in terms as nearly comparable as can be to the expected results; in terms, in other words, which make it possible for the proprietors to judge whether the business is a 'success' and fulfils those expectations in the light of which they invested their capital, and which they alone are ultimately capable of deciding.
>
> (1955: 67, 68)

The managers of Short-Term Exploitation Plc plan a return of 77.2 per cent over the three-year period, they achieve a return of 77.2 per cent over the three-year period, and the venture accounts report a return of 77.2 per cent over the three-year period. The venture accounts give a similarly 'true and fair view' of the return over the three-year period planned and actually achieved by the managers of Long-Run Development Plc 'on the resources under their control'. The venture accounts in Table 3.2 fulfil both of the major objectives of accounting identified in the Introduction: (1) stewardship reporting on the 'safekeeping' of resources, and (2) performance reporting on their 'efficient use'.

There is, however, a fairly obvious drawback. Although venture accounting may have been acceptable for mediaeval voyages of relatively short duration, it is not a practical solution for modern business. The 'voyage' (upon which a typical limited liability company ventures the capital of what may be several generations of investors) does not normally come to an end until the company has been liquidated, its assets realized, and the capital returned to investors. Strict application of the principle of venture accounting would mean having to wait until the end of a firm's life.

That is the reason why modern accounting is no longer a relatively simple matter of counting beans. 'Because of the requirement to prepare periodic financial statements, it is necessary to break up the entity's operating cycle into artificial periods' (Ernst & Young, 2004: 1453).

MODERN 'PERIODIC' ACCOUNTING

The necessity for regular up-to-date information dictates the artificial division of the firm's life into arbitrary periods of no more than a year. This is reflected in the custom of drawing up business accounts at annual intervals and the legal requirement for their publication by public companies. The mediaeval venture accounts of Table 3.2 have therefore evolved into the modern annual accounts of Table 3.4.

The figures are derived from Table 3.1 which shows that, in Year 1, Short-Term Exploitation Plc buys inputs for and sells three batches of Lo-Vals. That is reflected in the Year 1 'cost of sales' in Table 3.4 of (£1,000,000 + £1,100,000 + £1,210,000 =)

Table 3.4 *Modern 'Periodic' accounts for Year 1*

Balance sheet at the end of Year 1	Short-Term Exploitation Plc		Long-Run Development Plc	
Equities	£		£	
Capital (at the beginning of the year)	1,000,000		1,000,000	
Revenue from sales *	3,641,000	(First	1,200,000	(First
Less: Cost of sales *	(3,310,000)	three	(1,000,000)	batch
		batches)		only)
Profit (for the year)	331,000		200,000	
Total equities	1,331,000		1,200,000	
Assets	£		£	
Cash	1,331,000		1,200,000	
Total assets	1,331,000		1,200,000	
Accountant's rate of profit (ARP)				
Accounting Return = $\dfrac{\text{Profit}}{\text{Capital}}$	$\dfrac{£331,000}{£1,000,000}$ = 33.1%		$\dfrac{£200,000}{£1,000,000}$ = 20.0%	

* These details would normally appear in a separate profit and loss account.

£3,310,000 and 'revenue from sales' of (£1,100,000 + £1,210,000 + £1,331,000 =) £3,641,000. Table 3.1 shows that, in Year 1, Long-Run Development Plc manufactures and sells only one batch of Hi-Vals. That is reflected in the Year 1 'cost of sales' in Table 3.4 of £1,000,000 and 'revenue from sales' of £1,200,000.

The modern 'periodic' accounts for Year 1 give a message that is unmistakable. Short-Term Exploitation Plc has a larger balance sheet value than Long-Run Development Plc, and it has a higher accounting return. The picture presented as a 'true and fair view' by the accounts indicates clearly and unambiguously that Short-Term Exploitation is more successful than Long-Run Development.

The economic reality, however, is quite the opposite. The investment of £1 million in Long-Run Development Plc produces £2,985,984 at the end of three years; the same investment in Short-Term Exploitation Plc produces only £1,771,561. As an economic investment, Long-Run Development Plc is undoubtedly superior because it promises *and delivers to the investors* larger returns with exactly the same time pattern and with exactly the same degree of risk.

How 'true and fair' is the view presented by the modern 'periodic' accounts?

As *stewardship* reports on the 'safekeeping' of resources, the modern 'periodic' accounts in Table 3.4 are perfectly accurate. As *performance* reports on the 'efficient use' of resources, they are totally misleading. They are misleading for the purpose of comparing the two firms with each other; and they are misleading for the purpose of comparing investment in either of the firms with other forms of investment. They therefore fail to meet the IASB's requirement 'to provide information . . . that is useful to a wide range of users in making economic decisions' (2005: 36).

According to the 'Kaldor criterion', if 21 per cent per annum is the return on capital planned for Short-Term Exploitation Plc over its three-year life, and if 21 per cent per annum is the return actually achieved, then there is only one 'true and fair' view. During the course of that achievement, the return on capital indicated by the published accounts should be 21 per cent per annum. The same applies to the 44 per cent per annum planned and delivered by Long-Run Development Plc.

However, even though they are drawn up in strict conformity with the highest accounting standards (according to which every £ is valued precisely at a £), the accounts in Table 3.4 paint a very different picture. They are seriously misleading as a guide to the return on capital invested in either firm. Yet this is one of the few instances where there is no controversy over accounting standards. There are none of the normal problems of asset valuation, changing prices, or business uncertainty. The only asset is cash; there are no price changes of any kind; and everything turns out precisely according to plan.

The fact that strict compliance with modern accounting standards can lead to the publication of information known to be seriously misleading raises fundamental ethical problems. The root cause of the dilemma is the misuse of the accounting system for a purpose for which it was not designed.

Conventional accounts are excellent for cataloguing resources in the physical dimension. Backward-looking symbols of volume are ideal for reporting on stewardship

– for keeping track of the lottery tickets. But they cannot be interpreted as forward-looking estimates of value. In the value dimension of performance reporting, their use is highly dangerous.

INTO A BLIND ALLEY?

The first *Statement of Financial Accounting Concepts* issued by the FASB as part of its 'conceptual framework project' is entitled 'Objectives of Financial Reporting by Business Enterprises'. It contains the reassurance that 'no conclusions [are implied] about the identity, number, or form of financial statements because those matters are yet to be considered in the conceptual framework project' (1978: 4).

A quarter of a century later, those matters are still to be considered. For most of the subsequent research has been devoted, not to investigating new types of accounting system, but to improving the five-centuries-old system inherited from Pacioli. A great deal of effort has been expended in an attempt to stretch the principles of economic theory in order to justify the use of conventional *stewardship* accounts in the role of *performance* reports.

There are two basic mistakes in this approach. The first mistake is failure to recognize that the conventional system of accounting is simply the wrong vehicle for the purpose. The second mistake is failure to recognize that, both in the measurement of income and in the valuation of assets, economic theory itself has serious flaws.

These mistakes have combined to lead the profession up a theoretical blind alley. The misguided attempt to introduce current values into an inappropriate system produced the inflation accounting debacle of the 1970s, and it has been held responsible for setting back the cause of financial reporting in the latter part of the twentieth century. In its latest 'fair value' disguise, it remains one of the most dangerous threats to progress at the start of the twenty-first.

For a proper understanding of the reasons for the muddle into which the accounting standards process has degenerated, however, it is necessary to re-examine some of the 'ancient' controversies over income and value.

The measurement of income and value

INTRODUCTION

Of all economic statistics, income is probably the most vital. For it is by the size of income that economic performance is commonly measured.

> Income plays an important rôle in all economic problems; it is income for which capital exists; it is income for which labor is exerted; and it is the distribution of income which constitutes the disparity between rich and poor.
>
> (Fisher, 1906: viii)

> Individual income calculations . . . have an important influence on individual economic conduct; [and] calculations of social income . . . play . . . an important part in social statistics, and in welfare economics.
>
> (Hicks, 1939: 180)

In the allocation of economic resources, business income is particularly crucial, and business accounts have become a fruitful source of raw material for national income statistics.

That income is an important economic concept, therefore, is not in dispute.

> Income is the alpha and omega of economics.
>
> (Fisher, 1930: 13)

The unanimity of opinion as to the importance of income, however, is in sharp contrast to the diversity of opinion as to its exact nature.

Writing in 1929, Professor J.B. Canning complained that 'a diligent search of the literature of accounting discloses an astonishing lack of discussion of the nature of income'.

One could hardly expect that the profession which, above all others, is most constantly engaged in the statistical treatment of income should have found almost nothing at all to say about the nature of the thing they measure so carefully. Nor could one have expected that the academic writers on accounting, many of whom are economists and statisticians as well as students of accounting, should have paid so little attention to this lack of definition and should, apparently, have made little effort to supply the wanting proposition.

(1929: 93)

Today, it requires a diligent search of the literature of accounting to discover any self-respecting work on financial reporting which does *not* contain a discussion of the nature of income. There are, however, some interesting and important exceptions, of which perhaps the most interesting and important are the UK Accounting Standards Board, the US Financial Accounting Standards Board, and the International Accounting Standards Board.

The work of the accounting standards bodies and their predecessors seems to have proceeded by what Canning calls 'a sort of patchwork and tinkering'.

To be sure, the patching [is] often shrewdly planned and executed, but it [is] patchwork nevertheless in the sense that there [is] little going back to fundamentals for a fresh start.

(1929: 9)

Part II is an attempt to sift through what has become a rather untidy pile of jumble.

Chapter 4

Economic income and accounting profit

If 'income' is to be a measure of economic performance, it must relate to the object for which economic activity takes place. The object of economic activity is one of the few issues on which there seems to be general agreement.

> Consumption is the sole end and purpose of all production.
>
> (Smith, 1776: vol. 2, 159)

> Human effort and human consumption are the ultimate matters from which alone economic transactions are capable of deriving any significance.
>
> (Keynes, 1930: vol. 1, 134)

> All production is for the purpose of ultimately satisfying a consumer. . . . Consumption – to repeat the obvious – is the sole end and object of all economic activity.
>
> (Keynes, 1936: 46 and 104)

Economic performance cannot therefore be measured without reference to the change in consumption for which the productive activity is responsible. That is why, in one way or another, all concepts of income relate to consumption.

> There is general agreement on the definition of income among the various schools of thought: Income is the difference between wealth at two points in time plus consumption during the period. The problem centers around the method of determining the wealth or well-offness.
>
> (Sterling, 1970: 19; cf. Edwards, 1938; Alexander, 1948; Solomons, 1961; Sandilands, 1975)

There appear to be two quite distinct approaches towards the determination of 'well-offness'. Fisher (1906) develops his concept of income in terms of an individual's *actual* stream of consumption. Hicks (1939) develops his concept in terms of some *hypothetical* standard stream. To accountants, faced with the problem of measuring the income of a business enterprise, the relevance of what appears to be an ancient controversy is two-fold. There is, in the literature of accounting, extensive support for the Hicksian concept – at least as a theoretical ideal. Secondly, the current movement in the direction of 'fair value accounting' is justified on grounds of consistency with 'the economic concept of income' (Joint Working Group of Standard Setters, 2000: 233).

INCOME AS POTENTIAL CONSUMPTION

Depending on the interpretation of 'well-offness', 'there are two rival concepts of standard income'. '[There is] standard income . . . which would maintain its capital-value at a constant level . . . [and] standard income as a perpetual and uniform flow' (Fisher, 1906: 396). These are what Hicks calls 'Income No.1' and 'Income No.2' respectively. 'Income No. 1 is . . . the maximum amount which can be spent during a period if there is to be an expectation of maintaining intact the capital value of prospective receipts (in money terms)' (1939: 173).

The various income calculations can be illustrated by means of a simple two-year investment. The initial cash outlay is £10,000; and the prospective receipts are a single cash inflow of £13,200 at the end of two years. The rate of interest (at which it is possible to borrow or lend) is expected to be 10 per cent per annum during the first year. During the second and subsequent years, the rate of interest is expected to be 20 per cent per annum. All expectations turn out exactly according to plan.

At the beginning of the first year, the 'capital value of prospective receipts' is equal to the present value of the expected returns (discounted for two years):

$$\frac{£13,200}{1.1 \times 1.2} = £10,000$$

At the end of the first year, the 'capital value of prospective receipts' is equal to the present value of the expected returns (discounted for one year):

$$\frac{£13,200}{1.2} = £11,000$$

'Income No.1' for the first year is equal to £1,000, because that is the maximum amount which can be spent during the year 'if there is to be an expectation of maintaining intact the capital value of prospective receipts (in money terms)' – at the initial level of £10,000.

As Hicks points out, 'Income No.1 . . . is probably the definition which most people do implicitly use in their private affairs' (1939: 173). It is, however, not necessarily a good approximation to what he calls the 'central concept'. 'A person's income is what he can consume during the week and still expect to be as well off at the end of the week as he was at the beginning' (1939: 176).

Hicks explains the difficulty that arises 'if interest rates are expected to change'.

> If the rate of interest . . . which is expected to rule in one future [period] is not the same as that which is expected to rule in another future [period], then a definition based upon constancy of money capital becomes unsatisfactory.
>
> (1939: 174)

The case for Income No.2 is argued by Hicks on the following grounds. The owner of the two-year investment in the illustration can spend no more than £1,000 at the end of the first year, 'if he is to expect to have £10,000 again at his disposal at the end of the [year]';

> but if he desires to have the same sum available at the end of the second [year], he will be able to spend £2,000 at the end of the second [year], not £1,000 only. The same sum (£10,000) available at the beginning of the first [year] makes possible a stream of expenditures
>
> £1,000, £2,000, £2,000, £2,000, . . . ,
>
> while if it is available at the beginning of the second [year] it makes possible a stream
>
> £2,000, £2,000, £2,000, £2,000, ...

It will ordinarily be reasonable to say that a person with the latter prospect is better off than one with the former.

This leads us to the definition of Income No.2 . . . as the maximum amount the individual can spend this [year], and still expect to be able to spend the same amount in each ensuing [year]. . . . When the rate of interest is expected to change, . . . Income No.2 is . . . a closer approximation to the central concept than Income No.1 is.

(1939: 174, *mutatis mutandis*)

For the owner of the two-year investment in the illustration, Income No.2 in the first year amounts to £1,833.33. Although the prospective receipts are not due until the end of the second year, the investor can borrow for consumption £1,833.33 at the end of the first year. Together with 20 per cent interest for the second year, this loan accumulates to (£1,833.33 + £366.67 =) £2,200 at the end of the second year. After this loan has been repaid out of the £13,200 received from the investment at the end of the second year, £11,000 remains. Out of this, the investor can consume £1,833.33 again at the end of the second year – leaving a capital sum of £9,166.67. The 20 per cent annual interest in subsequent years of £1,833.33 enables the investor to consume 'the same amount in each ensuing year'.

39

A CIRCULAR ARGUMENT?

At this point, a digression may be appropriate for the expression of some misgivings. The 'proof' of the superiority of Income No.2 over Income No.1 can be repeated in almost exactly the same terms in order to 'prove' the superiority of Income No.1 over Income No.2.

Suppose, given the same rates of interest as in the previous illustration, the investor owns a perpetual annuity of £1,833.33. Income No.2 is clearly the annual receipt of £1,833.33, since that is what the investor can spend at the end of the year and still expect to be able to spend £1,833.33 at the end of each ensuing year.

At the beginning of the first year, however, the investor can spend £10,000 (the present value of the annuity) immediately; but if he has the same perpetuity available at the end of the year, he will be able to spend only £9,166.67 immediately at the end of the first year, not £10,000.

The same perpetuity (£1,833.33 per annum) available at the beginning of the first year makes possible (given the interest rates in the illustration) a stream of expenditures

£10,000.00 (immediately), £0, £0, £0, . . .,

while if it is available at the beginning of the second year it makes possible a stream

£9,166.67 (immediately), £0, £0, £0, ...

It will ordinarily be reasonable to say that a person with the latter prospect is worse off (by £833.33) than one with the former. This leads us to the definition of Income No.1 (£1,833.33 − £833.33 = £1,000), which is then a closer approximation to the central concept than Income No.2 is.

The fact that it is possible to 'prove' the superiority of *both* 'rival concepts of standard income' suggests that Fisher's objection (1906: 396) should not be lightly dismissed. All versions of the Hicksian concept of income are based on a stream of potential consumption which is purely hypothetical. 'Well-offness' is identified with the ability to consume. At the beginning of any period, an individual has the opportunity of consuming at various different levels according to various different time patterns. His 'income' for the period is what he can *potentially* consume during the period and still be able to look forward to the same *hypothetical* consumption prospect at the end of the period as he could at the beginning. Consequently, any number of 'hypothetical consumption concepts' of income can be developed depending on which particular hypothetical consumption prospect is chosen as the standard to be maintained (see Appendix A).

It is, in fact, the hypothetical aspect that Fisher finds particularly objectionable.

40

> To reckon what one *ought* to save [or spend] in order to maintain capital is not to save [or spend] it, and a definition of income which depends upon an ideal reckoning instead of a real payment is to that extent inadequate.
>
> (Fisher, 1906: 111, 112)

Fisher's alternative to the 'hypothetical consumption concepts' of income is an 'actual consumption concept'.

INCOME AS ACTUAL CONSUMPTION

As human enjoyment is the ultimate end of all economic activity, Fisher argues that income ought to be identified with the actual enjoyment derived from consumption.

> Intermediate stages [of production and exchange] are merely preparatory to the final use or so-called 'consumption' of wealth.
>
> (1906: 152)

> Income . . . resolves itself in final analysis into a flow of psychic enjoyments or satisfactions during a period of time.
>
> (1930: 453)

This is, as its author declares, a 'consumption concept of income' (1930: 454), and it is consistent with the view that 'pleasure and pain are undoubtedly the ultimate objects of the Calculus of Economics' (Jevons, 1871: 37).

Using the analogy of 'capital' as the tree which produces 'income' as the fruit, Fisher defines income as the *actual* 'flow of services' from which the source – the stock of capital – derives its value. 'A *stock of wealth* existing at an *instant* of time is called *capital*. A *flow of services* through a *period* of time is called *income*' (1906: 52).

In the 'final net income' the 'interactions' of intermediate services during production and exchange 'drop out'. 'The only items which survive are the final personal uses of wealth, ordinarily called "consumption"' (1906: 165). In this scenario, the 'firm' is merely an intermediary in the economic process, standing between the pain of labour and the enjoyment of pleasure. It is 'a fictitious person . . . a mere bookkeeping dummy' (1906: 92). Because it cannot consume, the firm itself cannot enjoy an income.

> A corporation is a fictitious, not a real, person. . . . Its stockholders may get income from it, but the corporation itself, considered as a separate person apart from these stockholders, receives none.
>
> (1930: 23)

> A corporation, as an entity distinct from its stockholders, cannot enjoy income.
>
> (1906: 138)

41

Whatever the merits of this argument, it has to be admitted that it is highly inconvenient for accountants engaged in the measurement of 'business income'.

But there is a more serious and obvious difficulty; and it lies in the fact Fisher uses the term 'income' for what, on his own admission, is 'ordinarily called consumption' (1906: 165). The trouble with 'income-as-consumption' is that it may vary between periods in a way which has nothing to do with the productive activity which made the consumption possible. In calculating current income, however, Fisher insists that no account is to be taken of a fall or rise in future consumption. Changes of that nature are to be recognized only in the period when they actually occur. There is no question of 'maintaining capital intact'. On the contrary, in Fisher's view, 'capital gains . . . are merely capitalization of future income' (1930: 25). To include them as present income would be 'double counting'. The services of capital would 'have been counted as income in anticipation as well as in realization' (1906: 108).

By the normal rules of language, Fisher's 'actual consumption concept' of income looks a clear failure; and Kaldor's objection seems unanswerable. 'If we reserved the term Income for Consumption we should still need another term for what would otherwise be called Income' (1955: 57).

The implication of Fisher's approach is that different incomes need to be calculated for different investors in the same company, depending on the actual stream of consumption derived from their investment.

From an accountant's point of view, Fisher's concept looks theoretically unsound and practically impossible. It is also a century old. So why bother discussing it – even as an historical curiosity?

The answer (which will become apparent in Chapter 9) is that a major obstacle to progress in modern accounting is failure to recognize that Fisher's argument is essentially correct and is highly relevant for accounting reform in a market economy.

On the face of it, however, Fisher's approach appears to have little to offer. It is no surprise, therefore, that there is a clear preference in the literature of accounting in favour of the Hicksian alternative. There are, nevertheless, enormous problems in making the transition from economic theory to accounting practice. Not the least of these is the fact that Hicks's income is defined in terms of personal consumption.

THE PROBLEM OF SUBJECTIVITY

An aggregate of the incomes of individual shareholders is vulnerable to the objection voiced by Hicks 'when we pass from the consideration of individual income . . . to the consideration of social income'.

> Individual income . . . is a subjective concept, dependent on the particular expectations of the individual in question. . . . There is no reason why the expectations of different individuals should be consistent. . . . An aggregate of their incomes has little meaning.
>
> (1939: 177, 178)

Although this appears to shut the door on 'business income', Hicks offers, as a means of escape, the definition of 'income *ex post*'.

All the definitions of income . . . hitherto discussed are *ex ante* definitions – they are concerned with what a person can consume during a week and still *expect* to be as well off as he was. . . . If [the expectation] is not realized exactly, the value of his prospect at the end of the week will be greater or less than it was expected to be, so that he makes a 'windfall' profit or loss.

(1939: 178)

This gives rise to 'a new set of definitions, definitions of "income including windfalls" or "income *ex post*"'.

Income No.1 *ex post* equals the value of the individual's consumption *plus* the increment in the money value of his prospect which has accrued during the week; it equals Consumption *plus* Capital accumulation.

(1939: 178)

This appears to remove the problem of subjectivity.

Income No.1 *ex post* is not a subjective affair, like other kinds of income; it is almost completely objective. The capital value of the individual's property at the beginning of the week is an assessable figure; so is the capital value of his property at the end of the week. . . . The incomes *ex post* of all individuals composing the community can be aggregated without difficulty; and the same rule, that Income No.1 *ex post* equals Consumption *plus* Capital accumulation, will hold for the community as a whole. . . . *Ex post* calculations of capital accumulation . . . are a useful measuring-rod for economic progress.

(1939: 178, 179)

THE ACCOUNTING IDEAL

For purposes of accounting, however, the consumption that individual investors may or may not be able to enjoy is still too subjective. The focus of attention has therefore been shifted to the amounts that a business firm is able to distribute.

We might define a company's profit for the year by adapting Sir John Hicks' definition as follows:
    'A company's profit for the year is the maximum value which the company can distribute during the year, and still expect to be as well off at the end of the year as it was at the beginning.'

(Sandilands, 1975: 29; cf. Solomons, 1961: 376;
Stamp, 1971: 284; Edwards *et al.*, 1987: 2)

43

This *ex ante* definition raises problems already discussed. There is one profit concept corresponding to 'Income No.1' and another corresponding to 'Income No.2'. If the two-year investment in the previous illustration is the only asset held by a firm, 'Profit No.1' for the first year is equal to £1,000, because that is the amount it can distribute while maintaining the capital value of its assets in money terms. 'Profit No.2' is equal to £1,833.33, because that is the amount it can distribute at the end of the first year and still be able to distribute the same amount at the end of every ensuing year.

Once again, the solution (advocated by Stamp, 1971: 284, among others) is to take refuge in the analogy with 'Income No.1 *ex post*'.

> Profit No.1 *ex post* equals the value of a firm's distributions *plus* the increment in the money value of its prospect which has accrued during the period; it equals Distributions (*minus* Contributions) *plus* Capital accumulation. . . . The incomes *ex post* of all investors in the company can be aggregated without difficulty; and the same rule, that Profit No.1 *ex post* equals Distributions (*minus* Contributions) *plus* Capital accumulation, will hold for the firm as a whole. . . . *Ex post* calculations of capital accumulation . . . are a useful measuring-rod for business progress.
>
> (Hicks, 1939: 178, 179, *mutatis mutandis*)

The good news is that this corresponds very closely to the traditional definition of accounting profit, namely, the change in a firm's balance sheet value after allowing for contributions from and distributions to its owners. The bad news is that conventional balance sheet values are normally based on historical cost.

Chapter 5

The inflation accounting 'debate'

Table 5.1 is an indication of the rapid price inflation suffered by the United Kingdom during the 1970s and early 1980s. Table 5.2 indicates that the United Kingdom was not alone. When price changes continue at significant rates over significant periods of time, they pose problems for traditional historical accounts which rely on money as the unit of account and on historical acquisition cost as the basis of valuation. At low levels of inflation, 'inflation accounting' tends to remain a subject of academic interest. At higher levels, it becomes a matter of serious professional and public concern.

> Accounting grew up as a day-by-day record of business dealings. Its figures are a series of snapshots, each a glimpse of some event as it happened. They are faithful history. But usually they are left as historical records; the accountant does not touch them up when conditions change at later times. For instance, he continues to measure assets and inputs at their original cost, no matter how far their current values have moved. Particularly during inflation, the values are apt to move a long way. So now the question is whether the accountant should not try to update his figures.
>
> (Baxter, 1975: v)

Table 5.1 *Annual percentage change in consumer prices in the United Kingdom: 1960–2004*

Year Decade	0	1	2	3	4	5	6	7	8	9	Average for decade
	%	%	%	%	%	%	%	%	%	%	%
1960s	1.0	3.6	4.1	2.1	3.2	4.8	3.9	2.4	4.7	5.5	3.5
1970s	6.4	9.4	7.1	9.2	15.9	24.2	16.5	15.9	8.2	13.5	12.5
1980s	18.0	11.9	8.6	4.6	5.0	6.1	3.4	4.1	4.9	7.8	7.4
1990s	9.5	5.9	3.7	1.6	2.5	3.4	2.4	3.1	3.4	1.6	3.7
2000–04	2.9	1.8	1.6	2.9	3.0						2.5

Source: International Financial Statistics website, Washington, DC: International Monetary Fund.

Table 5.2 *Average annual percentage change in consumer prices in the Group of Seven: 1960 to 2004*

	1960s	1970s	1980s	1990s	2000–04
	%	%	%	%	%
United Kingdom	3.5	12.5	7.4	3.7	2.5
Canada	2.5	7.3	6.5	2.2	2.4
France	3.9	8.9	7.3	1.9	1.9
Germany	2.4	4.9	2.9	2.3	1.5
Italy	3.4	12.2	11.0	4.1	2.5
Japan	5.4	9.0	2.5	1.2	−0.5
United States	2.3	7.1	5.5	3.0	2.5

Source: International Financial Statistics website, Washington, DC: International Monetary Fund.

THE IRRESISTIBLE CASE FOR INFLATION ACCOUNTING

Suppose that Tweedledum buys a Nice New Rattle for £100 cash. He subsequently sells the rattle for £150 cash. The conventional 'historical' accounting profit is £50.

Irrespective of any controversy over the accounting return, the £50 historical profit unequivocally represents a cash increase during the period of £50. If there have been no price changes of any kind during the period, the extra £50 cash represents an extra £50 of immediate purchasing power. If, however, *all* prices have risen by 50 per cent during the period, then his purchasing power has not increased by a single penny.

A £50 cash increase during a period of price stability is very different from a £50 cash increase against the background of a 50 per cent increase in all prices. The fact that the conventional historical accounts report £50 as a 'true and fair view' of the profit in *both* cases is responsible for public scepticism over the reliability of financial information. How true is 'true' and how fair is 'fair'? When 'profit' is the basis of business taxation, scepticism can turn into outrage. Taxpayers are not noted for anxiety over the finer points of accounting theory, but they are liable to become very agitated at the injustice of having to pay tax on what they consider to be non-existent gains.

It is when the rate of price inflation is at its highest that the public clamour for 'something to be done' is at its loudest. Exactly what that 'something' should be is not always obvious.

The accounting literature provides a veritable cornucopia of solutions. In this chapter, however, it is impossible to do justice to all the many variations on the alternative inflation accounting themes. A full account of the history and theoretical background of the 'inflation accounting debate' is given by Whittington (1983) and Tweedie and Whittington (1984). What follows here is no more than a brief outline.

INFLATION ACCOUNTING: THE BASIC ALTERNATIVES

According to the traditional textbook analysis, there are two distinct accounting problems arising from the phenomenon of changing prices. It follows, therefore, that there are two distinct solutions.

Problem number one:

Changes in the *general level of prices* may cause the monetary unit of account to become 'out of date' in terms of purchasing power.

Solution number one:

The *unit of account* should be 'updated' by switching from the nominal monetary unit to the current purchasing power equivalent by using an appropriate general price index (GPI).

Problem number two:

Changes in the *specific prices* of items actually acquired may (if there is a 'time-lag' before use or sale) cause costs charged as expenses in the profit and loss account and costs included as assets in the balance sheet to become 'out of date'.

Solution number two:

The *valuation basis* should be 'updated' by switching from historical cost to the current cost equivalent by using appropriate specific price indices (SPIs).

Depending on which, if any, of the solutions are implemented, there are four basic alternative systems of accounting. Their main features are summarized in Table 5.3.

The accounting implications can be demonstrated by the application of each alternative to the adventures (summarized in Table 5.4) of Tweedledum and his Nice New Rattle. Four versions of Tweedledum's operating profit are shown in Table 5.5.

In the language of Chapter 2, each alternative system has its own 'accounting code'. By the historical cost accounting (HC) 'code', no adjustment at all is made for price

Table 5.3 *Summary of the basic alternatives*

Name of system	Nature of system	Unit of account	Basis of valuation
Historical cost accounting (HC)	Unadjusted historical cost	Money	Historical cost
Current purchasing power accounting (CPP)	'Updated' historical cost	Current purchasing power	Historical cost
Current cost accounting (CCA)	Unadjusted current cost	Money	Current cost
'Full stabilization' (CPP/CCA)	'Updated' current cost	Current purchasing power	Current cost

Table 5.4 *The purchase and sale of Tweedledum's Nice New Rattle*

	Beginning of period	Date of sale of rattle	End of period
Tweedledum's transactions	£100 cash ↓ [buy] ↓ 1 rattle → [hold] →	£150 cash → [hold] → ↑ [sell] ↑ 1 rattle	£150 cash
Specific (cost) price index of Nice New Rattles (SPI)	100	120	150
General price index (GPI)	100	110	121

Table 5.5 *Monetary symbols according to four different 'accounting codes'*

Name of 'code'	Nature of 'code'	Cost of sales (1 rattle 'out')	Sales revenue (£150 cash 'in')	Operating profit (£150 cash 'in' – 1 rattle 'out')
HC	Unadjusted historical cost	£100 = £100	£150 = £150	£50
CPP	"Updated" historical cost	$£100 \times \dfrac{121}{100} = £121$	$£150 \times \dfrac{121}{110} = £165$	£44
CCA	Unadjusted current cost	£120 = £120	£150 = £150	£30
CPP/CCA	"Updated" current cost	$£120 \times \dfrac{121}{110} = £132$	$£150 \times \dfrac{121}{110} = £165$	£33

changes: Tweedledum's operating profit is reported as £50. By the current purchasing power accounting (CPP) 'code', the monetary unit is converted into a unit of constant purchasing power using the GPI only: Tweedledum's operating profit is reported as £44. By the current cost accounting (CCA) 'code', the valuation basis is shifted from historical cost to current cost using SPIs only: Tweedledum's operating profit is reported as £30. By the CPP/CCA 'code', both types of adjustments are made: Tweedledum's operating profit is reported as £33. (In the case of both CPP methods, the operating profit is offset by a 'loss on monetary assets' of £15 due to holding the £150 sales proceeds as prices rise by 10 per cent.)

Because it incorporates both types of adjustment, CPP/CCA is often referred to as 'full stabilization' to distinguish it from the 'partial stabilization' of the CPP or CCA alternatives. Tweedie and Whittington call the combination of 'the CCA valuation base with CPP adjustment' 'a real terms, RT, system'.

This combines the CCA revaluation of individual assets with reference to specific price changes with a general index adjustment of capital, to yield the CPP gain on borrowing or loss on holding monetary assets. . . . The Real Terms (RT) approach . . . combines information from the CPP (general price-level changes) and CCA (specific price changes) systems.

(1984: 8, 11)

This gives the impression that inflation accounting is a progression (even a pilgrimage) from the 'dark ages' of historical cost accounting by way of partial 'revelations' like current purchasing power accounting and current cost accounting (which make only one type of adjustment) to the ultimate 'enlightenment' of CPP/CCA (which makes both). The weakness of this approach is that inflation accounting is treated purely as a technique – capable of being justified on technical grounds alone. The various rival systems are compared, not by testing the quality of the information to the consumer, but by demonstrating the alleged superiority of their respective production techniques.

INFLATION ACCOUNTING AND UK ACCOUNTING STANDARDS

In January 1974, a Committee of Enquiry was set up under the chairmanship of F.E.P. Sandilands to consider the question of inflation accounting. The Accounting Standards Steering Committee (representing the British professional accountancy bodies) had been on the point of issuing *Statement of Standard Accounting Practice No. 7 (SSAP 7)*, entitled 'Accounting for changes in the purchasing power of money'. One of the features of its recommended system of 'current purchasing power accounting' would have been to report the effect of what is criticized as 'taxation by currency depreciation' (Keynes, 1923: 9) and 'a hidden tax' (Friedman, 1974: 13). It was feared by the tax authorities that, if companies were allowed to deduct purchasing-power losses on monetary assets from their taxable profits, personal savers would demand the same deductions from their taxable income. As a result of the appointment of the Sandilands Committee, *SSAP 7* was published as a 'provisional' standard, when it appeared in May 1974.

The danger feared by the tax authorities was eventually removed by the publication of the Sandilands Report in September 1975 which recommended the CCA system. In November 1976, an exposure draft based on the Sandilands Report was issued by the Accounting Standards Committee. Entitled 'Current cost accounting', *ED 18* represented a valiant attempt to implement CCA in practice. Not the least of the problems was the treatment of technological change.

Where there has been marked technological advance so that it would in practice be more economical for a company to replace the existing asset with an alternative replacement rather than a substantially identical one, it will be appropriate to reflect

49

the effect of the advent of a technologically improved alternative asset on the value of the existing asset owned and to reduce the gross current replacement cost to the lower cost of the modern equivalent asset. . . . To estimate the cost of the modern equivalent asset, the gross capital cost of the modern alternative asset should be adjusted by:

(a) the present value of any material differences in operating costs over its whole life;

(b) any material differences in output capacity, as long as any increased output from the modern machine is usable by the company; and

(c) material differences in the total life of the modern machine, compared with the substantially identical replacement.

(*ED 18*, 1976: 45, 61)

Academics, presented with an endless supply of calculations to set for their students, were ecstatic. Professionals, responsible for doing the calculations themselves, were less enthusiastic. *ED 18* was rejected (by 15,512 votes to 13,184 of 46 per cent of members voting) in July 1977 at a Special Meeting of the Institute of Chartered Accountants in England and Wales called by two members in practice at Burgess Hill, David Keymer and Martin Haslam (see Tweedie and Whittington, 1984: 136). Following the interim publication of 'the Hyde Guidelines' in November 1977, a new standard, *SSAP 16*, emerged in March 1980, under the old title 'Current cost accounting'.

The new standard included an attempt to recognize the loss of purchasing power suffered by business firms without extending the privilege to private savers. Adjustments to profit were to be made for the purpose of maintaining a firm's purchasing power to replace its fixed assets (through 'backlog depreciation') and its current assets (through a 'monetary working capital adjustment') in conjunction with a 'gearing adjustment' (to restrict the effect to equity capital).

The general effect was to convert 'pure' CCA, not so much into CPP/CCA, as into CCA/CCA – by 'updating' the currency unit for changes, not in the general level of prices (GPI), but in the specific prices of items intended to be representative of a firm's purchases.

At another special meeting of the ICAEW instigated by Keymer and Haslam in July 1982, *SSAP 16* was accepted – but by such a narrow majority (15,745 votes to 14,812 of 41 per cent of members voting) that it was obvious that opposition within the profession remained substantial. During the 1980s, as the rate of inflation began to fall, much of the pressure for a system of inflation accounting evaporated; and, in July 1988, *SSAP 16* was finally withdrawn. Full details are given by Tweedie and Whittington (1984). For purposes of the present argument, however, the details are less important than the general nature of the controversy.

THE NATURE OF THE CONTROVERSY

The purchasing power of money depends on the prices of the items on which it is spent. Not only do different individuals (or firms) spend on different items, but their spending patterns are liable to change. The subjective nature of 'purchasing power' is recognized in the very construction of the price indices themselves. They are normally based on a 'basket' of items carefully chosen to be representative of the spending pattern of those for whom the index is constructed.

Suppose that Tweedledee has a half-share in Tweedledum's rattle firm and that they wind up the firm and split the £150 cash between them at the end of the period. Each brother has increased his £50 cash investment by 50 per cent during the period. If Tweedledum spends his share on items which have risen in price by *less than* 50 per cent, then his purchasing power has *increased*. If Tweedledee spends his share on items which have risen in price by *more than* 50 per cent, then his purchasing power has *fallen*. It is clear, therefore, that it is impossible *in principle* to devise a measure of purchasing-power change that applies to all the investors in a firm.

On one side of the inflation accounting controversy are those who maintain the pretence that it is possible to devise a single measure to tell a varied assortment of investors how their purchasing power has changed. On the other side are those (including the author) who accept the reality that the most that can be done is to provide investors with relevant information to enable them to work it out for themselves.

The question then arises: what exactly do the alternative inflation-adjusted figures (in Table 5.5, for example) actually mean? The answer is the same as the one given in Chapter 2. They are 'backward-looking symbols of volume'. The £50 historical figure of operating profit symbolizes '£150 cash IN *minus* one rattle OUT'. The inflation-adjusted versions say the same thing in three different languages (or 'accounting codes'). The first says it in CPP, the second says it in CCA, and the third says it in CPP/CCA. But, however sophisticated the language into which it is translated, the underlying message remains the same: '£150 cash IN *minus* one rattle OUT'.

In their role as *stewardship* reports on the *safekeeping* of resources, historical accounts are perfectly adequate as symbols of the existence of assets without the need for any adjustment. That is a significance they have never lost.

As *performance* reports on the *efficient use* of resources in earning a return on investors' capital, however, historical accounts are unreliable, even when prices are stable – and that is something generally acknowledged on both sides of the controversy (see Chapter 7). It follows that index number gymnastics, however spectacular, are insufficient to convert the historical figures into accurate measures of the return on investors' capital in a going concern. That is a significance they have never had.

The case against inflation accounting is quite simple. For stewardship reporting it is unnecessary; for performance reporting it is inadequate. If the historical return can be reported accurately (like the 50 per cent in Tweedledum's rattle firm), investors are able to evaluate it in the light of their own individual circumstances. They are also able to compare it with the return from alternative investments. Not only are inflation-adjusted versions (like those in Table 5.5) unnecessary, they can make evaluation and comparison more difficult rather than less. If, on the other hand, the historical return is liable to be inaccurate in the first place, how can adjusting it for price changes 'restore' an accuracy it does not have even when prices are stable?

THE TREATMENT OF DISSENT

The account given by Tweedie and Whittington (1984) is entitled *The Debate on Inflation Accounting*. 'Debate' implies more than one side. The case in favour of inflation accounting occupies most of the text. Apart from references to '"agitators" such as Messrs Keymer and Haslam who led the rebellion against CCA in the UK' (1984: 313), however, the case against inflation accounting – that the underlying theory is fundamentally flawed – is not even mentioned. The impression is given that dissent is a sign of ignorance. 'The education of many accountants is woefully deficient. . . . Many of the leaders of the profession . . . have not had a university education in the subject' (Tweedie and Whittington, 1984: 318).

The trouble with the 'Emperor's New Standards' reaction is that it has stifled debate. Problems have not been solved; they have simply been swept under the carpet.

Chapter 6

Historical cost or current value?

In retrospect, the excursion into inflation accounting may appear to have been an expensive, and perhaps unnecessary, distraction. Instead of straying into the quicksand of 'purchasing-power change', it is possible to reach more or less the same objective by a route that is theoretically safer and more direct. It is the one indicated at the end of Chapter 4.

Conventional accounting profit is the change in a firm's balance sheet value (after allowing for contributions from and distributions to its owners). This is tolerably close to Hicks's definition of 'Income No.1' *ex post*, which 'when modified . . . to suit the situation of the corporation as distinct from that of the individual . . . equals distribution plus capital accumulation' (Stamp, 1971: 284).

The major difference is that balance sheet figures are traditionally based on historical cost, whereas Hicks's capital accumulation is based on current value. A move from historical cost to current value can therefore be recommended without the need to venture anywhere near the theoretical quicksand of inflation accounting. Command of the theoretical high ground can be secured simply by arguing that current value is more 'relevant' than historical cost. It is a more effective argument for convincing supporters and silencing critics.

Although the concept of value is far from simple, a ready-made definition is available – honed to apparent perfection during the inflation accounting debate. It is based on the common-sense principle that, if you lose something which is worth replacing, then it makes sense to replace it. That way, your loss is limited to the cost of replacement.

DEPRIVAL VALUE: THE ASB FORMULA

The definition of 'value to the business' which lives on in the *Statement of Principles for Financial Reporting* (ASB, 2005: 59) is the one given by Bonbright in *The Valuation of Property* (1937: 71). It has strong support from some of the most distinguished writers on accounting theory, and it is the one that is quoted in the Sandilands Report.

The value of a property to its owner is identical in amount with the adverse value of the entire loss, direct and indirect, that the owner might expect to suffer if he were to be deprived of the property.

(1975: 58; cf. Solomons, 1966: 123; Baxter, 1975: 126)

Bonbright's statement that an 'asset must be valued at the discounted adverse value of the loss . . . that the *whole enterprise* would suffer, were it to be deprived of the particular asset in question' (1937: 227) remains the guiding principle.

Its basic method is to establish the minimum loss which a firm would suffer if it were deprived of an asset: this is taken as a measure of the value of the benefits conferred by ownership of the asset.

(Whittington, 1983: 131; cf. Edwards *et al.*, 1987: 39)

That is the approach adopted in the Sandilands Report.

There are only three alternative general bases of the valuation of an asset:
(i)   The current purchase price (replacement cost) of the asset (RC);
(ii) The net realisable value (or current disposal value) of the asset (NRV); and
(iii) The present value of the expected future earnings from the asset or 'economic value' (PV).

(1975: 58)

These three bases describe the complete range of possible bases of estimating the 'value' of an asset, reflecting the fact that it may be either bought, disposed of, or held.

(1975: 26)

In cases where NRV is higher than PV, 'the firm would be better off by disposing of the asset' (1975: 59). In cases where PV is higher than NRV, 'the firm would be better off by using the asset' (1975: 59). Since the benefit of ownership of an asset (its 'net revenue') is the higher of PV from use or NRV from disposal, the loss of this benefit – or 'netback value' (Stamp, 1971: 285) – can be described as the 'net revenue loss' (NRL); so that

NRL = NRV or PV, whichever is higher.

Loss of an asset, however, does not necessarily involve a loss as great as the NRL.

The amount required to purchase another asset is the maximum loss the firm would suffer if it were suddenly deprived of the existing asset, . . . since by purchasing another asset of the same type the firm will restore the opportunity to gain the NRV by disposing of it . . . [or] the opportunity to use it to generate earnings to the amount denoted by PV.

(Sandilands, 1975: 59; cf. Solomons, 1966: 123, 124;
Parker and Harcourt, 1969: 17; Stamp, 1971: 285)

If, on the other hand, the replacement cost is *greater* than the net revenue loss, 'the firm cannot gain as much by either using the asset or disposing of it as it would cost to replace it. If the firm were suddenly deprived of the asset, the maximum loss it would suffer . . . will be the higher of PV and NRV' (Sandilands, 1975: 59).

Any individual asset could be valued on each of these three alternative bases (RC, NRV and PV). However, there are six, and only six, ways in which valuations of an asset on these three bases can be ranked in order of magnitude.

(1975: 58; see Table 6.1)

In its *Statement of Principles for Financial Reporting*, the Accounting Standards Board expresses the same view.

The current value of an asset could be determined by reference to entry value (replacement cost), exit value (net realisable value) or value in use (discounted present value of the cash flows expected from continuing use and ultimate sale by the present owner). . . . Current value is at its most relevant when it reflects the loss that the entity would suffer if it were deprived of the asset involved. That measure, which is often referred to as the 'deprival value' or the 'value to the business', will depend on the circumstances involved. . . . This can be portrayed diagrammatically as follows:

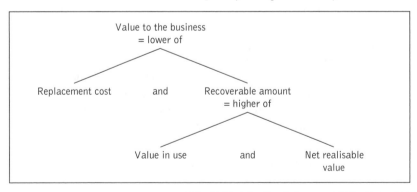

(ASB, 2005: 59, 60; cf. Baxter, 1975: 126, 131)

In terms introduced earlier in this chapter, 'value to the business' according to the ASB deprival value formula, is equal to

replacement cost (RC) or net revenue loss (NRL), whichever is lower.

Table 6.1 *Basis of valuation of assets (per Sandilands, 1975: 58)*

Six possible cases					Consequence			Deprival value
1	NRV*	>	PV	>	RC	NRL	>	RC	RC
2	NRV*	>	RC	>	PV	NRL	>	RC	RC
3	PV*	>	RC	>	NRV	NRL	>	RC	RC
4	PV*	>	NRV	>	RC	NRL	>	RC	RC
5	RC	>	PV*	>	NRV	RC	>	NRL	NRL (= PV)
6	RC	>	NRV*	>	PV	RC	>	NRL	NRL (= NRV)

* Indicates NRL (i.e. higher of NRV or PV).

This bears a very strong resemblance to the traditional 'lower of cost or market value' accounting rule:

historical cost (HC) or net revenue loss (NRL), whichever is lower.

A switch from historical cost (HC) to current replacement cost (RC) as the basis of asset valuation can conveniently be presented as a simple process of 'evolution rather than revolution'. 'We should emphasise that our proposals are evolutionary rather than revolutionary. They represent a development of the existing conventions of accounting . . . and . . . do not involve any fundamentally new principles of accounting' (Sandilands, 1975: 160).

The evolutionary nature of the proposals is a refrain of the various exposure drafts leading up to the final version of the *Statement of Principles for Financial Reporting* (ASB, 2005: 13–99). It is still regarded as one of the most powerful arguments in favour of a system of accounting based on current cost. The beauty of the ASB version of deprival value is that it appears to achieve a perfect combination of practical convenience and theoretical respectability. In that perspective, the rejection of *SSAP 16* (discussed in the previous chapter) can be seen as the throwing out of the deprival value baby with the inflation accounting bathwater; and it is a fertile source of recrimination. 'There is widespread ignorance of the work of early writers on inflation accounting, and many of those participating in the debate do not know the origins of the ideas which they are discussing' (Tweedie and Whittington, 1984: 318).

This is, however, a dangerous stone to throw – particularly when one's own house is so conspicuously made of glass. 'The origins of [what is variously known as "value to the owner", "opportunity value" or "deprival value"] appear to be in the United States in the 1920s' (Whittington, 1983: 131; cf. Edwards *et al.*, 1987: 39).

Since the deprival value concept is particularly associated with the work of the 'Austrians', Menger, Böhm-Bawerk and Wieser in the 1870s and 1880s, the conventional academic wisdom is out by several thousand miles and at least half a century. 'Ignorance of the work of early writers' is probably the single most important source of error in the ASB's corruption of the concept.

DEPRIVAL VALUE: THE NINETEENTH-CENTURY ORIGINAL

Menger attributes 'the circumstance that a good has value . . . to the fact that command of it has for us the significance of satisfying a need that would not be provided for if we did not have command of the good' (1871: 119). The value of a good to its owner is therefore measurable by reference to the consequences 'if some accident were to deprive him of one of his . . . goods' (1871: 132).

Where assets are replaceable at will, measurement of the consequences of their deprival is fairly simple, even if they are 'complementary goods'.

> Where some individual members of the group are . . . replaceable by other goods of the same kind . . . , [they] are [in the event of their loss] simply replaced by others. . . . Even if they are needed as complements, [they] can never obtain any higher than their 'substitution value' – viz. [in modern terminology, the lower of their cost of reproduction or the loss of their contribution] in those branches of employment from which the replacing goods are obtained.
>
> (Böhm-Bawerk, 1888: 172, 173)

But that is dependent on the assumption that 'the great majority [of assets] are marketable commodities, and replaceable at will' (1888: 175).

Where individual complementary assets are not 'replaceable at will', it may be necessary to resort to the method of imputation suggested by Wieser.

> If we take . . . accurately into account . . . the amount of the products, their value, and the amount of the means of production employed at the time, . . . we obtain a number of equations . . . according to the number of individual productive combinations.
>
> (1889: 87, 88)

In modern terminology, the 'productive contributions' imputed to scarce factors by Wieser are the 'shadow prices' which emerge as a by-product of the linear programming solution (see Baumol, 1961: ch. 5). However, the complications of shadow pricing arise only where there is more than one scarce factor. They are mentioned simply as an indication that the nineteenth-century writers recognized the possibility of a loss of revenue *greater than* the net realizable value from the disposal of the item itself. Where no replacement or substitute can be acquired, other than by being withdrawn from employment in a less profitable opportunity, the net revenue loss arising from curtailment of the other opportunity (the so-called 'opportunity cost') is part of the 'adverse consequences of deprival'.

There are two later contributions to the 'nineteenth-century' version of deprival value: Canning's 'service principle' and Bonbright's 'incidental-loss factor'.

According to Canning's 'service principle', the consequence of deprival is not so much the absence of the asset itself but the loss of its services. 'It is the assured, separable service-series, not the agent rendering them, that constitutes the essence of enterprise assets' (1929: 188). Consequently, the 'upper limit' is not necessarily as great as the cost of an identical replacement asset. It may be the cost of obtaining the lost services 'by the most economical alternative means' (1929: 243). The service principle is emphasized by Solomons.

> The loss which results to an owner from being deprived of his asset . . . is the minimum cost of replacing the *services rendered by his asset*. . . . Replacement cost, as now defined, sets an upper limit on the value of an asset to its owner.
>
> (Solomons, 1966: 124)

The importance of this redefinition is widely recognized. 'It is essential . . . to interpret current replacement cost not as the cost of replacing the actual physical asset used by the firm but as the cost of currently acquiring the *services* provided by the asset' (Parker and Harcourt, 1969: 19; cf. Baxter, 1975: 131). In that case, the deprival value (DV) is equal to the net substitution cost (NSC) even though the replacement cost (RC) is higher.

Although the 'service principle' is well understood (e.g. Whittington, 1983: 118), the complexity associated with *ED 18*'s 'modern equivalent asset' (mentioned in the previous chapter) is an indication of the practical difficulties involved. The *Statement of Principles for Financial Reporting* (ASB, 2005: 13–99) is remarkably quiet on the subject.

Bonbright's 'incidental-loss factor' indicates that the inference that property cannot be worth more than its replacement cost 'is not invariably valid'.

> Owners and prospective buyers of property cannot secure substitutes instantaneously; sometimes the delay is serious, not to say fatal. In consequence, property which is now available may be worth much more than the cost of a substitute which would be quite as satisfactory save for the fact that it cannot be secured until a future date.
>
> (1937: 157)

The cost of reproduction constitutes the upper limit of the value of an asset only 'so long as its reproduction is possible and the satisfaction of want is not prejudiced by the delay' (Wieser, 1889: 177). A clear example is 'a haberdasher . . . deprived of his supply of straw hats, irreplaceable until the end of the summer' (Bonbright, 1937: 158).

> In extreme cases, the time factor is so important that, were the . . . owner to be deprived of the property, he would not find it worth while to secure a substitute. In such cases, replacement cost should be completely ignored . . . , and the property must be valued as if it were unique.
>
> (1937: 158)

In that case, the deprival value (DV) is equal to the net revenue loss (NRL) even though the replacement cost (RC) is lower.

The nineteenth-century original, therefore, gives rise to the following formula for deprival value (DV):

DV = net substitution cost (NSC) + net revenue loss (NRL).

Before contrasting this with the ASB version, however, it is instructive to consider the role of deprival value.

DEPRIVAL VALUE AS A GUIDE TO ECONOMIC DECISIONS

As its name implies, deprival value is a measure of the consequences of deprivation. It is therefore relevant in the event of deprivation and at the date of deprivation. The calculation of fair compensation for insurance purposes is an obvious case. There is also a very important type of economic activity which involves a deliberate decision in favour of self-deprivation.

> Deprival value . . . has the great advantage of being the right figure for many everyday management decisions. . . . The owner['s] . . . two alternative courses are: (1) to continue in possession; or (2) not to continue in possession, e.g., to deprive himself of the asset by using it up on a job.
>
> (Baxter, 1975: 126)

The use of resources in production, as inputs for conversion into output, is, in effect, 'planned deprivation'. A decision whether or not to use a firm's assets must be guided by their deprival value in order to ensure that the cost of their use is justified by the benefit of the anticipated returns.

> Any error in valuation, *no matter in which direction*, misleads the management to their harm.
>
> (Canning, 1929: 259)

> Control will be at fault, as it will induce . . . either . . . a too limited or a too extensive employment.
>
> (Wieser, 1889: 93)

59

THE TWO VERSIONS COMPARED

According to the ASB deprival value formula (given earlier in this chapter),

> DV = replacement cost (RC) *OR* net revenue loss (NRL),
> whichever is lower.

According to the nineteenth-century original,

> DV = net substitution cost (NSC) *PLUS* net revenue loss (NRL),
> that would actually be incurred.

Suppose a firm owns a widget, which originally cost £120 to acquire. Its current replacement cost (RC) is £140, and its net realizable value on disposal (NRV) is £80. It can be used in either of two ways depending on how early it is introduced into the manufacturing process:

1 Early introduction: present value of subsequent net revenue (PV1) = £250.
2 Late introduction: present value of subsequent net revenue (PV2) = £225.

Equivalent services of the widget can be obtained in either of three ways:

1 Cheaper substitute: present value of acquisition cost (NSC1)   = £100.
2 Identical replacement: present value of acquisition cost (NSC2)   = £140.
3 Dearer substitute: present value of acquisition cost (NSC3)   = £170.

In all cases, PV > RC > NRV. This corresponds to Case 3 in Table 6.1. Consequently, according to the ASB formula, deprival value is equal to the replacement cost of £140.

The nineteenth-century version is dependent on the actual circumstances. Even in Case 3, there are many possibilities. The following five subcases are examples:

Case 3a: The cheaper substitute is available in time for early introduction into the manufacturing process:

> DV = NSC (£100) + NRL (£0) = £100.

Case 3b: The cheaper substitute is available but only in time for late introduction into the manufacturing process:

> DV = NSC (£100) + NRL (£25) = £125.

Case 3c: The only replacement available is the dearer substitute, but it can be obtained in time for early introduction into the manufacturing process:

> DV = NSC (£170) + NRL (£0) = £170.

Case 3d: The only replacement available is the dearer substitute, but it can be obtained in time only for late introduction into the manufacturing process:

$$DV = NSC\ (£170) + NRL\ (£25) = £195.$$

Case 3e: A replacement is available, but not in time even for late introduction into the manufacturing process:

$$DV = NSC\ (£0) + NRL\ (£250) = £250.$$

Suppose the firm's managers are considering an activity that requires the use of one widget. If the expected net revenue from the activity is £135 (and there are no other considerations), the ASB deprival value formula signals *rejection* of the activity on the ground that the net revenue is insufficient to cover the widget's 'value to the business' of £140. The nineteenth-century formula, by contrast, signals *acceptance* in Cases 3a and 3b.

If the expected net revenue from the activity is £145, the ASB deprival value formula signals *acceptance* of the activity on the ground that the net revenue is sufficient to cover the widget's 'value to the business' of £140. The nineteenth-century formula, by contrast, signals *rejection* in Cases 3c, 3d, and 3e.

In the majority of cases, it may well be that the cost of obtaining the lost services of the widget 'by the most economical alternative means' (Canning, 1929: 243) is the cost of a replacement that will be available in time to avoid any loss of net revenue. If so, the NSC = the RC of £140, and the NRL is zero, so that the DV = £140, whichever version is used. It is true that some of these subcases may be unlikely, but they are by no means unknown. There is also the possibility of a whole series of additional subcases where the NRL is based on the opportunity cost of withdrawing the widget from other activities (either present or future).

When it is compared with the nineteenth-century version, it is evident that the deprival value formula presented in the ASB's *Statement of Principles* (2005: 60) is not a reliable measure of 'value to the business'.

WHAT'S WRONG WITH THE ASB FORMULA?

It is true that 'there are six, and only six, ways in which valuations of an asset on these three bases [RC, NRV and PV] can be ranked in order of magnitude' (Sandilands, 1975: 58; see Table 6.1). 'The six cases listed exhaust all of the possible relationships between the three values so that the rules deal with all possible contingencies' (Whittington, 1983: 132).

The conclusion that 'the rules deal with all possible contingencies' is, however, a non-sequitur based on the false assumption that the three bases and their rankings are themselves exhaustive. The subcases in the previous illustration are ample evidence of the possibility of other contingencies.

61

It simply does not follow that 'by purchasing another asset of the same type the firm will restore the opportunity to gain the NRV by disposing of it . . . [or] the opportunity to use it to generate earnings to the amount denoted by PV' (Sandilands, 1975: 59). It is generally true, only on the false assumption that the services of assets are *always* 'replaceable at will' so that delays causing loss of revenue can *never* occur. The substance of what may be called the 'replaceability fallacy' is the mistaken belief that the replacement of the services of a lost asset is the same thing as the replacement of a lost opportunity.

The replaceability fallacy has been allowed to creep in, probably because the bases of valuation are presented by the Sandilands Report as purely hypothetical.

> It must be strongly emphasised that the choice of any of the three bases of valuation . . . does not imply any intention on the part of the company. In cases where written down replacement cost is the correct measure of asset valuation to adopt, there is no implication that the company intends to replace the asset. Equally, in cases where net realisable value is the correct measure of the value of an asset to a business, no intention to sell the asset is implied.
>
> (Sandilands, 1975: 60)

This is extremely odd, in view of the fact that the stated objective is to implement Bonbright's definition of value to the owner as 'the adverse value of the entire loss, direct and indirect, that the owner might expect to suffer if he were to be deprived of the property' (quoted by Sandilands, 1975: 58). If the owner has 'no intention' of acting on the 'bases of valuation', how can the 'bases of valuation' be considered relevant for measuring the expected consequences? 'Present costs of replacement have nothing to do with present valuations unless present replacements are contemplated' (Canning, 1929: 253).

Situations where replacements are possible, but not without some loss of net revenue, are fairly common, if not routine. It is, however, easy to see why the ASB may have chosen to disregard them.

It is the assumption that assets are 'replaceable at will' which provides replacement cost with its legitimacy as the 'upper limit' on deprival value. Without it, the modern version of deprival value as set out by the Sandilands Committee (1975: 58–60) and confirmed by the Accounting Standards Board (2005: 59, 60) loses both of its principal justifications: practical convenience and theoretical respectability.

In its proper role as a measure of the consequences of deprivation, deprival value is a useful tool for economic decisions. But it is essential that the consequences of deprivation are calculated accurately. The difference between the expected net revenue from an economic opportunity and the deprival value of any assets to be consumed is a reliable measure of the financial consequences of accepting that opportunity, however, *only if* deprival value is calculated according to the nineteenth-century original. If it is calculated according to the modern ASB corruption, there is a serious danger that it may 'mislead the management to their harm' (Canning, 1929: 259).

The fact that the ASB's 'modern corruption' of deprival value is liable to be misleading in its proper role as a guide to economic decisions is regrettable. But there is an objection that is far more serious than any inaccuracies in the method of calculation. It is the assumption that the deprival value concept is relevant for reporting financial performance.

DEPRIVAL VALUE AS A GUIDE TO FINANCIAL PERFORMANCE

Far more pertinent than any doubts over the accuracy of its calculation is the question: does 'deprival value' have any relevance for financial reporting *even if it is measured accurately*? Coming, as it does, from some of the most distinguished authorities on the subject, the answer is quite astonishing.

> Value to the owner has never been demonstrated to arise out of a particular information requirement of a potential user of financial reports, other than that of an insurer.
>
> (Whittington, 1983: 136; cf. Kay, 1977: 301)

Precisely!

In spite of all the controversy over which method of measuring 'value to the business' is 'relevant' for financial reporting, it has never been demonstrated that 'value to the business' has any relevance at all. It has simply been taken for granted.

> The Statement envisages that all gains and losses will be recognised in a performance statement. Furthermore, . . . realised profits may conceivably be shown alongside unrealised profits. . . . The terms 'gains' and 'losses' . . . include . . . gains and losses arising from . . . the remeasurement of assets and liabilities.
>
> (ASB, 2005: 95 and 47)

According to the ASB, 'the financial performance of an entity' includes 'the return it obtains on the resources it controls' (2005: 27). 'Under the accounting model described by the Statement . . . any surplus of gains over losses during a period represents a return *on* capital for that period' (2005: 66). Yet no serious attempt seems to have been made to substantiate the claim beyond repeating the self-evident fact that current values are more 'relevant' than historical costs for making economic decisions. Their exact relevance for financial reporting is never properly explained.

This is in spite of the fact that the dangers of using current costs have been well advertised over a long period. 'Without altering the selling situation at all any one of the items could, legitimately, be higher if the buying present or future position were *worse*' (Canning, 1929: 241).

An increase in costs could be reported as a 'gain', even if accompanied by an expected fall in revenues. This is a well-known absurdity of systems based on current cost.

'Suppose the sales remain the same,
  But input costs all rise,
There's one thing,' the Accountants said,
  'Which may cause some surprise:
We have to *raise* the value of
  The business enterprise!
            (*Accountancy*, April 1980: 126)

Throughout the inflation accounting debate, the absence of any convincing explanation became a standing joke within the profession.

The 'backwoodsmen' are reactionaries with the irritating habit of asking impertinent questions like 'what are inflation adjusted accounts actually supposed to mean?'. The 'inflation accounting experts' are progressives who, by virtue of much sophisticated argument, have so far managed to avoid giving an answer.

            (*Financial Times*, 16 January 1980)

The question is still unanswered in the ASB's *Statement of Principles for Financial Reporting* (2005: 13–99).

The reason why no answer is forthcoming may be that no answer is thought to be necessary. After all, a consensus appears to be well established. 'There is general agreement on the definition of income among the various schools of thought. . . . The problem centers around the method of determining wealth or well-offness' (Sterling, 1970: 19). The implication is that a change in economic value is the same thing as a change in economic well-offness. This is so obviously true that it seems pointless to question it. But, if it turns out to be false, then there is a new question that needs to be answered.

Is the quest for more accurate methods of measuring value the way forward; or is it a blind alley?

Part III

A theoretical blind alley*

INTRODUCTION

On the subject of performance reporting, perhaps the most highly regarded book published during the past half-century is *The Theory and Measurement of Business Income* (1961) by Edgar O. Edwards and Philip W. Bell.

The shift away from the 'revenue and expense view' towards the 'asset and liability view', which has been discernible from the start of the Financial Accounting Standards Board's 'Conceptual Framework Project' in the mid-1970s, probably owes much to the influence of Edwards and Bell. Within the bodies responsible for setting accounting standards, the so-called 'balance sheet perspective' seems to have become firmly entrenched.

> The IASB's conceptual framework adopts a balance sheet approach to recognition, whereby all the elements of financial statements are defined in terms of assets and liabilities, with the consequence that income recognition is a function of increases and decreases in net assets rather than the completion of acts of performance.
>
> (Ernst & Young, 2004: 73)

The core of *The Theory and Measurement of Business Income* is an extremely plausible argument equating business performance with value change. There is, however, no concept of the *nature* of income independent of its *measurement*. This leaves the impression of income measurement without an income concept. It is therefore entirely understandable that the standard-setting bodies have no concept of income. Accounting, once criticized as a practice without a theory, is in danger of becoming a *theory* without a theory.

---

* The reference to a 'blind alley' is borrowed from the title of the Sir Julian Hodge Accounting Lecture by R. Paterson of Ernst & Young (1998).

As a practical measure of a firm's performance, however, the change in the value of its net assets seems to offer welcome relief from endless academic controversy over the concept of income. For the past thirty years, accounting standards bodies have been engaged in a quest for a practical measure of asset value that is both 'reliable' and 'relevant'. The end of the line which has passed through current cost and current value may have been reached with the advent of 'fair value'.

Part III explains how a wrong turning into the theoretical blind alley of value change has finished up in the dead end of 'fair value accounting'.

Chapter 7

Value change: a wrong turning?

One of the most significant features of *The Theory and Measurement of Business Income* is the clean break that it makes with the tradition of seeking justification for the measurement of accounting profit by reference to the so-called 'economic concept of income'. 'Being subjective, this concept is by definition not susceptible to objective measurement' (Edwards and Bell, 1961: 25).

The approach adopted by Edwards and Bell is based on the view that the object of business enterprise is to create 'added value' by converting inputs into outputs of higher market value. Success implies the ability to create or seize opportunities ahead of the rest of the market, with the object, as Keynes remarked in a slightly different context, 'of securing profit from knowing better than the market what the future will bring forth' (1936: 170).

> Each asset arrangement or plan of operation signifies a series of expected dividends including, as a 'final dividend,' the expected market value of the assets remaining in the possession of the firm on the horizon date. . . . The firm's valuation of each dividend stream is a *subjective value*. . . . If the firm seeks to maximize profit, it is clear that the firm should select that composition of assets which, in the eyes of management, has the greatest subjective value.
>
> (Edwards and Bell, 1961: 34, 35)

Success depends on how far the subjective expectations receive ultimate confirmation in the form of objective market values.

'If these subjective expectations are correct . . . [they] will be converted into market value by the end of the plan; the market will then recognize the correctness of the subjective expectations by sharing them' (1961: 48). The conclusion follows with what appears to be inexorable logic.

> A concept of profit which measures truly and realistically the extent to which past decisions have been right or wrong and thus aids in the formulation of new ones is required. And since rightness or wrongness must, eventually, be checked in the

market place, it is changes in market values of one kind or another which should dominate accounting objectives.

(1961: 25)

The implication for performance reporting is clear. Since the ultimate destination of business activity is an objective market value, what could be more obvious in measuring progress towards that destination than the change in market value?

Edwards and Bell acknowledge that 'change in the market values of a firm's assets' is often suggested as a practical approximation to the subjective 'ideal'. 'Economists recognize that this deficiency cannot be remedied and suggest only that the change in the market values of a firm's assets is perhaps the best approximation' (1961: 25). Edwards and Bell themselves, however, go a great deal further. 'The change in market value, appropriately defined, is much more than an approximation; it is the ideal concept of short-run profit itself . . . [and can] be modified for long-run purposes' (1961: 25).

Irrespective of the precise interpretation of the term 'appropriately defined', measurement of business performance in terms of 'the change in market value' marks a switch of emphasis from the profit and loss account to the balance sheet.

THE BALANCE SHEET PERSPECTIVE

A shift away from the 'revenue and expense view' towards the 'asset and liability view' (FASB, 1976: 19) – from 'matching costs against revenues' towards 'an equity-change concept' (Alexander, 1948: 139, 140) – has been discernible from the start of the Financial Accounting Standards Board's 'Conceptual Framework Project' in the mid-1970s. That it is no longer considered necessary even to pay lip-service to the 'economic ideal' owes a great deal to the influence of Edwards and Bell. Within the bodies responsible for setting accounting standards, the balance sheet perspective seems to have become firmly entrenched. 'The overall profit or income for a period is equal to the change in recorded equity (net assets), after adjusting for transactions with owners' (Johnson and Lennard, 1998: 3).

The 'relevance' of asset values is a major preoccupation of the Accounting Standards Board's *Statement of Principles for Financial Reporting*.

Ownership interest is the residual amount found by deducting all of the entity's liabilities from all of the entity's assets. Gains are increases in ownership interest not resulting from contributions from owners. Losses are decreases in ownership interest not resulting from distributions to owners.

(ASB, 2005: 41)

The International Accounting Standards Board defines some gains and losses in terms of changes in 'fair value' (realizable in the market place). 'A gain or loss on a financial asset or financial liability classified as at fair value through profit or loss shall be recognised in profit or loss' (IASB, 2005: 1684; cf. JWG, 2000: 150).

The characteristic of the 'balance sheet perspective' is the notion that business performance can be measured in terms of 'the change in market value, appropriately defined' (Edwards and Bell, 1961: 25).

> What has emerged is the adoption of a particular balance sheet orientated model by the IASB and the FASB. It seems likely that this model has been adopted because it supports the use of fair values, the goal towards which it appears the IASB wants to move financial reporting.
>
> (Ernst & Young, 2004: 126)

'Fair value accounting' (which is the subject of Chapter 9) is just one of a rich variety of possibilities which depend on the particular choice of market value. The menu of *entry* and *exit* values for assets in different forms (initial, present, and ultimate) and at different dates (past, current, and future), offered by Edwards and Bell (1961: 77), fills an array of eighteen 'value concepts'. However, it is not necessary to examine details of the various alternatives to 'fair value', since they are all subject to the same fallacy.

A selling-point used by the Accounting Standards Board in its *Statement of Principles for Financial Reporting* is that accounts drawn up in accordance with their standards provide useful information on the rate of return obtained by an enterprise on the resources under its control.

> The objective of financial statements is to provide information about the reporting entity's financial performance and financial position that is useful . . . for making economic decisions. . . . The financial performance of an entity comprises the return it obtains on the resources it controls.
>
> (ASB, 2005: 24 and 27)

A similar claim is made by Edwards and Bell. 'The current operating profit rate . . . indicates the firm's true rate of return from operating net assets having a recognized current value' (Edwards and Bell, 1961: 267, 268).

An acid test for this type of claim has already been proposed in Chapter 3. If no assets are held other than cash, then *all* systems of accounting produce exactly the same result. It makes no difference whether they are based on entry, exit, historical, or current prices. This test can be used to demonstrate that the claims made on behalf of 'current cost', 'current cash equivalent', 'deprival value', 'value to the business', or 'fair value' are totally false.

THE ACID TEST

The flaw in the theory can be exposed by re-examining the accounts of Short-Term Exploitation Plc and Long-Run Development Plc in Chapter 3. The salient feature is that the managers of both firms intend to operate for three years and then to wind up their respective firms with a first and final cash distribution to investors. Based on the expected results of operations, the planned distributions at the end of the three years are £1,771,561 to investors in Short-Term Exploitation Plc and £2,985,984 to investors in Long-Run Development Plc.

During the three years, everything goes according to plan for both firms, and throughout the economy there are no price changes. Over the lifetime of their investment of £1 million, the rate of return realized by investors in Short-Term Exploitation Plc is therefore exactly 21 per cent per annum. For investors in Long-Run Development Plc, the rate of return is exactly 44 per cent per annum.

THE 'INTERNAL RATE OF RETURN' (IRR)

The rate of return over the lifetime of an investment is commonly known as the 'internal rate of return' or IRR.

> Bound up in the very structure of any net revenue series there is a rate of return which pertains to it, and which can be calculated if we know all the terms of the net revenue series and nothing else.
>
> (Boulding, 1935: 482)

> The rate of return in the enterprise is that rate of interest which will make the present values at any date of the revenues equal to the present value of the costs at the same date.
>
> (1935: 492)

It is equal to r in the equation:

$$\sum_{t=0}^{n} \frac{x_t}{(1+r)^t} = 0$$

where $x_0, {}_1, {}_2, {}_3, \ldots, {}_n$, is the net revenue series or equity cash flow.

A well-known difficulty with this equation is the possibility of multiple solutions. Provided that the series contains negative terms followed by positive terms, the solution is unique. Difficulties arise if the series contains either no change of sign or more than one change of sign. 'There may be no value which satisfies this equation . . . on the

Table 7.1 *Cash flow ('net revenue series') to investors*

	End of Year 0	End of Year 1	End of Year 2	End of Year 3
	£	£	£	£
Short-Term Exploitation Plc	−1,000,000	0	0	+1,771,561
Long-Run Development Plc	−1,000,000	0	0	+2,985,984

other hand . . . there may be a multiplicity of solutions of this equation' (Samuelson, 1937: 475).

In the case of the flow of contributions from and distributions to shareholders in a limited company, however, it is normally legitimate to adopt the assumption that 'the early terms of the series will in general be negative . . . the later terms of the series will normally be positive' (Boulding, 1935: 477, 478).

In the case of the two firms in the illustration, the 'net revenue series' is shown in Table 7.1.

For Short-Term Exploitation Plc, the IRR is therefore equal to ($\sqrt[3]{1.771561} - 1 =$) 0.21, or 21 per cent per annum. For Long-Run Development Plc, it is equal to ($\sqrt[3]{2.985984} - 1 =$) 0.44, or 44 per cent per annum.

It is important to emphasize that, in the choice between alternative investments of different risks and time shapes, the internal rate of return is *NOT* a magnitude which a rational investor should necessarily attempt to maximize (see Appendix B). The internal rate of return is, however, an accurate *description* of the average rate of return per period over the life of the investment (see Table 3.3).

Since 21 per cent per annum is the rate of return that has been both planned and achieved by Short-Term Exploitation Plc, any system of accounting which does *not* report the return on investors' capital as 21 per cent per annum for three years is neither 'true' nor 'fair'; and it fails by the 'Kaldor criterion' (see p. 4). A reported return for Short-Term Exploitation Plc of less than 21 per cent per annum is misleadingly low; a reported return of more than 21 per cent per annum is misleadingly high. Similarly, since 44 per cent per annum is the rate of return that has been both planned and achieved by Long-Run Development Plc, 44 per cent per annum is the rate that should be reported in its accounts.

That is why the internal rate of return is often described as the 'true yield' (Solomon, 1971: 165) or the 'true rate of return' (Kay, 1976: 459).

THE 'ACCOUNTANT'S RATE OF PROFIT' (ARP)

By contrast with the IRR, the conventional accounting return (otherwise known as the 'accountant's rate of profit' or ARP) is liable to be influenced by the time pattern of the firm's activity.

Table 7.2 *Expected and actual operations of two firms*

Batch	Short-Term Exploitation Plc		Long-Run Development Plc	
	Cash purchase of inputs	Cash sales of Lo-Vals	Cash purchase of inputs	Cash sales of Hi-Vals
	£	£	£	£
First	1,000,000	1,100,000	1,000,000 } Year 1	1,200,000
Second	1,100,000 }Year 1	1,210,000	1,200,000 } Year 2	1,440,000
Third	1,210,000	1,331,000	1,440,000	1,728,000
Fourth	1,331,000 } Year 2	1,464,100	1,728,000	2,073,600
Fifth	1,464,100	1,610,510	2,073,600 }Year 3	2,488,320
Sixth	1,610,510 } Year 3	1,771,561	2,488,320	2,985,984
Total	7,715,610	8,487,171	9,929,920	11,915,904

Details of each firm's activity (which are, revealingly, not necessary for the calculation of the IRR) are given in Table 3.1. They are reproduced in Table 7.2.

Over the three years, both firms achieve the same volume of activity – the manufacture and sale of six batches. The reason why the return on capital invested in Long-Run Development Plc – the IRR – is higher than the return on capital invested in Short-Term Exploitation Plc is that Hi-Vals with a 20 per cent margin are twice as profitable as Lo-Vals with a 10 per cent margin. (Owing to the reinvestment of the whole of the sale proceeds, however, Long-Run Development's IRR is *more* than twice as high as Short-Term Exploitation's.)

All purchases and sales are for cash, and there are no other revenues or expenses. Because there are no price changes of any kind, and because the only asset held at the balance sheet date is cash, it makes no difference whether the accounts are drawn up in terms of historical cost, current cost, deprival value, or fair value. *They all come to the same thing.*

Both firms' accounts for each of the three years are presented in Table 7.3. The accounts for Year 1 have already been given in Table 3.4; but they are accompanied by the accounts of Year 2 and Year 3.

The first-year accounts have already been criticized for presenting (as 'true and fair') a view that is seriously misleading. They show Short-Term Exploitation Plc with a greater balance sheet value and a higher accounting return than Long-Run Development Plc, even though the economic reality is quite the opposite. The investment of £1 million in Short-Term Exploitation is on its planned course of producing £1,771,561 at the end of three years; the same investment in Long-Run Development is on its planned course of producing £2,985,984. As an economic investment, Long-Run Development is undoubtedly superior because it promises *and delivers* larger returns to investors with

Table 7.3 The Accounting Return (ARP) reported in the accounts of Years 1, 2, and 3

Balance sheet at the end of Year 1	Short-Term Exploitation Plc		Long-Run Development Plc	
Equities	£		£	
Capital (at the beginning of the year)	1,000,000		1,000,000	
Revenue from sales *	3,641,000	(First	1,200,000	(First
Less: Cost of sales *	(3,310,000)	three batches)	(1,000,000)	batch only)
Profit (for the year)	331,000		200,000	
Total equities	1,331,000		1,200,000	
Assets	£		£	
Cash	1,331,000		1,200,000	
Total assets	1,331,000		1,200,000	

Accountant's rate of profit (ARP)

Accounting Return = $\dfrac{\text{Profit}}{\text{Capital}}$

$$\frac{£331,000}{£1,000,000} = 33.1\% \qquad \frac{£200,000}{£1,000,000} = 20.0\%$$

Balance sheet at the end of Year 2	Short-Term Exploitation Plc		Long-Run Development Plc	
Equities	£		£	
Capital and retained profit	1,331,000		1,200,000	
Revenue from sales *	3,074,610	(Next	3,168,000	(Next
Less : Cost of sales *	(2,795,100)	two batches)	(2,640,000)	two batches)
Profit (for the year)	279,510		528,000	
Total Equities	1,610,510		1,728,000	
Assets	£		£	
Cash	1,610,510		1,728,000	
Total assets	1,610,510		1,728,000	

Accountant's rate of profit (ARP)

Accounting Return = $\dfrac{\text{Profit}}{\text{Capital}}$

$$\frac{£279,510}{£1,331,000} = 21.0\% \qquad \frac{£528,000}{£1,200,000} = 44.0\%$$

■ **Table 7.3** *(Continued)*

Balance sheet at the end of Year 3†	Short-Term Exploitation Plc		Long-Run Development Plc	
Equities	£		£	
Capital and retained profit	1,610,510		1,728,000	
Revenue from sales *	1,771,561	(Last	7,547,904	(Last
Less: Cost of sales *	(1,610,510)	batch only)	(6,289,920)	three batches)
Profit (for the year)	161,051		1,257,984	
Total equities	1,771,561		2,985,984	
Assets	£		£	
Cash	1,771,561		2,985,984	
Total assets	1,771,561		2,985,984	
Accountant's rate of profit (ARP)				
Accounting Return = $\dfrac{\text{Profit}}{\text{Capital}}$	$\dfrac{£161,051}{£1,610,510} = 10.0\%$		$\dfrac{£1,257,984}{£1,728,000} = 72.8\%$	

* These details would normally appear in a separate profit and loss account.
† Immediately prior to the final distribution to investors.

exactly the same time pattern (at the end of three years) and with exactly the same degree of risk.

There is only one possible verdict: the first-year accounts give a totally misleading picture of what the ASB calls 'the return it obtains on the resources it controls' (2005: 27) – and, since the only balance sheet asset is cash, the method of valuation makes no difference.

THE SHORT-RUN IMPORTANCE OF THE ACCOUNTING RETURN

It is perfectly true that discrepancies between the ARP and the IRR will be 'ironed out' over the lifetime of an investment.

> Distortions in one year will be offset in due course by opposite distortions, so that it is essentially the timing of changes which is in error. The accountant's rate of profit, measured over a period of years, will be an acceptable indicator of the true rate of return: it is over a single year that it may prove seriously misleading.
>
> (Kay, 1976: 459)

Ample confirmation of this view is provided by Table 7.3 which covers all three years of both firms' life. Short-Term Exploitation's ARP in Year 1 which is *above* the IRR is 'offset' by its ARP in Year 3 which is *below* the IRR.

Over the whole three-year life of the firm, its discounted average ARP ($\sqrt[3]{(1.331 \times 1.21 \times 1.1)} - 1$) is exactly equal to the IRR of 21 per cent. (That is because the assumption of reinvestment of all profit creates a *special case* where a simple discounted average of the ARPs gives an accurate measure of the IRR. In the general case, it is necessary to employ the iterative procedure described by Edwards *et al.* (1987: 26) and discussed in Appendix B.) The same applies to Long-Run Development Plc. In Year 1, its ARP is *below* the IRR; in Year 3, it is *above* the IRR; over the whole three years, the discounted average ARP is exactly equal to the IRR of 44 per cent.

But it is precisely because information about each single year is regarded as crucially important that accounts are produced annually. Accountants, of all people, cannot take refuge in the long run.

> This *long run* is a misleading guide to current affairs. *In the long run* we are all dead. Economists set themselves too easy, too useless a task if in tempestuous seasons they can only tell us that when the storm is long past the ocean is flat again.
>
> (Keynes, 1923: 80)

On the basis of the first part of this passage taken out of context, Keynes is sometimes unfairly accused of disregarding the importance of the long run. It is clear, however, that the passage is simply a warning of the folly of overlooking the importance of the short run where decisions need to be made in the short run.

If the Year 1 accounts in Table 7.3 are used as a guide 'for making reasoned choices among alternative uses of scarce resources in the conduct of business and economic activities' (FASB, 1978: 5), they are so grossly misleading that resources are liable to be diverted from Long-Run Development of the Hi-Val business to Short-Term Exploitation of the Lo-Val business. By the time of the eventual 'correction' in Year 3, it is too late; the damage has been done.

Furthermore, the expectations of both firms' managers have been *confirmed* by the first year's operations. To report as 'true and fair' anything other than 21 per cent per annum for Short-Term Exploitation and 44 per cent per annum for Long-Run Development raises serious ethical questions, not only for managers and auditors, but also for standard setters.

The argument that, in the long run, the ARP for Year 1 will eventually be 'corrected' in the accounts of a subsequent period can be used to justify *any* figure – 50 per cent, 100 per cent, or even 500 per cent – as long as it is reversed at some date in the future. It still leaves the accounting return of 33.1 per cent without an explanation in its own right.

> Many types of error in ARR (viewed as an approximation to IRR) can be expected to average out . . .; but [this argument] does not purport to be a valid defence of ARR

as a measure of the performance of an individual firm in a single year. It is thus not of direct relevance to the problem of producing annual financial reports to the shareholders or other interested parties of a particular firm.

(Whittington, 1983: 46)

'Corrections' in the accounts of future periods are too late to be of much assistance to those who have already relied upon the accounts to mean what the accounting standards bodies say that they mean.

The first of the 'the objectives of the IASB', set out in the Preface to *International Financial Reporting Standards 2005*, is

to develop, in the public interest, a single set of high quality, understandable and enforceable global accounting standards that require high quality, transparent and comparable information in financial statements and other financial reporting to help participants in the various capital markets of the world and other users of the information to make economic decisions.

(IASB, 2005: 24)

This is amplified in the IASB's *Framework for the Preparation and Presentation of Financial Statements*.

The objective of financial statements is to provide information about the financial position, performance and changes in financial position of an entity that is useful to a wide range of users in making economic decisions. . . . To be useful, information must be relevant to the decision-making needs of users. . . . If there is undue delay in the reporting of information it may lose its relevance.

(2005: 36, 38, and 41)

'Corrections' in the accounts of subsequent periods hardly meet the IASB's requirement of 'timeliness', nor do they match the expectations of users.

The assessment of the performance of the business within each separate period is one of the main concerns of periodic accounts.

(Whittington, 1983: 59)

Accounting rates of profit are thus widely used, by economists and others, to assess the performance of activities such as firms, industries and entire sectors.

(Edwards *et al.*, 1987: 4)

Yet, for the conventional one-year accounting period, the accountant's rate of profit (ARP) – otherwise known as the 'book yield' – is liable to differ from the internal rate of return (IRR) – otherwise known as the 'true yield' or 'true rate of return'. As a consequence, the ARP is widely criticized for its inaccuracy as a measure of the return on capital.

> Any[one] . . . who compares rates of profit of different industries, or of the same industry in different countries, and draws inferences from their magnitudes as to the relative profitability of investments in different uses or countries, does so at his own peril.
>
> (Harcourt, 1965: 325)

Much of the blame for this sorry state of affairs has traditionally been placed on the difficulties of asset valuation; and it cannot be denied that asset valuation is often to blame. The peril encountered with a simple comparison between two firms with no assets other than cash, however, suggests that the obsession with asset valuation has been allowed to distract attention from a more fundamental weakness.

Chapter 8

Asset valuation: a convenient distraction?

The admission that the rates of return reported in published accounts are liable to be misleading, and that anyone who 'draws inferences from their magnitudes as to the relative profitability of investments in different uses or countries, does so at his own peril' (Harcourt, 1965: 325) is a source of considerable embarrassment to those engaged in the theory and practice of financial reporting. After all, a firm's published accounts are supposed to give 'a true and fair view' of its financial performance. 'Financial accounts are intended to report the economic performance of the firm to the individual shareholder or proprietor' (Whittington, 1983: 89, 90).

Since accounting standards bodies and academic theorists have spent at least half a century trying to improve the implementation of the system, it is not easy to accept that the effort may have been largely wasted because there is a serious flaw in the system itself. It is far more comforting to believe that the fault lies elsewhere. 'The principal difficulties in using accounting data are the result, not of fundamental deficiencies in accounting concepts, but in the practical application of these concepts' (Kay and Mayer, 1986: 206). It cannot be denied that 'the practical application of these concepts' is fraught with difficulty. But practical difficulties should not be used as an excuse to distract attention from 'fundamental deficiencies' in the concepts themselves. Placing the blame on practical difficulties serves two purposes. It implies that the theoretical basis is sound. It also keeps the standard-setting bodies in business, so to speak – as suppliers of solutions to the practical difficulties of valuation.

ECONOMY WITH THE TRUTH?

It has become something of a tradition to put the blame for discrepancies between the 'accountant's rate of profit' (ARP) and the 'true rate of return' (IRR) on the practical difficulties of asset valuation. Top of the list is the depreciation of fixed assets (including a choice between the straight-line, reducing balance, and several other methods).

The problems involved in using the ARP to assess the performance of an investment . . . arise from one particular feature of the accountant's method of measuring profitability, namely the use of more or less arbitrary depreciation charges in arriving at accounting profits and book value of capital employed.

(Edwards *et al.*, 1987: 20; cf. Hotelling, 1925; Preinreich, 1938; Lutz and Lutz, 1951: ch. 19; Wright, 1964; Harcourt, 1965)

Stock valuation (including a choice of fifo, lifo, and average cost) comes a close second.

It should be remembered that the valuation of stocks and work-in-progress is potentially an important source of such discrepancies: the existing literature tends to concentrate on the problems raised by the accounting valuation of fixed assets.

(Whittington, 1979: 208n)

A further complication is the question of whether overhead costs should be carried forward as part of the balance sheet value of stocks and work-in-progress or charged against profit as expenses of the accounting period. Controversy over the treatment of expenditure on research and development or on goodwill adds to the problems of asset valuation.

An object of particular criticism in the late 1960s and early 1970s was the discretion allowed in the choice of accounting method for the valuation of assets. The 'view' presented by published accounts could be seriously distorted by innocent mistakes, by legitimate differences of opinion, by a form of manipulation euphemistically known as 'creative accounting', or by deliberate fraud. 'The root of the problem lies in the wide range of choice open to management in the selection of accounting principles' (Stamp and Marley, 1970: 131).

Concern over the 'multiplicity of accounting principles' (and the opportunities thereby created for the unscrupulous) was a powerful stimulus to the establishment of the first accounting standards bodies. Most of the questions of asset valuation are now covered by accounting standards, but this may give a spurious impression of accuracy. Compliance with accounting standards cannot guarantee the accuracy of values which depend on the outcome of subsequent events; and (as Table 7.3 clearly demonstrates) accurate values cannot guarantee the reliability of conventional accounts as performance reports.

In addition to the valuation problems peculiar to different types of asset, the phenomenon of changing prices is a problem that affects them all. During the rapid inflation experienced in the 1970s, the focus of attention was on the danger that balance sheet values were getting 'out of date', and various alternative methods of 'inflation accounting' (discussed in Chapter 5) were proposed for stabilizing accounts.

All these arguments are, of course, perfectly valid. It is undeniable that the problem of asset valuation – particularly in a world of risk, uncertainty, imperfect markets, and changing prices – is a serious obstacle to a 'true and fair view'. Their 'economy with the truth' lies in the failure to mention that accounts could not be relied upon for a 'true and fair' view, *even if the problem of asset valuation did not exist.*

On closer examination, it turns out that conventional accounts depend for their truth and fairness as performance reports on a 'hidden assumption'.

THE HIDDEN ASSUMPTION: PERPETUAL REPETITION

The assumption behind the use of conventional accounts as performance reports is generally so well concealed that it escapes attention entirely. On rare occasions, however, it can be spotted.

> Present accounting practices would be fully valid only if prices, quantities, and qualities of both factors and products were unchanging over time, i.e., if there were a stable general price level (the first assumption), stable individual prices (the second assumption), and perfect certainty about the future (the third assumption). But this is a situation clearly akin to the stationary state.
>
> (Edwards and Bell, 1961: 9)

The first part of that passage is perfectly correct: there must be no change in prices, quantities, and qualities of either factors or products. But the list of assumptions is one short. There is a missing fourth assumption which is necessary to reproduce 'a situation clearly akin to the stationary state'. 'A stable volume of activity' is the assumption that has to be added to the other three in order to fulfil the proviso that 'quantities and qualities of both factors and products' must be 'unchanging over time'.

The missing assumption is, however, of crucial importance. It implies that, throughout the life of the firm, each accounting period will be an exact replica of every other: with a constant population of assets and the *perpetual repetition* of identical transactions. That would, indeed, be 'a situation clearly akin to the stationary state'.

The two firms in the previous chapter's illustration provide a clear example. In every accounting period, Short-Term Exploitation Plc would have to repeat the manufacture and sale of three batches of Lo-Vals and the distribution to investors of £331,000. Long-Run Development Plc would have to repeat the manufacture and sale of one batch of Hi-Vals and the distribution to investors of £200,000. The accounts of *every* period would then be a replica of those of the first year; and the ARP of each period would coincide exactly with the lifetime IRR.

The maintenance of a constant population of assets, guaranteed by the 'perpetual repetition' assumption, would prevent accounting conventions, however arbitrary, from distorting the accounts. As long as accounting practices were not altered between periods, the result would be an unchanging balance sheet and a perpetually repeating profit and loss account.

It is evident, therefore, that the ARP is a reliable measure of the return on an investment only if the 'perpetual repetition' assumption is fulfilled throughout the lifetime of the investment, so that each accounting period is a replica of every other.

Where the lifetime of the investment is exactly the same length as the accounting period, the 'perpetual repetition' assumption is automatically fulfilled (i.e. throughout the whole of the investment's single-period life). That is a special case where the ARP is equal to the IRR.

The origins of the modern system of accounting have been traced to the merchants of mediaeval Venice who chartered ships for their export–import business. Chapter 3 gives an illustration of 'venture accounts', which were not split into artificial accounting periods but covered the whole period of a voyage even if it lasted for several years (Roover, 1956: 156, 157).

If the two firms in the previous chapter's illustration had been wound up at the end of the first year and their assets (consisting entirely of cash) had been distributed to the investors, the accounting period could legitimately have been regarded as a 'single investment'. The ARP in Year 1 for both firms would be an accurate measure of the return on investors' capital. In the normal case, however, firms are 'going concerns' with a life beyond the end of the accounting period. To treat each accounting period as if it were a single investment would be to ascribe to the investors a discretion (to withdraw their capital *from the firm* at the end of the period) which they do not normally possess.

It is precisely because the hidden assumption of a stable volume of activity is *not* fulfilled that the discrepancy arises in Table 7.3 between the IRR and the ARP. In Year 1, for example, the manufacture and sale of the first three batches of Lo-Vals gives Short-Term Exploitation Plc an asset turnover of (£3,310,000/£1,000,000 =) 3.31 times. Since the margin of profit on Lo-Vals is 10 per cent, the accounting return is equal to 10 per cent multiplied by 3.31, or 33.1 per cent.

The influence of the volume of activity on the accounting return of both companies is explained by the calculations in Table 8.1. Since the margin of profit on Lo-Vals remains constant at 10 per cent, it is the fall in asset turnover which is responsible for the decline in its ARP over the three years. For Long-Run Development Plc, the margin of profit on Hi-Vals remains constant at 20 per cent. Again, it is evident that the increase in asset turnover is responsible for the rise of its ARP over the three years.

Edwards and Bell are not alone in emphasizing the necessity of the 'stable volume' assumption and then conveniently ignoring it. This oversight is vitally important in providing the rationale for adjusting accounts for changing prices.

> Outside the unrealistic conditions of the 'stationary state' (in which all prices remain constant), . . . historical cost accounts fail, in the presence of relative price changes but the absence of general inflation, to provide measures of value and income which are likely to be of use in assessing the economic performance of the accounting entity.
>
> (Whittington, 1983: 194)

But a stationary state implies a stable volume of activity. Once the missing condition is restored, it is clear that the previous quotation misses the point. It would be equally true and far more pertinent if it were rephrased.

Table 8.1 The influence of the volume of activity on the accounting return (ARP)

	Short-Term Exploitation Plc				Long-Run Development Plc			
	Margin of added value	×	'Activity' (asset turnover)	= Accounting Return (ARP)	Margin of added value	×	'Activity' (asset turnover)	= Accounting Return (ARP)
Year 1	10%	×	3.31 [£3,310,000/£1,000,000]	= 33.1%	20%	×	1.00 [£1,000,000/£1,000,000]	= 20.0%
Year 2	10%	×	2.10 [£2,795,100/£1,331,000]	= 21.0%	20%	×	2.20 [£2,640,000/£1,200,000]	= 44.0%
Year 3	10%	×	1.00 [£1,610,510/£1,610,510]	= 10.0%	20%	×	3.64 [£6,289,920/£1,728,000]	= 72.8%

Outside the unrealistic conditions of the 'stationary state' (in which all prices *and volumes* remain constant), . . . historical cost accounts fail, in the presence of volume changes but the absence of both relative price changes and general inflation, to provide measures of value and income which are likely to be of use in assessing the economic performance of the accounting entity.

It is then clear that the problem still exists *even in the absence of any price changes at all* simply if there are changes in the volume of activity. Consequently, adjusting for price changes cannot be sufficient to solve the problem of accounts which 'fail . . . to provide measures of value and income which are likely to be of use in assessing the economic performance of the accounting entity' (Whittington, 1983: 194).

The necessary condition for 'present accounting practices to be fully valid' is therefore 'perpetual repetition'. But 'perpetual repetition' is so unusual that its assumption is totally unrealistic. Can there be any justification for its use?

UNCERTAINTY AND THE FALLACY OF 'BAXTER'S BIKE'

There is, in fact, no justification for reporting performance on the (usually undisclosed) assumption that 'quantities, and qualities of both factors and products [are] unchanging over time'. Instead of a justification, however, there is an excuse. The excuse is that, since the future is uncertain, the safest course is to assume continuation of the past.

It is sometimes implied that support for this approach can be found in Professor Baxter's famous advice for dealing with uncertainty. 'As long as one cannot tell to which side a wobbly cyclist is likely to swerve, one had better assume that he will come straight on' (1971: 9). The advice itself is perfectly sound, but it cannot apply in circumstances where the cyclist has deviated from his original course and is now wobbling in a completely different direction. To assume a stable volume of activity in the face of directly contradictory evidence is therefore a gross abuse of the 'principle of Baxter's bike'.

The two firms in the illustration are both on their planned path. Short-Term Exploitation Plc is on a planned path of decreasing volume; Long-Run Development Plc is on a planned path of increasing volume. The return on capital reported in the first year's accounts is accurate only if the volume remains unchanged. Why should the performance of either firm be reported on the assumption of an outcome which is *neither planned nor expected*?

Economic uncertainty means that all businesses are, to varying degrees, 'wobbly'; but that is no excuse for ignoring changes of direction and for pretending that the previous course will be maintained. Professor Baxter's advice remains sound; but perhaps it needs to be supplemented. As soon as one can tell to which side a wobbly cyclist is swerving, one had better assume that he will *not* come straight on. The 'hidden assumption' that the business 'will come straight on' is responsible for some of the most pernicious economic effects of the conventional system of accounting.

THE ACCOUNTANT'S CONTRIBUTION TO THE TRADE CYCLE

What Baxter (1955) calls the 'accountant's contribution to the trade cycle' is portrayed as a stock valuation problem caused by price changes during the period between acquisition and sale. But the accountant's 'contribution' is far more pervasive than that. It can occur even when no stocks are carried and no prices change. The effect in such simple circumstances is shown in Table 7.3: where the activity of the period is above the lifetime average, the ARP is greater than the IRR; where the activity of the period is the same as the lifetime average, the ARP is equal to the IRR; and where the activity of the period is below the lifetime average, the ARP is smaller than the IRR.

The standard setters have no excuse for ignoring this characteristic inherent in accounts, for it is very well known. It is discussed, for example, by Solomon (1971), Whittington (1979: 205), and Edwards *et al*. (1987: 36). It is a standard feature of the financial 'ratio analysis' routinely presented in introductory textbooks (illustrated in Table 8.1).

The over-reporting of the return on capital during periods of higher-than-average activity and its under-reporting during periods of lower-than-average activity is a built-in feature of the conventional system of accounting. It has the destabilizing macro-economic effect of encouraging over-investment during a boom and under-investment during a recession.

It also has a micro-economic effect which can be even more damaging to economic growth.

THE ACCOUNTING INCENTIVE TO 'SHORT-TERMISM'

The conventional system of accounting has the distorting micro-economic effect of diverting resources away from more profitable expanding firms (like Long-Run Development Plc) in growth industries (like Hi-Vals) towards less profitable contracting firms (like Short-Term Exploitation Plc) in industries which are declining (like Lo-Vals). The fact that changing prices may make matters even worse should not obscure the essential point that the problem can occur *even if prices are stable*.

This aspect of the conventional system of accounting is largely responsible for what has come to be known as 'short-termism', where the decisions of managers are influenced by the accounting appearance rather than by the economic reality. That is because published accounts are normally the main instrument for evaluating managerial performance.

A manager entrusted with £1 million of investors' money may have the choice between either of two options:

(a) to invest in the Lo-Val business, with the expectation of an activity pattern like Short-Term Exploitation's, so as to return £1,771,561 to investors in three years' time; or, alternatively,

(b)   to invest in the Hi-Val business, with the expectation of an activity pattern like Long-Run Development's, so as to return £2,985,984 to investors in three years' time.

There is no doubt that the choice of option (b) is in the best interests both of investors and of the whole economy. For the manager, however, there is a dilemma. If he chooses option (a), the first-year accounts will report a return (ARP) of 33.1 per cent; if he chooses option (b), they will report a return of only 20 per cent. Since his performance (and that of his potential replacements) is likely to be evaluated on the basis of the accounts, there is a strong temptation to choose option (a). If he chooses option (b), he may well be vindicated 'in the long run'. But there is a considerable risk that he will have already lost his job on the strength of the 'poor performance' reported by the first-year accounts. In the long run, it is his career that would be dead – literally.

Warning is rarely given of the fact that conventional accounts cannot be interpreted as reports on economic performance *except on the assumption of an unchanging volume of activity*. Failure to disclose the hidden assumption can lead to a serious misallocation of economic resources: they are liable to be directed into the wrong places, in the wrong quantities, at the wrong time.

There is, however, an almost insurmountable obstacle to disclosure of the truth. It is the formidable power of deeply entrenched vested intellectual interests.

THE VESTED INTELLECTUAL INTERESTS

Too much research has been devoted to the development of accounting standards; and too many reputations have been too deeply committed. In order to save face, it is essential that any shortcomings should be blamed, not on the system itself, but on its practical implementation. It is no surprise that this has become established as the conventional wisdom (already quoted at the beginning of this chapter). 'The principal difficulties in using accounting data are the result, not of fundamental deficiencies in accounting concepts, but in the practical application of these concepts' (Kay and Mayer, 1986: 206).

The truth – amply demonstrated by the two firms used to illustrate this chapter and the previous one – is precisely the opposite. *The principal difficulties in using accounting data are the result, not of deficiencies in the practical application of accounting concepts, but of fundamental deficiencies in the concepts themselves.*

In the case of both firms in the illustration, all transactions are for cash, and the only asset held at the balance sheet date is cash. There are therefore no depreciation provisions, no stock valuations, nor any other arbitrary accounting allocations. In addition, there are no price changes of any kind whatever, nor are there any disappointed expectations. Furthermore, the accounts have been drawn up in strict accordance with the highest accounting standards. *The possibility of 'creative' accounting through deliberate manipulation by dishonest individuals does not therefore arise.* Yet the rate of return reported in the accounts gives a totally misleading view of the rate of return actually earned on investors' capital.

85

This illustrates the danger of using conventional accounting information for performance reporting. *Even if there are no arbitrary accounting allocations, no creative accounting, no price changes, and no unfulfilled expectations, discrepancies between the ARP and the IRR can still occur.*

In short, the undoubted practical difficulties of asset valuation have been used almost as a cover-up to conceal fundamental flaws in the accounting system itself. However accurate the asset values may be, they are still liable to be seriously misleading if used for calculating gains and losses. For the fundamental flaw in the system is that value change is not appropriate as a measure of economic performance.

To strive after an ideal method of asset valuation, though worthwhile for its own sake, is to remain obstinately stuck in a theoretical blind alley. Even if the system of 'fair value accounting' being implemented by the International Accounting Standards Board achieves the goal of an economically ideal method of asset valuation, it is the wrong goal for performance measurement. It takes financial reporting into a dead end.

Chapter 9

Fair value accounting: a dead end?

Finding themselves in a blind alley, the accounting standards bodies are clearly determined to press on as far as they can. 'The use of fair values [is] the goal towards which it appears the IASB wants to move financial reporting' (Ernst & Young, 2004: 126). And 'fair value accounting' is about as far as it is possible to go. The fair value model relies on a concept of value that comes close to the 'theoretical ideal' of determination by the forces of a freely competitive market.

> *Fair value* is the amount for which an asset could be exchanged, or a liability settled, between knowledgeable, willing parties in an arm's length transaction.
>
> (IASB, 2005: 1672)

Since the IASB regards 'the existence of published price quotations in an active market [as] the best evidence of fair value' (2005: 1722), it is no surprise that high on the list of candidates for the fair value treatment are 'financial instruments'. *IAS 32* covers their 'Disclosure and Presentation' (IASB, 2005: 1231–1320), and *IAS 39* covers their 'Recognition and Measurement' (IASB, 2005: 1657–1939).

ACCOUNTING FOR FINANCIAL INSTRUMENTS

Financial instruments are financial rights or financial obligations defined by contract.

> A *financial instrument* is any contract that gives rise to a financial asset of one entity and a financial liability or equity instrument of another entity. . . . Financial instruments include primary instruments (such as receivables, payables and equity instruments).
>
> (*IAS 32*: 1241 and 1268)

Examples include 'cash', an 'equity instrument of another entity', 'a contractual right to receive cash . . . from another entity', and 'a contractual obligation to deliver cash . . . to another entity' (*IAS 32*: 1241, 1242).

The 'fair value' of a financial instrument is defined by reference to its current exit price in a competitive market: 'the amount for which an asset could be exchanged, or a

liability settled, between knowledgeable, willing parties in an arm's length transaction'
(*IAS 39*: 1672).

> The existence of published price quotations in an active market is the best evidence
> of fair value and when they exist they are used to measure the financial asset or financial
> liability.
>
> (*IAS 39*: 1722)

Where appropriate market information is not available, other techniques are allowed.

> If the market for a financial instrument is not active, an entity establishes fair value
> by using a valuation technique . . . [including] discounted cash flow analysis and option
> pricing models.
>
> (*IAS 39*: 1723)

In that case, however, there is some doubt on the exact nature of the result.

> What is described as a 'mark-to-market' basis, with all the relevance and reliability
> the term implies, is in reality a 'mark-to-model' basis, which is actually hypothetical.
> . . . Fair values attributed to assets that do not have readily available market prices,
> may be subjective to a degree that is not always understood.
>
> (Ernst & Young, 2004: 126 and 75)

It seems eminently reasonable that this should be recognized 'by choosing a different
term . . . for instance "calculated value"' (Ernst & Young, 2004: 125).

Whatever technique is used, however, the IASB takes the view that the measurement
of financial instruments should be a reflection of their exit value in a freely competitive
market.

> The objective of using a valuation technique is to establish what the transaction price
> would have been on the measurement date in an arm's length exchange motivated by
> normal business considerations.
>
> (*IAS 39*: 1723)

The claim traditionally made on behalf of current exit value is its 'relevance'.

> The single financial property which is uniformly relevant at a point of time for all
> possible future actions in markets is the market selling price or realizable price of any
> or all goods held. Realizable price may be described as *current cash equivalent*.
>
> (Chambers, 1966: 92)

> The present market price is relevant to all decision theories. . . . The periodic reports
> ought to show the current (exit) values at the time the report is prepared.
>
> (Sterling, 1970: 359 and 361)

Nevertheless, for the time being at least, the IASB seems to prefer the argument in favour of restricting 'fair value accounting' to financial instruments.

> Financial instruments represent contractual rights or obligations to receive or pay cash or other financial instruments or residual interests in the net assets of an enterprise. Non-financial items have a more indirect, non-contractual relationship to future cash flows. . . . They must be used in a productive activity, and effectively transformed into goods or services, which must be sold, before there is any right to receive cash.
>
> (Joint Working Group of Standard Setters, 2000: 167)

This is a purely practical consideration, however, and has no visible means of conceptual support.

> There is . . . no foundation in business or economic reasoning for drawing a distinction between 'fixed assets' and current assets on the ground that the former are 'not held for sale or for conversion into cash.' . . . The acquisition of any non-monetary asset is the initiation of a process which is consummated only when the asset is converted into cash, by the sale of the services or products of the asset or of the asset itself.
>
> (Chambers, 1966: 198 and 205)

Chambers is remarkable for the logical consistency of his approach. There is, however, one area in which he seems to depart from the principles of his 'continuously contemporary accounting' (affectionately known as CoCoA).

> The contractual amount of the bonds outstanding at any time is the amount of the debt then to be shown. . . . The company . . . may buy in its bonds to its advantage. But, until it does so, the market price may be regarded only as indicating a possibility of gain.
>
> (Chambers, 1966: 290)

Since this is the one area avoided by the strongest claimant to the title of 'father' of fair value accounting, it is odd that the IASB has chosen to plunge in with both feet. It has done so in defiance of a clear warning of the absurdity that is likely to result.

> One of the more controversial aspects of the fair value option is that in determining the fair value of a financial liability, the credit risk associated with the instrument should be taken into account. This can result in the rather counter-intuitive result of a financially distressed entity reporting significant gains as the fair value of its debt deteriorates (and vice versa).
>
> (Ernst & Young, 2004: 1028)

89

For the purpose of this chapter, however, there is no need to become involved in the argument over what should or should not be included. Even if fair value accounting is restricted to financial instruments over which there is no controversy, the flaw in the fair value model can clearly be identified.

FAIR VALUE ACCOUNTING AND THE ACID TEST

The essence of 'fair value accounting' is that changes in the fair value of financial instruments classified as 'at fair value through profit or loss' are to be reported as 'income'.

> Interest, dividends, losses and gains relating to a financial instrument or a component that is a financial liability shall be recognised as income or expense in profit or loss.
>
> *(IAS 32*: 1249)

> A gain or loss on a financial asset or financial liability classified as at fair value through profit or loss shall be recognised in profit or loss.
>
> *(IAS 39*: 1684)

The crucial question is whether or not fair value accounting can achieve its stated objective 'to enhance financial statement users' understanding of the significance of financial instruments to an entity's financial position, performance and cash flows' (*IAS 32*: 1239).

The two firms used to illustrate the previous two chapters, once again, provide the acid test. They have no assets other than cash; and cash is the 'financial instrument' *par excellence* whose 'fair value' is never in doubt. The conventional accounts in Table 7.3 therefore require no alteration whatsoever to convert them to fair value.

Consequently, the verdict of the previous two chapters applies to accounts drawn up on the basis of fair value: they are liable to report a return on capital that may be seriously misleading, and they create a positive incentive to 'short-termism' because the reported 'fair value' return is distorted by the volume of activity.

But why should this be so? After all, fair value accounting is about as close as it is possible to get to what has become established as the theoretical ideal. 'Ultimately, the assessment of profitability depends on being able to measure the present value of expected future returns from a collection of assets, and attaches significance to the difference between consecutive estimates of this' (Kay, 1977: 307). This, however, is a manifestation of the 'present value fallacy' which is based on a false inference from investment theory.

THE PRESENT VALUE FALLACY

In a perfect capital market, where it is possible to borrow or lend without restriction at the market rate of interest, a higher present value can be converted into a greater consumption stream *of any time shape* than can a lower present value. *Irrespective of individual subjective preferences*, therefore, the optimal investment strategy is to choose the investment with the highest net present value.

Although the net present value decision rule is frequently misapplied (as explained in the next chapter), the rule itself is perfectly valid. What is false, however, is the inference (frequently, but mistakenly, drawn) that growth in present value *over a period* is a reliable measure of economic performance. Because an investor is better off with a bigger present value than with a smaller present value *at any given moment*, it does not *necessarily* follow that the investor becomes better off as a result of an increase in present value *over a period of time*.

Geometric proof of the present value fallacy is provided in Appendix C by means of 'Fisher diagrams'. However, for purposes of the present argument, a simple illustration is sufficient.

The Fair Value Company operates in an economic utopia of perfectly competitive markets. It is therefore possible 'to obtain present values by observing prices in these markets' (Whittington, 1983: 128), and subjective present values are equal to objective market values. In the terminology used by Edwards and Bell (1961: 77), there are no differences between *entry* and *exit* prices in any market. Asset valuation is greatly simplified by the fact that, in these (totally unreal) perfect market conditions, all values are 'fair values'.

With the (perfect) market rate of interest at 8 per cent per annum, the Fair Value Company invests the whole of its investors' capital of £100 million in various equity shareholdings. The cash returns expected by the market from these 'financial instruments' total £8 million per annum. The company has no other assets or liabilities.

At the current market rate of interest of 8 per cent per annum, the 'fair' market value of the expected cash returns of £8 million per annum is equal to their present value of (£8m/0.08 =) £100 million.

Suppose an 'event' occurs – perhaps fear of a previously unexpected economic recession. Suppose this event causes (1) the market expectation of the annual dividends to be revised downwards to £5.5 million, and (2) the monetary authority to lower the rate of interest to 5 per cent per annum. As a consequence, the market value of the company's financial instruments rises from (£8m/0.08 =) £100 million to (£5.5m/0.05 =) £110 million.

The £10 million 'windfall' increase in the fair value of the company's 'financial instruments' is based on observable market prices. According to *IAS 39*: 1684, it is to be reported as a 'gain'.

Since these financial instruments constitute the whole of the company's net assets, the market value of the company's share capital also rises from £100 million to £110 million. Investors in the Fair Value Company therefore have the opportunity of selling their shares and spending £10 million more than they could before the 'event'.

From every point of view, it looks like an open-and-shut case in favour of *IAS 39* and reporting a gain of £10 million – but appearances can be deceptive.

Only if the investors *actually* take the opportunity of realizing the market value and spending it immediately, are they able to spend £10 million more than they could before the 'event'. If they save for one year before actually spending, the extra spending made possible by the 'event' is only £7.5 million; and the equivalent present sum (at 5 per cent per annum) at the balance sheet date is £7.1 million.

Table 9.1 (adapted from Rayman, 2004: 82, 83) shows that the effect of the 'event' on investors depends on how long they choose to save. For investors intending to save for more than $3\frac{1}{2}$ years, the effect of the fall in the rate of interest from 8 per cent per annum to 5 per cent per annum outweighs the initial increase in fair value.

The right-hand column of Table 9.1 indicates how the 'windfall' gain or loss varies with the length of the chosen saving period.

If all the investors intend to save for, say, three years, the 'event' increases the amount available for spending at the end of the third year by £1.4 million. To produce this increase without the 'event', the 'windfall' that would be required at the balance sheet date (in order to accumulate at 5 per cent per annum for three years) amounts to £1.2 million.

If all the investors intend to save for eight years, the 'event' reduces the amount available for spending at the end of the eighth year by £22.6 million. To cover this shortfall, the compensation that would be required at the balance sheet date (in order to accumulate at 5 per cent per annum for eight years) amounts to no less than £15.3 million.

To report a gain of £10 million in such circumstances is neither true nor fair.

THE IRRELEVANCE OF VALUE CHANGE

The fair value approach suffers from the same flaw as all the value-change approaches to performance reporting. It has nothing to do with the accuracy or 'fairness' of the valuation. It is failure to appreciate that a market value, however 'fair', simply represents an opportunity. If the opportunity is not actually taken, then it is a rejected opportunity; and, however good or bad it might have been, it has no economic relevance once it has been rejected.

The fact that investors in the Fair Value Company have the *opportunity* of consuming an extra £10 million, *if they choose to consume the whole present value immediately*, has no effect whatsoever on their 'well-offness' if they choose *not* to do so. It is also a reason why the current basis for taxing so-called 'capital gains' is both economically inefficient and socially inequitable.

Nevertheless, the argument in favour of current market value sounds extremely persuasive. 'The single financial property which is uniformly relevant at a point of time for all possible future actions in markets is the market selling price or realizable price of any or all goods held' (Chambers, 1966: 92). Once that 'point in time' has passed, however, the market price represents a rejected opportunity – a transaction that could have happened, but didn't. The very fact that an item appears in a firm's balance sheet is incontrovertible proof that it has *not* been exchanged.

This point is so crucial for financial reporting that it is worth repeating the nature of the fallacy.

> Because an investor is better off with a bigger present value than with a smaller present value *at any given moment*, it does not *necessarily* follow that the investor becomes better off as a result of an increase in present value *over a period of time*.

That is the reason why an increase in fair value cannot necessarily be reported as a 'gain': some investors may be worse off as a result.

It is important to make clear the reason for criticizing fair value accounting. The *disclosure* of fair values (in the balance sheet, for example) is a development to be welcomed; the objection is to reporting *changes* in fair value as gains or losses (whether through profit and loss, direct to equity, or in any other way). An accounting standard which generates a fair value 'gain' of £10 million in response to a fall in the expected annual returns from the Fair Value Company's net assets from £8 million to £5.5 million does not inspire confidence. The 'event' is certainly responsible for an increase in the fair value of the company's net assets from £100 to £110 million. But a gain of £10 million is a 'true and fair view' of the result *on one assumption only*: that the fair value is realized and *actually* consumed at the balance sheet date. The most common reason for investing, however, is to save for the future. *Of all the assumptions that could have been chosen, immediate consumption is the least likely.* It is ruled out almost by definition.

The possibility that 'movements in opposite directions of the market value of the securities and their yield will cause some shareholders to feel better off and others worse' (Paish, 1977: 181) should not be dismissed as a curiosity. It has extremely serious practical implications for pensions and savings. 'Although this has the one-off effect of raising the value of outstanding bonds, it forces insurers to reinvest maturing bonds and new premiums at lower yields' (*The Economist*, 16 January 1999: 77).

'Fair value accounting' is about as far as it is possible to go down the theoretical blind alley of value change as a measure of performance – and it has turned out to be a dead end. But that is not all. The nature of the dead end makes it clear that the journey has also been circular. The unresolved problems of financial reporting have their origin in the theoretical controversy discussed in Chapter 4 and thought to have been settled decades ago.

Table 9.1 The effect on investors of a reported fair value 'gain' of £10 million

Length of saving period	Actual spending prospect before the 'event' £ million	Actual spending prospect after the 'event' £ million	Change in actual spending caused by the 'event' £ million	Present value at the balance sheet date of the change £ million
If spent immediately	100.0	110.0	+ 10.0	+ 10.0
Interest for 1st year	+ 8.0	+5.5		
If saved until end of 1st year	108.0	115.5	+ 7.5	+ 7.1
Interest for 2nd year	+ 8.6	+ 5.8		
If saved until end of 2nd year	116.6	121.3	+ 4.7	+ 4.2
Interest for 3rd year	+ 9.3	+ 6.0		
If saved until end of 3rd year	125.9	127.3	+ 1.4	+ 1.2
Interest for 4th year	+10.1	+ 6.4		
If saved until end of 4th year	136.0	133.7	– 2.3	– 1.9
Interest for 5th year	+ 10.9	+ 6.7		
If saved until end of 5th year	146.9	140.4	– 6.5	– 5.1
Interest for 6th year	+ 11.8	+ 7.0		
If saved until end of 6th year	158.7	147.4	– 11.3	– 8.4
Interest for 7th year	+ 12.7	+ 7.4		
If saved until end of 7th year	171.4	154.8	– 16.6	– 11.8
Interest for 8th year	+ 13.7	+7.7		
If saved until end of 8th year	185.1	162.5	– 22.6	– 15.3

Note: Whether investors choose to finance their spending

(1) by selling their shares immediately and reinvesting the proceeds at the market rate of 5 per cent per annum;

or (2) by continuing to hold them until the date of actual spending,

it makes no difference to the impact on their *actual* spending as shown in the table.

Mathematical note:

Since patterns of consumption vary widely, there is no general formula for calculating the time beyond which an initial change in present ('fair') value is outweighed by an opposite change in the rate of interest at which it accumulates. If the intention of investors is to defer consumption of the whole amount for *n* periods, however, the 'crossover point' occurs when

$$\frac{r_1}{i_1} \times (1 + i_1)^n = \frac{r_2}{i_2} \times (1 + i_2)^n.$$

Before the 'event', the investment rate, r_1, and the rate of interest, i_1, both = 8 per cent per annum.
After the 'event', the investment rate, r_2, = 5.5 per cent per annum, and the rate of interest, i_2, = 5 per cent per annum.
Following Fisher (1896: 19–22):

$$n = \frac{\log\left(\dfrac{r_2}{i_2}\right)}{\log\left(\dfrac{1 + i_1}{1 + i_2}\right)} = \frac{\log 1.1000}{\log 1.0286} = \frac{0.0414}{0.0122} = 3.4.$$

The 'crossover' point, in this case, is therefore just under 3½ years (when the actual spending prospect both before and after the 'event' amounts to £129,742,480).

Geometric proof of the present value fallacy is provided in Appendix C by means of 'Fisher diagrams'.

THE RIVAL CONCEPTS OF INCOME

According to both Fisher and Hicks, the economic impact of an event can be measured by calculating how much the individual concerned can consume and still be as 'well off' as before the event. For Hicks, 'well-offness' is defined in terms of maintaining a 'standard' *hypothetical* consumption prospect. For Fisher, by contrast, 'well-offness' is defined in terms of maintaining the *actual* consumption prospect.

Hicks's approach gives different answers according to the consumption prospect chosen as the hypothetical standard. According to his constant capital concept (Income No.1), all investors in the Fair Value Company are 'better off' as the result of the 'event' because the amount they can consume *immediately* has risen by £10 million from £100 million to £110 million. According to his constant consumption concept (Income No.2), all investors are 'worse off' because the constant amount they can consume *every year* has fallen by £2.5 million from (8 per cent on £100m =) £8 million to (5 per cent on £110m =) £5.5 million.

Fisher's approach requires the answer to a more pertinent question: what would it take to restore each investor's *actual* consumption prospect to what it was before the 'event'? The answer, which is the *change in the value of capital* (1906: ch. 14), depends on the subjective choice of each individual investor. If they all choose immediate spending, they are collectively 'better off' by £10 million, because that is the amount they can afford to give away without reducing their *actual* immediate consumption prospect. If they all choose to save for five years, however, they are 'worse off' by £5.1 million, because (as shown in Table 9.1) that is the amount of immediate compensation (at the balance sheet date) necessary to restore their *actual* consumption prospect at the end of five years to what it was before the 'event'. If they all choose to save for eight years, they are collectively 'worse off' by £15.3 million, because that is the amount of immediate compensation necessary to restore their *actual* consumption prospect at the end of eight years to what it was before the 'event'.

Fisher's approach is summarized in Table 9.2.

It is unfortunate that Fisher's approach appears to have fallen victim to the verdict (quoted on page 42) pronounced by Kaldor. 'If we reserved the term Income for Consumption we should still need another term for what would otherwise be called Income' (1955: 57). Whatever the merits of this objection on grounds of terminology, it should not be allowed to obscure the fundamental validity of Fisher's argument. The financial impact of an event on any investor depends on the consumption pattern chosen by that particular individual; and that is so, *even if markets are perfect*.

This conclusion is clearly at odds with the approach adopted by Edwards and Bell (discussed in Chapter 7). Yet their use of objective market value is supposed to avoid all the difficulties associated with 'the economic concept of income'.

96

Table 9.2 *Fisher's measure of change in 'well-offness'*

	If all investors are immediate spenders	If all investors are five-year savers	If all investors are eight-year savers
Income (actual consumption prospect) before the 'event'	£100 million immediately	£146.9 million in five years' time	£185.1 million in eight years' time
Income (actual consumption prospect) after the 'event'	£110 million immediately	£140.4 million in five years' time	£162.5 million in eight years' time
Change in income caused by the 'event'	+ £10 million immediately	− £6.5 million in five years' time	− £22.6 million in eight years' time
Change in the value of capital caused by the 'event'	+ £10 million at Balance Sheet date	− £5.1 million at Balance Sheet date	− £15.3 million at Balance Sheet date

SUBJECTIVE VALUE AND ITS CONVERSION INTO OBJECTIVE MARKET VALUE

One of the oddities of *The Theory and Measurement of Business Income* is that Edwards and Bell never establish why 'change in market value . . . is the ideal concept of short-run profit itself' (1961: 25); they simply assume that, because market value is the ultimate destination, change in market value is an appropriate measure of progress along the way. Not only is this assumption fallacious, but it seems to be in conflict with their own basic philosophy.

In their scenario, an essential feature of managerial expertise in 'beating the market' is to be ahead of the rest of the market in spotting or creating economic opportunities. The hallmark of success lies in gaining eventual recognition from the market that the manager's own initial subjective value was right and the objective market value of the rest of the market was wrong. 'The market will then recognize the correctness of the subjective expectations by sharing them' (Edwards and Bell, 1961: 48). Until the rest of the market 'catches up', it is the objective market value that is 'wrong' in the sense of being based on incorrect expectations. This raises an awkward question. *Why should the 'wrong value' be set up as a criterion of managerial performance?*

The answer given by Edwards and Bell is that the 'right value' is subjective.

The subjective value of a firm's assets represents how well off the firm is in the eyes of its management. A sensible definition of expected profit is immediately suggested. It is the amount that could be paid out as dividends in any period without impairing subjective value.

(1961: 38)

97

But it has a serious defect. 'Subjective profit . . . must be discarded as the ideal concept for accounting measurement because . . . it cannot be measured objectively' (1961: 43).

That is a perfectly legitimate reason for discarding 'change in subjective value' on practical grounds; but it does nothing at all to establish a positive case for adopting 'change in objective market value'. The fact that present values based on management expectations are *subjective* does not constitute evidence that objective market values are *relevant*.

To achieve long-term economic success, managers sometimes have to make a bold advance ahead of *or even in conflict with* conventional 'expert opinion'. Ventures into uncharted territory may require the deliberate sacrifice of present market values in the hope of future reward. To report the return on capital on the basis of current market values is like declaring, during the course of a long-distance race, that the leader over the current lap is 'the winner'. Early pace-makers often burn themselves out; and ultimate victory may go to those whose stamina and strategic judgement enables them to decide when to hold back and when to exert the maximum effort. 'It makes no sense to judge a marathon on the results of the first 50 yards' (*Financial Times*, 12 December 2002).

The use of 'change in market value' as a measure of performance encourages the type of 'short-termism' discussed in the previous chapter. It provides an incentive to reject the higher three-year *real return* of the Hi-Val business in favour of the higher first-year *accounting return* of the Lo-Val business. There is an obvious danger that the economic reality may be sacrificed for the sake of the accounting appearance.

In the measurement of economic progress, it is essential to distinguish between movement *of* the destination (the seizing of opportunities) and movement *towards* the destination (their subsequent implementation). In the language of Edwards and Bell, the former represents the creation of subjective value; the latter represents the conversion of subjective value into objective market value. If profit is defined as 'change in market value', this vital distinction is obscured.

The two firms in the illustration used in previous chapters provide a classic example. Long-Run Development's most significant economic achievement in Year 1 is the setting up of the six-consignment Hi-Val project which 'moves the firm's destination' setting it on course for an average return of 44 per cent per annum over the three years. The fact that progress towards that destination – the change in objective market (or 'fair') value during the first year – is no more than 20 per cent is a reflection of the timing. It depends on how the manufacture and sale of the six consignments happen to be distributed over the three accounting periods. Had the pattern of activity been two consignments a year, the first year's accounting return (*the appearance*) would have been 44 per cent; but the actual return at the end of the third year (*the reality*) would not have been affected.

Long-Run Development's managers are clearly more successful than Short-Term Exploitation's in selecting 'that composition of assets which . . . has the greatest subjective value' (Edwards and Bell, 1961: 35). Suppose that what Edwards and Bell call the 'target rate of interest' (1961: 36) is 5 per cent per annum for both firms.

The subjective present value of Short-Term Exploitation's expected distribution of £1,771,561 in three years' time is only (£1,771,561/1.05^3 =) £1,530,341; whereas the subjective present value of Long-Run Development's £2,985,984 is (£2,985,984/ 1.05^3 =) £2,579,405.

Whether or not the expectations are translated into reality depends on how closely the subsequent performance matches the initial plan. In the case of the two firms in the illustration, all expectations *do* turn out exactly according to plan. The subjective value is therefore fully realized in the form of objective market value. It is the ultimate vindication of the foresight of both firms' managers.

The results can be summarized in accordance with the scenario presented by Edwards and Bell. In the *choice* of economic opportunities, Long-Run Development Plc is far superior to Short-Term Exploitation Plc; its plan has a much greater subjective value. In the *implementation* of their chosen opportunity, there is no difference between them; both firms are 100 per cent successful in converting subjective present value into objective market value.

THE SIGNIFICANCE OF MARKET VALUE CHANGES

This does not, of course, imply that changes in market value are of no consequence. On the contrary, for any given eventual real return, a pattern of activity which produces an earlier increase in market value is generally preferable to one which produces a later increase. Other things being equal, the quicker the two firms in the illustration can manufacture and sell their six consignments, the better. Earlier progress towards a given destination normally implies less risk, in the sense that a greater proportion of the total journey has already been accomplished. But, in that case, the 'quick route' is preferable, not because it is more profitable, but because there is less exposure to risk.

Insofar as an earlier increase in the fair market value means that it lags less far behind the (normally undisclosed) subjective value of the managers, however, shareholders may

Table 9.3 Subjective present value 'validated' by objective market value

	Short-Term Exploitation Plc		Long-Run Development Plc	
	Subjective present value £	Objective market value £	Subjective present value £	Objective market value £
Beginning of Year 1	1,530,341	1,000,000	2,579,405	1,000,000
End of Year 1	1,606,858	1,331,000	2,708,375	1,200,000
End of Year 2	1,687,201	1,610,510	2,843,794	1,728,000
End of Year 3	1,771,561	1,771,561	2,985,984	2,985,984

be able to realize a greater amount for the sale of their shares. At the end of Year 1, shareholders in Short-Term Exploitation Plc can sell their shares at a price reflecting the market value of £1,331,000 (see Table 9.3). For any shareholder who exercises that choice, a higher market value is preferable to a lower market value. Knowledge of the current (fair) market value is vital to the decision; *but it is not sufficient*. Although Short-Term Exploitation's first year ARP of 33.1 per cent considerably overstates its lifetime IRR of 21 per cent per annum, a shareholder, who *in ignorance of the managers' expectations* sells shares, may be misled by the fair value of the firm's assets into selling the shares too cheaply.

On its own, unaccompanied by any other information, the fair value of a firm's assets (however accurate) can be grossly misleading. The two firms in the illustration are cases in point. As a result of the incorrect expectations of the market, not only are *both* firms seriously undervalued at the end of Year 1, but they are also wrongly ranked relatively to each other. Yet the claims made on behalf of performance reporting on the basis of current market values appear to ignore this problem. 'The income for the firm related to the current cash equivalent of its net assets will give the rate of return for comparison with other opportunities' (Chambers, 1966: 307). Even when applied to nothing other than financial instruments, however, it is evident that these claims cannot be sustained.

The conventional wisdom implies that performance reporting is mainly a question of accuracy in asset valuation.

> There is general agreement on the definition of income among the various schools of thought: Income is the difference between wealth at two points in time plus consumption during the period. The problem centers around the method of determining wealth or well-offness.
>
> (Sterling, 1970: 19)

Yet, in all the illustrations used in this and the preceding chapters, no valuation problems exist. Either markets are perfectly competitive, or else no assets are held at the balance sheet date other than cash. There can be no dispute over the balance sheet values. It is therefore manifestly clear that the problem has nothing to do with the accuracy of the values; it has everything to do with their relevance for *performance reporting*.

Certainly, there is no doubt about their relevance for *decision making*. 'The present market price is relevant to all decision theories' (Sterling, 1970: 359). Subject to any effect on the observable market price of attempts to realize large holdings, 'current values are relevant information because they represent the value of opportunities which are currently available' (Whittington, 1983: 110).

For decision making, accurate information on current opportunities is absolutely vital; and balance sheets that give an accurate indication of the opportunities currently available at the balance sheet date are to be welcomed. The objection is to *changes* in the aggregate of these (by definition rejected) opportunities being reported as gains or losses in the profit and loss account. 'If the aggregate of value to the owner of individual assets is an arbitrary sum of dubious significance . . . , what can be the significance of an aggregate income measure derived from the same valuation?' (Whittington, 1983: 135).

TOWARDS AN ALTERNATIVE

In the quest for 'truth in accounting', the search for relevant market values has turned out to be a theoretical blind alley. As a measure of economic progress, 'change in market value' does not live up to claim made by Edwards and Bell (1961: 25) that it is an 'ideal concept of profit'. The blind alley also appears to be circular. Whether the object is to measure a flow of income or to compare two stocks of value, the same problem keeps recurring. The measures may be influenced by *hypothetical* transactions which have no *actual* economic significance whatsoever.

Perhaps the only way of escape is by following Canning's advice and 'going back to fundamentals for a fresh start' (1929: 9).

That is the nature of journey to be undertaken in Part IV.

Part IV

Back to basics

INTRODUCTION

The conclusion reached in Part III is that accounting has been led into a blind alley. The only logical way out is to retrace one's steps; and there can be few better places to return for a fresh start than the 'Kaldor criterion'.

> The main purpose of accounting is to exhibit, for the proprietors of the business, the actual results in terms as nearly comparable as can be to the expected results; in terms, in other words, which make it possible for the proprietors to judge whether the business is a 'success' and fulfils those expectations in the light of which they invested their capital, and which they alone are ultimately capable of deciding.
>
> (Kaldor, 1955: 67, 68)

The 'Kaldor criterion' is a useful reminder that financial planning and financial reporting are two sides of the same coin. Both are concerned with measuring investment performance – the first in prospect, the second in retrospect.

To repair the flaws in modern accounting practice, the first essential is to identify the flaws in modern investment theory.

Chapter 10

What's wrong with investment theory?

Investment appraisal is a question of measuring economic performance in advance. For this purpose, modern investment theory makes extensive use of discounted cash flow (DCF) analysis. Although the principle goes back to ancient times, its modern form turns out to be a corruption of Fisher's development of the nineteenth-century version.

FISHER'S NINETEENTH-CENTURY VERSION

Chapter 4 of Irving Fisher's *Appreciation and Interest* (1896) is entitled 'Present value'.

> The ordinary definition of the 'present value' of a given sum due at a future date is 'that sum which put at interest to-day will "amount" to the given sum at that future date'. . . . In fact, we may extend the preceding definition to include the present value of *past* sums as the accumulated 'amount' to-day of the past sum put at interest then.
>
> (1896: 19)

It is apparent from his *Elementary Principles of Economics* (1912) that the principle was well established in nineteenth-century schoolbooks.

> In general we may obtain the present worth of any sum due one year hence by dividing that sum by *one plus the rate of interest*. This latter operation is what we learned in our school arithmetics [sic] as 'discounting,' by which is meant finding the 'present worth' of a given future sum.
>
> (1912: 105)

Compounding and discounting were even more common in accounting practice. 'The rate of interest may be used either for computing from present to future values, or from future to present values. . . . Accountants, of course, are constantly computing in both directions' (1912: 107).

Perhaps the best known of Fisher's works on the subject, however, is *The Rate of Interest* (1907) – particularly in its revised version as *The Theory of Interest* (1930). It includes the rationale for choosing the option with the highest net present value. 'Since any time-shape may be transformed into any other no one need be deterred from selecting an income because of its time-shape, but may choose it exclusively on the basis of maximum present value' (1907: 144; cf. 1930: 138, 139).

Subjective preferences do not make any difference to the rule.

> Each person, after or while first choosing the option of greatest present worth, will then modify it by exchange so as to convert it into that particular form most wanted by him.
>
> (1930: 148; cf. 1907: 174)

> It will then happen that his income as finally transformed will be larger than it could have been if he had chosen some other use which afforded that same time-shape.
>
> (1907: 144)

However, the ability to transform one time shape into another is dependent on the assumption of unrestricted access to a perfect capital market, so that 'after the most valuable option has been chosen, it is possible to borrow and lend or to buy and sell *ad libitum*' (1907: 144).

> If this assumption is not true, if a person were cut off from a free loan market, the choice among optional income streams might or might not fall upon that one having the maximum present value, depending on the other circumstances involved, particularly his preferences as regards time shape.
>
> (1930: 139)

The argument is presented in 'geometric terms' by Fisher (1907, 1930). 'Fisher diagrams' are commonly encountered in modern textbooks on investment theory. Many are derived from Hirshleifer's article 'On the theory of optimal investment decision' (1958) which is now regarded as 'the classic reference' (Edwards *et al.*, 1987: 28n).

Figure C.1 in Appendix C, for example, indicates that, where there is unrestricted access to a perfect capital market, a higher present (or future) value is preferable to a lower present (or future) value *irrespective of subjective time preferences*. Provided that the individual's activities have no significant influence on the market rate of interest, a higher present (or future) value can be converted into a greater consumption stream *of any time shape* than can a lower present (or future) value.

Fisher's nineteenth-century version of the 'NPV decision rule' is therefore perfectly valid. The question to be considered is whether or not the same can be said of the modern corruption.

THE MODERN CORRUPTION

An argument that looks very similar to Fisher's was used by Samuelson in the 1930s to secure victory for the net present value criterion over the rival internal rate of return.

> *Given an interest rate at which all can lend or borrow . . . each entrepreneur will select that value of the variable under his control which maximizes the present value of the investment account, the present value being computed by capitalization of the income stream at the market rate of interest.* This follows from the fact that under our ideal conditions, the investment account necessarily has a market value equal to the capitalized value, and is equivalent to an equal money sum, *and a larger initial sum of money is always to be preferred to a smaller one.*

> (Samuelson, 1937: 482)

That is still the rationale behind modern investment theory.

> A perfect market allows any preferred pattern of cash flows over time which can be generated from a given set of future cash flows to be achieved. Any set of cash flows can be converted to any other having the same present value in the market.

> (Bromwich, 1992: 35)

Samuelson's observation of the possibility of conflict between the two criteria and his objections to the IRR are now part of the modern textbook routine.

> *The internal rate of interest is that rate [if it exists] corresponding to which, the initial value of the investment account is equal to zero. . . .* There may be no value which satisfies this equation. . . . On the other hand . . . there may be a multiplicity of solutions of this equation.

> (Samuelson, 1937: 475)

An 'NPV decision rule', which looks indistinguishable from the nineteenth-century original, has become firmly entrenched as part of the conventional wisdom. 'It is now generally accepted that if capital markets are perfect, a firm acting in its shareholders' interests should assess investments on the basis of their net present value' (Edwards *et al.*, 1987: 12). Even the method of calculation does not seem to have changed since the days of Böhm-Bawerk's description of the declining present-value method of calculating depreciation (1888: 342–346). 'The present value of an investment is given by discounting all the net cash flows it generates over its life at a rate given by the appropriate opportunity cost of capital' (Edwards *et al.*, 1987: 13).

In the real world of risk and uncertainty, however, net cash flows cannot normally be forecast with absolute certainty; and, in imperfect markets where different investors have different preferences and access to different opportunities, ascertaining a single 'appropriate opportunity cost of capital' is not only practically difficult but also theoretically impossible.

For purposes of demonstrating the validity of the 'NPV decision rule', however, it is normal to make the helpful assumptions that 'the appropriate cost of capital is known' and that 'there is perfect certainty' (Edwards *et al.*, 1987: 14). Because these assumptions provide the most favourable conditions for the modern version, they are even more useful in demonstrating that the modern version *is not valid* even when the real-life problems are assumed away!

THE FLAW IN THE MODERN VERSION OF THE 'NPV DECISION RULE'

The net cash flows associated with three different investment projects are shown in Table 10.1. The net present value (NPV) at the beginning of the life of each project is calculated on the assumption that 'the appropriate cost of capital' for projects of this degree of risk is 25 per cent per annum. The internal rate of return (IRR) is calculated over the life of each project.

All three 'projects' have a *positive* NPV at the appropriate cost of capital, and all three have an IRR *greater* than the cost of capital. The possibility of conflict between the two criteria in certain cases is beside the point. In this case, *both* criteria give the same signal. The unequivocal message is that, in the economic interests of the investors, all three projects should be accepted.

Table 10.2 suggests precisely the opposite. Project A (financed by the initial contribution from investors) is undertaken at the beginning of the firm's life; Project B (financed out of the returns from Project A) is undertaken at the end of Year 1; and Project C is undertaken at the end of Year 2. Any other returns not distributed to investors are deposited by the firm to earn interest of 10 per cent per annum.

Table 10.2 indicates that the returns to investors on their £100,000 investment in the firm are distributions of £20,000 at the end of each of the first two years plus a final distribution of £120,000 at the end of the third. That represents a rate of return of

Table 10.1 *Net present value and internal rate of return of three 'investment projects'*

	Net cash flows				NPV (at the start of each Project) at 25% p.a.	IRR during the life of each Project
	End of Year 0	End of Year 1	End of Year 2	End of Year 3		
Project A	−£100,000	+£130,000			+£4,000	+30% p.a.
Project B		−£30,000	+£39,000		+£1,200	+30% p.a.
Project C			−£10,000	+£13,300	+£640	+33% p.a.

Table 10.2 Cash flows of the firm

Cash flows of firm { Inflows + ; Outflows – }		End of Year 0	End of Year 1	End of Year 2	End of Year 3
		£	£	£	£
Project A	Returns + Outlays –	–100,000	+130,000		
Project B	Returns + Outlays –		–30,000	+39,000	
Project C	Returns + Outlays –			–10,000	+13,300
Interest	at 10% per annum on opening bank balance	0	0	+8,000	+9,700
Net cash flow		–100,000	+100,000	+37,000	+23,000
Investors	Contributions + Distributions –	+100,000	–20,000	–20,000	–120,000
Bank	Deposits + Withdrawals –	0	+80,000	+17,000	–97,000
Opening bank balance		0	0	80,000	97,000
Closing bank balance		0	80,000	97,000	0

20 per cent per annum. Not only is it 5 per cent per annum *below* 'the appropriate cost of capital' but it results in a *negative* net present value (at 25 per cent per annum) of (– £100,000 + £16,000 + £12,800 + £61,440 =) –£9,760.

Both the NPV and IRR criteria seem to have failed quite spectacularly. The reason is not hard to find: those project returns which are not distributed to investors (or reinvested in other projects) earn a rate of interest of only 10 per cent per annum. Since all undistributed sums are reinvested at 10 per cent per annum, it might appear at first sight that 10 per cent per annum should be considered to be the 'appropriate opportunity cost of capital'. But that would only make matters worse. Lowering the 'cost of capital' from 25 per cent per annum to 10 per cent per annum would *increase* the net present value of all three projects. Both of the 'discounted cash flow' criteria would make them appear *even more profitable*.

Something is wrong somewhere.

There is nothing wrong with the discounting techniques themselves. They may be centuries old, but they are perfectly valid. It is the way they are applied in the textbooks of modern investment theory that is at fault. The error is traced, in Rayman (1972), to the classic articles in which the NPV/IRR controversy was fought out during the 1930s by Boulding and Samuelson.

THE 'SINGLE INVESTMENT' FALLACY

Preoccupation with the controversy over the two rival discounting criteria seems to have distracted attention from the more fundamental question of what precisely is to be discounted. The clue to the fallacy lies in the title of Boulding's (1935) article: 'The theory of a single investment'; and it lies also in Samuelson's response. 'Suffice it to define the Single Investment Account as a Source to which income is unequivocally imputed' (1937: 470). Both are in stark contrast with Fisher's analysis, in which the focus of attention is not the source but the recipient.

Fisher's analysis is based on a clear view that production and exchange are 'intermediate' processes. Business investment cannot be regarded as an end in itself.

> Neither these intermediate processes of creation and alteration nor the money transactions following them are of significance except as they are the necessary or helpful preliminaries to psychic income – human enjoyment. We must be careful lest, in fixing our eyes on such preliminaries, especially money transactions, we overlook the much more important enjoyment which it is their business to yield. . . . Money is of no use to us until it is spent. The ultimate wages are not paid in terms of money but in the enjoyments it buys.
>
> (Fisher, 1930: 5)

Superficially, modern investment theory is the same as Fisher's – complete with the same NPV criterion. Fundamentally, it is the polar opposite. Its error lies in focusing attention on the returns from *projects* rather than on the returns to *investors* – on the source rather than on the recipient.

> More recent works on investment decisions . . . suffer from the neglect of Fisher's great contributions – the attainment of an optimum through balancing consumption alternatives over time and the clear distinction between production opportunities and exchange opportunities. . . . Their common error lay in searching for a rule or formula which would indicate optimal investment decisions *independently of consumption decisions*. No such search can succeed, if Fisher's analysis is sound which regards investment not as an end in itself but rather a process for distributing consumption over time.
>
> (Hirshleifer, 1958: 329)

Modern investment theory has taken a wrong turning – and the wrong turning is often taken, not in the first chapter, not even in the first sentence, but in the title itself.

The unmistakable signs are words like 'capital projects' or 'investment projects' or even simply 'activities'.

If the stated object is to 'maximize the wealth of investors' (leaving aside, for the time being, the desirability and feasibility of such an objective), then the only flows which are relevant are the flows between the firm and the investors – not the flows between the projects and the firm.

The problem has nothing to do with discounting techniques; it has everything to do with what Fisher calls 'the threshold of measurement'.

Chapter 11

The 'threshold of measurement'

Those who criticize Irving Fisher for 'confusing' income with consumption miss the essential point of his argument. Business performance cannot be evaluated (either in prospect or in retrospect) without reference to the ultimate destination of all economic activity: consumption. That is why Fisher favours what he calls 'measuring at the domestic threshold' (1930: 9). 'At the end of production economics, or business economics, we find home economics. . . . The domestic threshold is, in general, a pretty good line of division' (1930: 10).

The reason for stopping at the domestic threshold rather than going on to 'the threshold of the . . . body . . . [and] beyond this point [to] include what the body communicates to the mind' (1906: 171) is purely practical. 'Enjoyment or psychic income, consisting of agreeable sensations and experiences . . . is the most fundamental. . . . [But it] is a psychological matter, and hence cannot be measured directly' (1930: 11, 12).

In that context, the difference between Fisher and the modern textbooks becomes clearer. Fisher measures the flow of consumption across what he calls the 'domestic threshold'; whereas the modern textbooks measure the flow of cash across what may be called the 'project threshold'. The difference is fundamental. They are measuring different flows across different thresholds.

Figure 11.1 represents the simple case of a firm run by an 'entrepreneur' who is both its owner and its manager. Although the 'entrepreneur' is both the 'investor' who owns

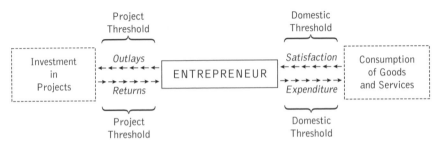

Figure 11.1 Ownership and control combined

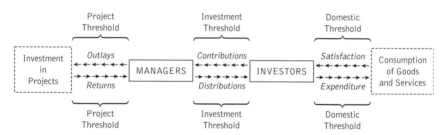

Figure 11.2 The divorce of ownership from control

the firm's equity and the 'manager' who controls its operations, these functions are quite distinct. In companies where ownership is divorced from control, the functions of shareholder/investors and director/managers are clearly separated, and the flow between investment and consumption must cross an additional threshold. This intermediate threshold may be called the 'investment threshold'. The flows across the different thresholds are not necessarily the same. Whether, for example, a flow of cash across the project threshold is translated into a flow of consumption across the domestic threshold depends on the managers' collective choice between distribution and retention and on the investors' individual choices between spending and saving.

Once the personal link between the manager and the investor is severed, the domestic threshold ceases to be 'a pretty good line of division'. Many business firms are corporate bodies with a large number of managers and a multitude of different individual share-holders with different consumption preferences and different economic opportunities. They rarely, if ever, meet. For theorists, Fisher's preference for 'measuring at the domestic threshold' of investors may be conceptually sound; but, for managers, that is not just impractical, it is impossible. The information is simply not available; and, even if it were, there is no way of reconciling the different consumption choices of different investors.

The choice of an alternative 'threshold of measurement' is therefore crucial.

THE THRESHOLD OF MEASUREMENT FOR FINANCIAL PLANNING

A useful guide to the choice of threshold can be obtained from a careful reading of part of the conventional 'NPV decision rule'. 'A firm acting in its shareholders' interests should assess investments on the basis of their net present value' (Edwards *et al.*, 1987: 12). That statement cannot make any sense unless it means their net present value *to the shareholders*; and 'net present value *to the shareholders*' cannot mean anything other than the net present value of the flow between the shareholders and the firm, which the investments generate across the *investment* threshold.

113

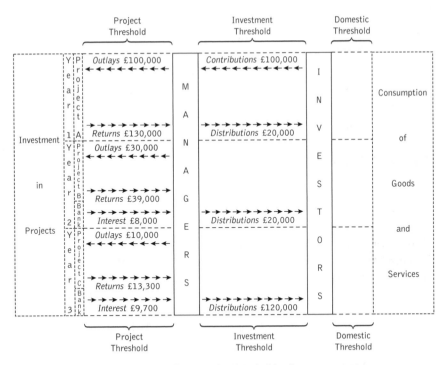

Figure 11.3 Cash flows analysed across the thresholds of measurement

Figure 11.3 (which analyses the data from Table 10.2 according to the thresholds that they cross) makes it clear that the flows across the *project* threshold are very different from flows across the *investment* threshold.

The figure is divided into three horizontal segments – one for each year. At the beginning of Year 1, the initial contributions of £100,000 from the firm's investors flow across the *investment* threshold to the firm's managers. The whole £100,000 is immediately invested as a flow of cash outlays across the *project* threshold to Project A. At the end of the year, the cash returns of £130,000 from Project A flow back across the *project* threshold to the firm's managers. Out of this sum, they make cash distributions of £20,000 which flow back across the *investment* threshold to the firm's investors.

At the end of Year 1, therefore, £110,000 cash remains in the hands of the firm's managers.

In the middle segment of the figure, at the beginning of Year 2, £30,000 is invested as a flow of cash outlays across the *project* threshold to Project B (with the remaining £80,000 held in a bank deposit earning interest at 10 per cent per annum). At the end of the year, cash returns of £39,000 from Project B flow back across the *project* threshold to the firm's managers. To this is added a flow of interest amounting to £8,000 from the bank deposit. Out of the total sum, cash distributions of £20,000 flow back across the *investment* threshold to the firm's investors.

At the end of Year 2, therefore, a further (£39,000 + £8,000 – £20,000 =) £27,000 cash remains in the hands of the firm's managers.

In the lower segment of the figure, at the beginning of Year 3, £10,000 is invested as a flow of cash outlays across the *project* threshold to Project C (with the remaining £17,000 added to the £80,000 held in the bank deposit earning interest at 10 per cent per annum). At the end of the year, cash returns of £13,300 from Project C flow back across the *project* threshold to the firm's managers. To this is added a flow of interest amounting to £9,700 from the bank deposit.

At the end of Year 3, therefore, a further (£13,300 + £9,700 =) £23,000 cash is in the hands of the firm's managers. The £97,000 held in the bank deposit is then withdrawn, and the total sum is paid by the managers as the final cash distributions of £120,000 which flow back across the *investment* threshold to the firm's investors.

When investors invest in a firm, the purpose behind their investment is to obtain a favourable return. The flows generated by projects across the *project* threshold are simply a means to that end. The only flows which have any ultimate economic significance for investors are the flows of contributions and distributions between the firm and themselves across the *investment* threshold. To the investors, the only relevance of the flows across the project threshold of the three projects in Figure 11.3, therefore, lies in their impact on the flows across the investment threshold. Insofar as discounting techniques are appropriate, it is to the flows across the *investment* threshold that they need to be applied.

On the basis of the assumed 'appropriate opportunity cost of capital' of 25 per cent per annum, the internal rate of return criterion and the net present value criterion both indicate that the investment projects undertaken by the firm would produce a result which is detrimental to the economic interests of the investors. The IRR across the *investment threshold* is 20 per cent per annum for three years which is *less than* the assumed opportunity cost of capital; and the NPV calculated at 25 per cent per annum is equal to (– £100,000 + £16,000 + £12,800 + £61,440 =) – £9,760, which is *negative*.

This does not mean, of course, that the projects should not be undertaken. What it means is that they should not be undertaken without focusing attention on the reinvestment of the proceeds before they are distributed to investors. This blind spot is unlikely to be removed until the importance of the 'investment threshold' is fully recognized.

In making the mistake of treating business projects as 'single investments' across the 'project threshold', modern investment theory has adopted the NPV baby but has failed to throw out the 'single investment' bathwater.

Table 11.1 *Cash flows of investors across the 'investment threshold'*

Cash flows of investors		End of Year 0	End of Year 1	End of Year 2	End of Year 3
		£	£	£	£
Investors	Contributions – Distributions +	–100,000	+20,000	+20,000	+120,000

What is overlooked is the two-dimensional aspect of capital investment. 'The *amount of investment of capital* . . . is a quantity of two dimensions, namely, the quantity of capital, and the length of time during which it remains invested' (Jevons, 1871: 229). Investors' capital is committed until it is returned over the *investment threshold*. It is because modern investment theory overlooks this essential characteristic that it measures the wrong flows across the wrong threshold; and modern financial reporting makes exactly the same mistake.

THE THRESHOLD OF MEASUREMENT FOR FINANCIAL REPORTING

Financial planning and financial reporting are different sides of the same coin. The first is concerned with the measurement of investment performance in prospect; the second is concerned with the measurement of investment performance in retrospect.

Financial reporting suffers from the equivalent of the 'single investment' fallacy due, possibly, to its origins in mediaeval 'venture' accounting (discussed in Chapter 3).

In principle, a 'true and fair view' of the return on invested capital is not possible by taking a single period in isolation – unless it is replicated exactly by every other period. The belief that the accounting return can be a reliable measure of the return on investors' capital is a manifestation of the 'single investment' fallacy. In financial planning, it takes the form of treating each *project* as a single investment. In financial reporting, it takes the form of treating each *accounting period* as a single investment. In both cases, the result is measurement of the wrong flows across the wrong threshold.

In Figure 11.4, the results of the activities of Short-Term Exploitation Plc (presented in Table 7.3) are analysed in the same way as the prospects of the investment projects in Figure 11.3.

In the upper (Year 1) segment of the figure, the initial contributions of £1 million from the firm's investors flow across the *investment* threshold to the firm's managers. The whole £1 million is immediately invested as a flow of cash outlays across the *project* threshold to purchase inputs for the first batch of Lo-Vals. The cash returns of £1,100,000 from the sale of the first batch flow back across the *project* threshold to the firm's managers. The whole of the returns are then used as outlays which flow across the *project* threshold to purchase inputs for the second batch. During Year 1, this process takes place for three batches of Lo-Vals.

The middle (Year 2) segment contains a similar representation of the outlays and returns that flow across the *project* threshold for the manufacture and sale of the fourth and fifth batches. The lower (Year 3) segment shows the flows resulting from the manufacture and sale of the sixth and final batch. This culminates in returns of £1,771,561 across the *project* threshold to the firm's managers. The whole amount is finally passed on as a flow of distributions across the *investment* threshold to investors at the end of Year 3.

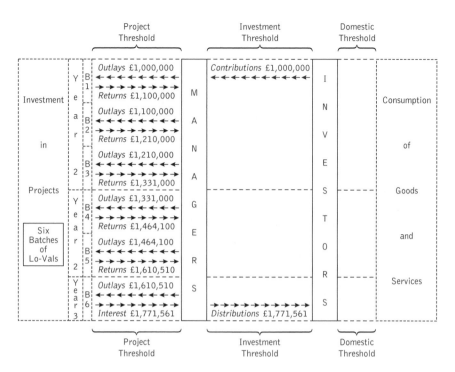

Figure 11.4 Activities of Short-Term Exploitation Plc analysed across the thresholds of measurement

The conventional profit and loss account measures the effect of flows across the 'project threshold'. Each accounting period is treated as a 'single investment'. Consequently, the accounting return is based, not on flows across the *investment* threshold between the firm and *investors*, but on the flows across the *project* threshold between the firm and *projects*.

Short-Term Exploitation's profit and loss account for Year 1 is a perfect example of the 'single investment' fallacy. It measures the flows (caused by the manufacture and sale of the first three batches of Lo-Vals) between the firm and *projects*. There can be no doubt that Year 1 makes a bigger contribution to the return on investors' capital than do either of the other two years. Figure 11.4 provides a graphical demonstration why the return to which it contributes cannot be measured by Year 1 – or any other accounting period – in isolation.

The only flows of relevance to investors are the flows across the *investment* threshold between themselves and the firm. The investors' capital of £1,000,000 is committed for three years. The return of £1,771,561 at the end of that time is the equivalent of an annual return of 21 per cent per annum.

By contrast, the accounting return is entirely dependent on flows across the *project* threshold during each accounting period. Conclusive proof of the irrelevance to investors of flows across the *project* threshold is provided by considering the effect of changes in timing of the six batches over the three years. The left-hand column of Figure 11.4 could be divided up in many different ways. This would make no difference whatever to the flows to investors across the *investment* threshold, but it could have a dramatic effect on the return reported in the annual accounts.

Because three batches are manufactured and sold in the first year, the accounting return for Year 1 – across the *project* threshold – has to be reported as (£1,331,000/ £1,000,000 =) 33.1 per cent. But, suppose the activities of the three periods are reversed – with one batch manufactured and sold in the first year, two in the second year, and three in the third year. Because only one batch is manufactured and sold in the first year, the accounting return for Year 1 – across the *project* threshold – has to be reported as (£1,100,000/£1,000,000 =) 10 per cent. Even if the managers (and the auditors) agree that the firm is on course for a planned return of 21 per cent per annum, the first year accounting return can vary, in these two cases, between 10 per cent and 33.1 per cent.

The reason why the accounting return cannot be relied upon to provide a 'true and fair' view of the return on investors' capital is clear from Figure 11.4. They are measures of different flows across different thresholds. The difference between the two arises from the difference in the 'threshold of measurement'. Based on the implicit assumption that each accounting period is a single investment project, the accounting return is the 'project rate' generated by flows during the accounting period across the *project* threshold. The return on investors' capital is the 'investment rate' generated by flows during the life of the investment across the *investment* threshold.

Modern investment appraisal and modern financial reporting are both involved in the same fundamental mistake. Neglect of the importance of Jevons's two dimensions of capital investment has obscured the central feature. Flows across the *project* threshold are simply the means to an end. The only flows that affect the economic position of investors are those across the *investment* threshold.

For both investment appraisal and financial reporting, it is not the *project* rate that needs to be estimated in advance and reported in retrospect, but the *investment* rate.

Switching the focus of attention from the project threshold to the investment threshold does not, in itself, provide a solution. On the contrary, it exposes a further problem which at first sight appears intractable.

A MISGUIDED IDEAL?

The necessity of tracing the progress of the flows between the project threshold and the investment threshold increases the practical difficulties of investment appraisal. It does not, however, introduce any new difficulty of principle. What is exposed as the insurmountable obstacle is the task of discovering the 'appropriate opportunity cost of capital'. For it is not simply a question of practical difficulty; it is a theoretical impossibility.

118

In a world where ownership is divorced from control and where markets are far from perfect, such a thing as a single 'appropriate opportunity cost of capital' cannot exist *even as a theoretical ideal*. The typical large company is owned by a multitude of different investors with a multiplicity of different opportunities and a multiplicity of different preferences. There cannot be a single 'cost of capital' which applies to them all.

> There is thus no unique cost of capital applicable to all the shareholders if their investment opportunities, tax status, dividend requirements, etc., vary widely.
>
> (Merrett and Sykes, 1963: 72)

> Imperfection of the market, which makes determination of the 'cost of capital' necessary in the first place, renders it impossible by severing the link between available market opportunities and subjective rates of time preference.
>
> (Rayman, 1972: 19n)

This calls into question the whole foundation of investment theory which is based on the idea of 'a firm acting in its shareholders' interests' (Edwards *et al.*, 1987: 12).

> It will be generally accepted that one of the main objectives of a firm's management is to maximize the profits of the owners, the equity shareholders.
>
> (Merrett and Sykes, 1963: 70)

It may be 'generally accepted' – even taken for granted – in the textbooks. On closer inspection, it turns out to be a dangerous myth: misleading in fact and misguided as an ideal.

The belief that one set of individuals can make choices in the (often conflicting) economic interests of another set of individuals is understandably popular with the advocates of state planning and control. It is extremely odd to find it adopted as a guiding principle for the management of private enterprise in a market economy.

Chapter 12

The fatal conceit of managerial capitalism

On the subject of the corporate governance of public companies, Adam Smith makes himself abundantly clear.

> The directors of such companies . . . being the managers rather of other people's money than of their own, it cannot well be expected, that they should watch over it with the same anxious vigilance with which the partners in a private copartnery frequently watch over their own. . . . Negligence and profusion, therefore, must always prevail, more or less, in the management of the affairs of such a company.
>
> (1776: vol. 2, 233)

'Fatal conceit' is the label applied by Hayek to the form of state capitalism practised in the name of socialism by the former communist dictatorships of Eastern Europe. The conceit lies in the belief that the managers of a centrally planned economy are able to act in the economic interests of millions of consumers whose preferences they cannot possibly know. Hayek's objection is short and to the point. 'What cannot be known cannot be planned' (1988: 85).

'Fatal conceit' is an equally appropriate label for the type of managerial capitalism practised in the name of free enterprise by the Western democracies. Hayek's objection is equally pertinent. However expert and well intentioned they may be, the managers of public companies are in no position to act in the economic interests of every one of the numerous investors whose (often conflicting) preferences they cannot possibly know.

In many former communist countries, the lesson has been learned and central planning seems to have gone out of fashion. It is widely recognized that one of the essential requirements for economic efficiency is the information about individual preferences that only a decentralized market can transmit. There are, however, pockets of determined resistance to market forces. They are to be found, not in the last redoubts of old-fashioned socialism, but in the citadels of modern managerial capitalism – the business school and the company boardroom. The most effective blueprints for central planning are laid out, not in the works of Marx and Engels, but in the textbooks of finance and accounting.

In the literature of investment theory, it is taken for granted, almost as a self-evident truth, that the objective of a company's directors is to act in the best economic interests of the shareholders. The difficulties of putting the theory into practice are widely acknowledged; but the theory itself is rarely challenged.

ALTRUISM OR SELF-INTEREST?

The notion of the altruistic company director sits awkwardly with the kind of free-market economics envisaged by Adam Smith.

> It is not from the benevolence of the butcher, the brewer, or the baker, that we expect our dinner, but from their regard to their own interest. We address ourselves, not to their humanity but to their self-love, and never talk to them of our own necessities but of their advantages.
>
> (1776: vol. 1, 16)

The faith which the literature of business investment professes in the idea that a company's directors should act selflessly for the common good of its shareholders is rather touching; but it is difficult to reconcile with Smith's scepticism. 'I have never known much good done by those who affected to trade for the public good' (1776: vol. 1, 421).

In a modern industrial economy characterized by the 'extensive division of labour' the belief that economic activity can be planned by any individual, however enlightened and however well intentioned, on behalf of the consumer is criticized by Hayek as the 'fatal conceit' of socialism.

> The individual can no longer know whose needs his efforts do or ought to serve, or what will be the effects of his actions on those unknown persons who do consume his products or products to which he has contributed. Directing his productive efforts altruistically thus becomes literally impossible for him.
>
> (1988: 81)

Although this criticism refers to planning for the whole economy, it applies with equal force to planning within a single company. The directors of public companies may have less acquaintance with their actual and potential shareholders than Smith's 'butcher, brewer, and baker' have with their actual and potential customers.

It is true, of course, that there may be considerable harmony of interest between shareholders and directors. Disaffected shareholders can be damaging – even fatal – to a director's career. But the harmony of interest between directors and actual and potential shareholders is not significantly different from the harmony of interest which exists between 'the butcher, the brewer, and the baker' and their actual and potential customers. The fact that there is a contract of employment in one case and not in the other does not alter the essential similarity of the fundamental economic relationship. If directors or shopkeepers wish to remain 'employed', they need to keep their customers satisfied. In a free market, that means offering better value than their competitors. What the 'customers' are after is a good return on their investment – whether the investment is in meat, beer, bread, or shares.

The whole point of Smith's free-market argument is that customers do *not* have to trust in the 'benevolence' of the shopkeeper; they can rely on his 'self-love'.

> He intends only his own gain, and he is in this, as in many other cases, led by an invisible hand to promote an end which was no part of his intention. . . . By pursuing his own interest he frequently promotes that of the society more effectually than when he really intends to promote it.
>
> (1776: vol. 1, 421)

In the literature of investment theory, however, the directors of limited companies are frequently assumed to act altruistically on behalf of others. But this is open to serious question.

> The assumption that management is in the best position to know what is in the best interests of investors disregards the consequence of the independent position of the management of corporations, namely that the management group has an interest of its own to promote and protect. Prestige, power, and perquisites are not wanted by corporations. They are wanted by the persons who manage them.
>
> (Chambers, 1966: 282)

Why should company directors, of all people, be singled out as an exception to Adam Smith's rule? If it is good enough for butchers, brewers, and bakers, it is good enough for the directors of limited companies.

> According to the normal rules of economic rationality, individuals attempt to maximize their own satisfaction. Managers of business enterprises are no exception. . . . There is no reason to expect that [they] should act in the interests of anyone but themselves. The fact that managers may be legally appointed by and on behalf of investors is hardly sufficient cause for suspending the normal rules of economic rationality and recommending on the part of management a policy of altruism rather than self-interest.
>
> (Rayman, 1972: 20)

Company directors are, in any case, not in a position to maximize satisfaction for shareholders, however much they may want to.

> The only person capable of maximizing the investor's satisfaction is the investor himself. Managers, who may not be aware of his preferences, cannot do it for him, however altruistic the motives by which they are inspired.
>
> (1972: 20)

The most they can do is to provide the information necessary to enable shareholders to do so for themselves.

Management is not expected to look after the interests of customers, employees or creditors. It is sufficient that adequate information about product, factor and capital markets is available to enable the participants to act in their own self-interest. The investor, too, can be expected to look after his own interests, provided that management, instead of attempting to maximize satisfaction for him, provides sufficient information to enable him to do so for himself. The 'invisible hand', insofar as it is effective, relies on information rather than altruism. After all, 'perfect information' is almost as good a description of the essential characteristics of a perfect market as 'perfect competition'.

(1972: 20)

This brings the argument full circle back to the question of accounting information.

The efficient allocation of resources according to the preferences of the investors to whom they belong requires . . . the development not of investment criteria for managers but of accounting information for investors.

(1972: 20)

The problem is to establish the precise nature of the accounting information which is necessary to enable the 'invisible hand' to function as effectively as possible in the real world.

INFORMATION AND MARKET FORCES

In the real world, information is seldom perfect. Nevertheless, when goods and services are bought and sold, the parties to the transactions usually have a fairly clear idea of what they are buying and selling. They may turn out to be disappointed or pleasantly surprised by the outcome; but they do not normally buy and sell sealed packages with unknown contents.

Shares in the equity capital of public companies can be bought directly from the company as part of a 'new issue' or they can be bought 'second-hand' in the stock market. Either way, the 'package' being bought and sold is the entitlement to a stream of distributions from the company – normally in the form of dividends and, occasionally, capital distributions.

Loan stock, too, can be bought directly from a company as part of a 'new issue' or it can be bought 'second-hand' in the stock market. Either way, the 'package' being bought and sold is also the entitlement to a stream of distributions – normally in the form of interest payments and, in the case of 'dated' stocks, capital repayment.

123

Shareholders are residual owners of the company, whereas the holders of its loan stock are creditors. Their *legal* relationship with the company is entirely different. Their *economic* relationship, however, is remarkably similar. Both are owners of a 'package' containing a stream of future distributions from the company.

The major difference is that the stream of distributions to holders of loan stock is specified at the date of issue: all participants in the market are told what the 'package' contains. By contrast, the stream of distributions to holders of shares is not specified at the date of issue: what the 'package' contains is a mystery.

On the face of it, there is a perfectly good reason. The stream of distributions payable to the holders of loan stock is fixed by contract. The stream payable to shareholders is at the discretion of the directors (subject to various legal constraints including rules to determine what is 'distributable' after all other interested parties have been paid). What is 'distributable' depends, not only on the skill and enterprise of the company's managers and employees, but also on the vagaries of the economic climate and on the slings and arrows of commercial fortune.

The ultimate effect is that participants in the market for loan stock, like the participants in any other market, know what they are buying and selling. Participants in the market for equity shares do not.

In the real world, however, nothing is certain. Even when there is information describing what the 'package' contains, there is always a risk that the description may turn out to be wrong. It is present in any type of market: one of the eggs may be bad – one of the oysters may contain a pearl. If a company suffers total collapse, holders of loan stock, like ordinary shareholders, can lose the whole of their investment. For all sorts of reasons, innocent or otherwise, there is always a possibility of default – of failure to deliver the 'package' according to specification. Nevertheless, there is normally a specification to be met.

Ordinary shares in public companies are in an unusual class of 'packages' (including mystery parcels at illegal mock auctions) where there is no specification at all. A share entitles the holder to a return from the company – but, in the terminology characteristic of the now outlawed 'bubble companies' of the 1720s, 'no one to know what it is'.

In those days, before John Harrison had perfected his marine chronometer, sea voyages could be as hazardous as any twenty-first-century dot.com enterprise. But that was never used as an excuse for keeping the passengers in the dark. There was no guarantee that they would arrive; but at least they were told where they were going. It is a courtesy rarely extended to twenty-first-century investors.

THE CONCEIT OF MANAGERIAL CAPITALISM

Apart from the publication of a prospectus on the occasion of a share issue, the captains of modern industry are under no obligation to say where they are taking their passengers. There is plenty of information in the published accounts about the structure of the ship and its contents; but the information on where it is heading is not normally specified in such a way that it can be subject to routine monitoring.

The preoccupation with means rather than ends is reflected in the fact that the only information considered relevant for either investment planning or financial reporting is concentrated on flows across the *project* threshold.

The textbooks of modern investment theory declare that it is in the interests of shareholders for managers to invest in projects with a positive net present value calculated at the shareholders' cost of capital, or with an internal rate of return higher than the shareholders' cost of capital. The practical difficulty (let alone theoretical impossibility) of determining the shareholders' cost of capital where markets are less than perfect is beside the point. Even if it were possible, the three projects discussed in the two previous chapters show clearly that the conventional wisdom is flawed. Investments that deliver a high return to managers (30 per cent, 30 per cent, and 33 per cent) in terms of flows across the *project* threshold may result in the delivery of a low return (20 per cent) to investors in terms of flows across the *investment* threshold. The flaw lies, not in the techniques of measurement, but in the choice of flows to be measured.

The major problem is confusion between the return across the *project* threshold to a firm's managers and the return across the *investment* threshold to its investors. The cause of the confusion is the abandonment of market principles – the conceit of planners and managers that they know better than the market.

The greatest contribution to eliminating confusion and to rendering managerial capitalism accountable to market forces would be the publication of information relevant to investors. That means disclosure of a piece of information without which capital markets cannot function efficiently – the investment rate.

The obvious place for the disclosure of a company's investment rate is its published financial report. Modern accounting practice is, however, unable to deliver because it is subject to the same flaws as modern investment theory.

The main obstacle to progress in financial reporting is the belief that there is nothing wrong with the accounting system that cannot be cured simply by improving the accounting standards by which it is implemented.

> The principal difficulties in using accounting data are the result, not of fundamental deficiencies in accounting concepts, but in the practical application of these concepts.
>
> (Kay and Mayer, 1986: 206)

That view is widely held; but, by placing all the blame on individuals, it diverts attention from flaws in the system itself. It is a principal reason for the failure of so many modern accounting standards to achieve their objective.

Chapter 13

What's wrong with accounting standards?

THE GUIDING PRINCIPLE: A 'TRUE AND FAIR VIEW'

Having made its debut in the Companies Act 1947, the principle of the 'true and fair view' has long been enshrined in company law.

> Every balance sheet of a company shall give a true and fair view of the state of affairs of the company as at the end of its financial year, and every profit and loss account of a company shall give a true and fair view of the profit or loss of the company for the financial year.
>
> (Companies Act 1948: section 149(1))

It is repeated in section 228(2) of the Companies Act 1985 and in section 226(2) of the Companies Act 1989; and it remains the first priority of the Accounting Standards Board.

> The primary focus of the Statement of Principles is on those financial statements that are required to give a true and fair view of the reporting entity's financial performance and financial position.
>
> (ASB, 2005: 20)

The focus is maintained in the wording of auditors' reports recommended by the Auditing Practices Board in its *Statements of Auditing Standards* (*SASs*) and *International Standards on Auditing* (*ISAs*).

> In our opinion, the financial statements give a true and fair view of (or 'present fairly, in all material respects,') the financial position of the Company as of . . ., and of the results of its operations and its cash flows for the year then ended in accordance with International Accounting Standards and comply with the Companies Act 1985.
>
> (APB, 2005: 588; cf. 2005: 910)

Auditing is not simply a matter of routine; it requires a thorough understanding of the operations of the entity and the exercise of a high degree of professional expertise and judgement.

> The auditor should obtain an understanding of the entity and its environment, including its internal control, sufficient to identify and assess the risks of material misstatement of the financial statements whether due to fraud or error, and sufficient to design and perform further audit procedures.
>
> (APB, 2005: 291; cf. 2005: 741)

One of the 'fundamental principles of independent auditing' described in the *Auditors' Code* is 'rigour'.

> Auditors approach their work with thoroughness and with an attitude of professional scepticism. They assess critically the information and explanations obtained in the course of their work and such additional evidence as they consider necessary for the purposes of their audit.
>
> (APB, 2005: 11; cf. 2005: 130 and 177)

One of the traditional strengths of the British profession is that 'professional scepticism' is taken very seriously. There is a great deal more to auditing than 'ticking invoices'. It demands an approach akin to forensic science.

> When planning the audit the auditors should assess the risk that fraud or error may cause the financial statements to contain material misstatements. . . . Conditions or events which increase the risk of fraud or error include . . . weakness in the design and operation of the accounting and internal control systems. . . . Based on their risk assessment, the auditors should design audit procedures so as to have a reasonable expectation of detecting misstatements arising from fraud or error which are material to the financial statements.
>
> (APB, 2005: 643)

Guidance in this area is covered in much greater detail in the recently issued *ISAs* (especially *200, 240, 300, 315, 320*, and *330*).

Whether accounting and auditing standards are appropriate depends on the precise nature of the view that is being presented as 'true and fair'. The problem is that conventional accounts are used in the two distinct roles discussed in Chapter 1:

1 *stewardship reporting* on 'the custody and safekeeping of enterprise resources'; and
2 *performance reporting* on 'their efficient and profitable use'.

STANDARDS FOR STEWARDSHIP REPORTING

The conventional system of accounting includes a comprehensive system for recording 'external' transactions between the 'firm' and 'outsiders'. The firm is treated as an entity separate from its owners. 'Outsiders' therefore include the firm's owner or owners. Because the conventional accounting records include *all* 'external' transactions – credit as well as cash – they contain a comprehensive record of the flows of *funds* that occur during the process of exchange.

'Funds' are defined as *current non-specific claims*, i.e. claims which are applicable to goods and services in general and not restricted to any particular item. This relationship – of current indebtedness between the firm and the outside world – manifests itself in a stock of current purchase potential both positive (claims by the firm against outsiders) and negative (claims by outsiders against the firm). The definition of 'funds' and the distinction between 'funds' and 'value' are discussed in more detail in Appendix D; but for present purposes a flow of funds can be regarded as the outcome of normal cash and credit transactions.

'Funds' *flow* between the firm and outsiders as current non-specific claims are created and cancelled. These claims accumulate in the form of a *stock* of 'funds' which represents the extent of the firm's 'purchase potential' either positive or negative. For a typical firm, positive items include cash, bank deposits, trade debtors, accrued income, etc. Negative items include overdrawn bank accounts, trade creditors, accrued expenses, etc. But these are the appearance rather than the substance. Just as it is not possible to point at 'value' (or 'service potential') in the abstract, so it is not possible to point at 'funds' (or 'purchase potential') in the abstract but only to items representing a stock of claims.

Table 13.1 provides a simple illustration of a firm's transactions (credit as well as cash) during a period of time.

In the normal course of events, transactions are recorded in the accounts on receipt of the objectively verifiable documentary evidence generated as a matter of routine. (The problem of recording transactions for which documentary evidence does not arrive before the end of the accounting period is discussed in Appendix D.)

Table 13.1 *Transactions during the period*

Nature of transaction	By cash	On credit
	£ million	£ million
Issue of ordinary shares	200	
Revenue from sales of 2m widgets	130	10
Variable manufacturing costs of 3m widgets	(75)	(15)
Purchase of manufacturing plant (with 3 years of expected life)	(180)	
Non-manufacturing expenses	(25)	(5)

Note: Figures in parenthesis ( ) are negative, representing outflows.

Table 13.2 *Funds flow statement for the period*

Funds flow during the period

	£m	£m
Operating activities		
Funds inflow from sales of 2m widgets (£130m + £10m)		140
Less:		
Variable manufacturing costs of 3m widgets (£75m + £15m)	(90)	
Non-manufacturing expenses (£25m + £5m)	(30)	(120)
Net funds inflow from operating activities		20
Capital expenditure		
Purchase of manufacturing plant		(180)
Net funds outflow before financing		(160)
Financing		
Issue of ordinary shares		200
NET FUNDS INFLOW during the period		40
FUNDS STOCK at beginning of period		0
FUNDS STOCK at end of period:		
Debtors for sales of widgets	10	
Cash balance	50	
less: Creditors for variable manufacturing costs	(5)	
less: Creditors for non-manufacturing expenses	(15)	
		40

The funds flow statement in Table 13.2 (compiled from the conventional accounting records) presents a comprehensive picture of the firm's 'external' transactions during the period. Because all transactions are included, funds accounting is the natural choice as the basis of the conventional system of accounting. A funds statement of the type presented in Table 13.2 is a pure record of external transactions. It contains the transactions, the whole of the transactions, and nothing but the transactions.

In principle, verifying the accuracy of a firm's external transactions is perfectly straightforward. The task of the auditor is normally helped by the availability of documentary evidence. It is a matter of making sure (1) that all transactions are genuine and (2) that the record includes every transaction that has actually taken place during the accounting period and excludes everything else.

In practice, it is not always easy. There are many reasons for trying to deceive an auditor and many ways of doing so. There may be people who wish to conceal transactions that have occurred, or to invent transactions that have not occurred, or to shift trans-actions from one period to another. Their ingenuity in manufacturing or doctoring the documentary evidence can make the auditor's task extremely difficult. Transactions that have actually occurred may not be genuinely at arm's length between independent parties. An ostensibly independent entity may in fact be under the influence of the company. Even if parties are genuinely independent, the transactions between them may turn out to be 'bogus swaps'. Firm A, for example, may agree to 'buy' white elephants from Firm B for umpteen £million – on the understanding that Firm B 'buys' flying pigs from Firm A for a similar sum.

That is why auditors cannot accept information at face value. The excuse of having been 'misled by management' is not so much a defence as an admission of guilt. The question is not whether representations made by management are misleading or false but whether the auditors have exercised 'due diligence' in verifying their truth.

The record of a firm's external transactions is a matter of objective fact rather than subjective opinion. Nevertheless, it may take a great deal of skill, judgement, and experience simply to establish the facts. There is, however, far more to 'stewardship accounting' (even in the narrow sense) than simply keeping records of external transactions. Internal operations present an additional degree of complexity precisely because they do not generate the same objectively verifiable evidence as external transactions.

The function of the conventional system as a financial 'cataloguing system' for tracing the stock and flow of resources has been described in Chapter 2. For this purpose, monetary symbols are used to represent the resources according to what may be called the 'accounting code'; and the most convenient source of these monetary symbols is the record of external transactions provided by the funds accounts.

The normal procedure is to 'attach' the cost of acquisition (the funds outflow) when resources are acquired and to accumulate these costs as 'symbols of volume' throughout the production process as the inputs go through the process of conversion into output. Outputs are recorded at selling price (the funds inflow) when they are eventually sold. At the end of the accounting period, the monetary symbols of resources *used up* or *sold* during the accounting period are charged in the profit and loss account as 'expenses'; the monetary symbols of resources *left over* at the end of the accounting period are shown on the balance sheet as 'assets'.

When resources are only *partly* used or sold by the end of the period, however, the 'accounting code' is liable to become more complicated. How should the monetary symbols be 'apportioned' – for partly used buildings? – for partly depreciated fixed assets? – for partly finished work-in-progress? – for unsold goods? – for partly eroded goodwill? – for the partly enjoyed benefits of research and development expenditure? Since these end-of-period apportionments represent a departure from the objectivity of the historical transactions record, it is no surprise that there can be controversy over the choice of 'accounting code'. (End-of-period adjustments to symbolize resources are different in principle from end-of-period adjustments to record transactions for which documentary evidence is not yet available; see Appendix D.)

Tables 13.3 and 13.4 illustrate the application of two different codes for tracing the manufacture and sale of the widgets detailed in Table 13.1. The conversion of inputs into an output of 3 million finished widgets is symbolized by the funds outflows in respect of variable manufacturing costs. As these costs accumulate during the productive process, so does the monetary symbol representing the widgets in progress. By the end of the period, the £90 million accumulated in this way is part of the monetary symbol for the output of 3 million widgets.

The use of the manufacturing plant is also symbolized by the funds outflow on its purchase. Since the year's use represents only a part of the plant's expected life of three years, only a portion of the initial funds outflow of £180 million is used as a symbol for its depreciation. The exact portion is a matter over which there may be legitimate differences of opinion. A common choice of 'depreciation code' is a simple *straight-line* proportion – in this case (assuming zero disposal value), one-third of the initial funds outflow, namely £60 million.

The balance sheet figure of £120 million (£180 million at cost less £60 million depreciation) is merely a monetary *symbol of the existence* of a one-year-old manufacturing plant with two more years of expected life. It is not a *measure of its value* (either in use or in exchange). That is why any other choice of 'depreciation code' will do equally well for keeping tabs on the firm's resources, provided that the auditor knows which code is being used.

The choice of 'accounting code' sometimes lies between attaching the monetary symbol either to the *product* or to the *period*.

According to the *full cost (or absorption cost)* 'code' illustrated in Table 13.3, the £60 million symbol for one year's use of the manufacturing plant is attached (as part of the process of conversion) to the product. Consequently, the 3 million finished widgets are symbolized by the 'full cost of manufacturing' of (£90m + £60m =) £150 million. It is then necessary to choose a 'code' for symbolizing the widgets that have been sold during the period and those that remain unsold at the end of the period. In Table 13.3 the *average cost* 'code' has been used. The 2 million widgets sold are symbolized by £100 million (charged in the profit and loss account as 'cost of sales'), and the unsold stock of 1 million widgets is symbolized by £50 million (carried forward in the balance sheet as a 'current asset').

According to the *marginal cost (or direct cost)* 'code' illustrated in Table 13.4, the £60 million symbol for one year's use of the manufacturing plant is attached (as part of the lapse of time) to the accounting period. Consequently, the £60 million is *not* included as part of the monetary symbol for the 3 million finished widgets, which are symbolized by the 'marginal cost of manufacturing' of £90 million. By the *average cost* 'code', the 2 million widgets sold are symbolized by £60 million (charged in the profit and loss account as 'cost of sales'), and the unsold stock of 1 million widgets is symbolized by £30 million (carried forward on the balance sheet as a 'current asset'). The use of one year's life of the plant during the period is (by the *straight-line depreciation* 'code') symbolized by £60 million and charged as an 'expense' in the profit and loss account.

The resource accounts in Tables 13.3 and 13.4 illustrate the use of three different 'accounting codes':

Table 13.3 *Resource accounts — by the* full cost *'code'*

Profit and loss account for the period

		£m	£m
Revenue			
Sales of 2m widgets (£130m + £10m)			140
Total revenue from sales			140
less: Cost of sales			
Variable manufacturing costs of 3m widgets (£75m + £15m)		(90)	
Fixed manufacturing costs per period (£180m ÷ 3)		(60)	
Full cost of manufacturing 3m widgets		(150)	
less: Unsold stock of 1m widgets (Full mfg. cost ÷ 3)		50	
Full cost of sales			(100)
Gross Profit			40
less: Expenses			
Non-manufacturing expenses (£25m + £5m)			(30)
Net Profit			10

Balance sheet at the end of the period

Assets	£m	£m	£m
Fixed assets			
Manufacturing plant: cost		180	
less: depreciation (£180m ÷ 3)		(60)	120
Current assets			
Unsold stock of 1m widgets	50		
Trade debtors for sales of widgets	10		
Cash balance	50	110	
less: Current liabilities			
Variable manufacturing costs (unpaid)	(15)		
Non-manufacturing expenses (unpaid)	(5)	(20)	
Working capital			90
			210

Equities	£m
Ordinary share capital	200
Accumulated profit	10
	210

Table 13.4   *Resource accounts — by the* marginal cost *'code'*

Profit and loss account for the period

	£m	£m
Revenue		
Sales of 2m widgets (£130m + £10m)		140
Total revenue from sales		140
less: Cost of sales		
Variable manufacturing costs of 3m widgets (£75m + £15m)	(90)	
Marginal cost of manufacturing 3m widgets	(90)	
less: Unsold stock of 1m widgets (Marginal mfg. cost ÷ 3)	30	
Marginal cost of sales		(60)
Gross Profit		80
less: Expenses		
Fixed manufacturing costs per period (£180m ÷ 3)	(60)	
Non-manufacturing expenses (£25m + £5m)	(30)	(90)
Net Loss		(10)

Balance sheet at the end of the period

Assets	£m	£m	£m
Fixed assets			
Manufacturing plant: cost		180	
less: depreciation (£180m ÷ 3)		(60)	120
Current assets			
Unsold stock of 1m widgets	30		
Trade debtors for sales of widgets	10		
Cash balance	50	90	
less: Current liabilities			
Variable manufacturing costs (unpaid)	(15)		
Non-manufacturing expenses (unpaid)	(5)	(20)	
Working capital			70
			190

Equities	£m
Ordinary share capital	200
Accumulated loss	(10)
	190

133

1 depreciation (in both tables) by the *straight-line* code;
2 cost attachment *either* by the *full cost* code (in Table 13.3) *or* by the *marginal cost* code (in Table 13.4); and
3 apportionment (in both tables) between sold and unsold widgets by the *average cost* code.

Viewed as resource accounts, Tables 13.3 and 13.4 are equally good at symbolizing the manufacture of 3 million widgets, the sale of 2 million widgets, and the holding of an unsold stock of 1 million widgets. The message is the same in both cases. It is just that the 'accounting code' – the language in which the message is expressed – happens to be different. By the *full cost* 'code', each widget is represented by £50; by the *marginal cost* 'code', each widget is represented by £30.

For keeping track of the stock and flow of resources, *the choice of code makes no difference*. There is no question of right or wrong. It does not matter whether the monetary symbol for one widget is £50 or £30; nor would it matter whether the monetary symbol for the partly used plant were £120 million or some other figure. As long as they are familiar with whatever 'code' is in use, the auditors are in a position to satisfy themselves *that all the resources entrusted to the firm by investors have been properly applied on the firm's business activities*. Although the monetary figures are different, both tables present an equally 'true and fair view' showing a period that starts with £200 million cash and ends with a one-year-old manufacturing plant, an unsold stock of 1 million widgets, and a stock of funds amounting to £40 million (represented by £10m trade debtors *plus* £50m cash *minus* £20m current liabilities).

The whole object of resource accounting is to ensure that all the firm's resources have been properly used on the firm's business. This object is served irrespective of the particular choice of monetary symbol. That is why the conventional system of accounting has proved to be such a successful instrument for stewardship reporting on the 'safe-keeping of resources' by managers and employees. Even though the conventional accounts lose their 'purity' as a record of external transactions, the monetary figures are perfectly adequate as symbols of volume.

There is therefore nothing wrong with the modern approach to setting standards for *stewardship reporting*. Since the accounting figures are symbols of volume, there can be no serious objection to accounting standards that impose a particular choice of 'accounting code' in the interests of uniformity. As long as 'due diligence' is exercised in following professional standards established by the various Boards, the accounts can (except in extreme cases of ingenious and elaborate fraud) be relied upon to present a 'true and fair view' of the stock and flow of the firm's resources. It is on the basis of the resource accounts that the auditors can report whether or not the firm's resources have been honestly applied on the firm's business.

To return to the question posed in the title to this chapter: there is nothing fundamentally wrong with modern accounting standards for *stewardship reporting*.

For *performance reporting*, however, the answer is entirely different.

STANDARDS FOR PERFORMANCE REPORTING

The fundamental flaw in modern accounting practice is the pretence that the resource accounts can be transformed into performance reports if the monetary *symbols of volume* are converted into *measures of value*. The fallacy has been encouraged by the standard-setting bodies themselves.

> The objective of financial statements is to provide information about the financial position, performance and changes in financial position of an entity that is useful to a wide range of users in making economic decisions.
>
> (IASB, 2005: 36; cf. FASB, 1978: 5; ASB, 2005: 24)

How this objective can be met by implementation of accounting standards is never properly explained. It is simply implied by the clever use of language. 'Many widely held beliefs live only implicitly in words or phrases implying them and may never become explicit; thus they are never exposed to the possibility of criticism' (Hayek, 1988: 106). The frequent repetition of the words 'relevance' and 'relevant' by the Accounting Standards Board in its *Statement of Principles* (2005: 13–99) and the use of the 'fair value' label by the International Accounting Standards Board are examples of this approach. Who can argue with 'relevance' or 'fair value'?

> 'Fair value' is a term that immediately inspires a degree of confidence, as the term draws much from the linguistic power, understood by all English speakers, of the words 'value' and 'fair', both of which carry very deep-seated, positive, essentially good, connotations. Quite whether the accounting outcomes of the technical term 'fair value' will actually reflect the linguistic undertones of its component words is an open question.
>
> (Ernst & Young, 2004: 123)

The implication that accounts would give a 'true and fair view' of economic performance, if only accounting values were 'relevant' and 'fair' is, however, highly economical with the truth. For (as demonstrated in Chapter 3 and Chapter 7) the conventional system of accounting is liable to be seriously misleading for performance reporting *even where there are no price changes, everything goes exactly according to plan, and there are no assets to value other than cash*. The practical difficulties of stock valuation, depreciation, overhead allocation, and all the rest, cannot be denied; but it is the *presence* of asset valuations in the accounts which is the cause of all the trouble rather than their *accuracy*.

Once end-of-period adjustments are admitted into the accounts as *measures of value* rather than *symbols of volume*, the figures become an unidentifiable mixture of records of fact and estimates of value, *and their validity is dependent on confirmation by subsequent events*.

135

To speak of accounting as if it included anticipatory calculations may lead to confusion among its exponents as well as its users. For it may result in the mixing of ascertained measures with hypothetical magnitudes in such a way that the mixture is deemed, mistakenly, to have the merit of objectivity.

(Chambers, 1966: 98)

This is implicit in the use of hindsight in cases where facts about a previous accounting period come to light after the accounts have been published. If the amounts are small enough, they are routinely tucked away in the accounts of the period in which the mistake comes to light. (Under-provisions are written off and over-provisions are written back.) This procedure has an eminently respectable title: it is called an 'accounting adjustment'. If the amounts happen to be too large to be conveniently buried in this way, the accounts of the period in which the original mistake occurred have to be reopened. This procedure has a far less respectable name: it often becomes known as a 'financial scandal'.

The validity of the conventional hybrid accounting figures is therefore at the mercy of future events – a point emphasized by a president of the Institute of Chartered Accountants in England and Wales. 'The assessment of profit of a going concern . . . calls largely for commercial judgment in evaluating the outcome of transactions not yet completed' (R.G. Leach, *The Times*, 22 September 1969).

As *performance reports*, therefore, conventional accounts are a hybrid mixture of funds and value accounting. No conceivable accounting standard can guarantee that forecasts will turn out to be correct. Not only are uniform accounting standards incapable, in principle, of converting conventional resource accounts into performance reports, but they run the risk of introducing problems of their own. The standard on stocks and long-term contracts (*SSAP* 9) is just one example.

Where management accounts are prepared on a marginal cost basis, it will be necessary to add to the figure of stocks so arrived at, the appropriate proportion of those production overheads not already included in the marginal cost.

(ASB, 2005: 143)

The ethical implications are appalling. Even though the *managers'* own accounts may show (per Table 13.4) a £10 million *loss*, the standard requires that the *shareholders* should receive accounts (per Table 13.3) showing – as 'a true and fair view' of their company's performance – a £10 million *profit*!

Fifty years ago, the profession was scrupulous in admitting that conventional financial statements were limited to the role of resource accounts.

It has long been accepted in accounting practice that a balance sheet . . . is an historical record and not a statement of current worth. Stated briefly its function is to show in monetary terms the capital, reserves and liabilities of a business at the date as at which it is prepared and the manner in which the total moneys representing them have been distributed over the several types of assets. Similarly a profit and loss account is an historical record.

(ICAEW, 1952: para. 1)

The truth of that statement has not diminished with time. Tables 13.3 and 13.4 are reliable as resource accounts. Although the balance sheets are different (due to the application of different accounting 'codes'), they both show the manner in which every penny of shareholders' money has been 'distributed over the several types of asset'. Neither balance sheet is reliable as a 'statement of current worth'. Similarly, the two profit and loss accounts show the operational movements in the volume of resources: neither the £10 million net profit nor the £10 million net loss is reliable as a measure of economic performance.

To return, once again, to the question posed in the title to this chapter: for *stewardship reporting*, there is nothing fundamentally wrong with modern accounting standards. For *performance reporting*, by contrast, there is nothing right. The presence of asset values succeeds in contaminating the accounts so that they lose their reliability as records of fact, but it fails to convert them into relevant measures of performance.

THE VERDICT ON MODERN ACCOUNTING STANDARDS

Superficially, the problem of valuation is a multiplicity of *accounting principles* – which can be easily cured. The real problem, however, is the possibility of a multiplicity of *economic outcomes*. Not even the most brilliantly designed accounting standard can guarantee that all balance sheet values will turn out to be correct. Even if it could, it would not solve the problem of measuring the return on capital employed in an ongoing business.

The real obstacle to presenting a 'true and fair view' of business performance is not that accounting reports can be seriously misleading if some of the asset values turn out to be wrong; it is that accounting reports can be seriously misleading even if all the asset values turn out to be right! Furthermore, they can be seriously misleading without any dishonesty or negligence on the part of individuals. The real culprit is the 'hybrid' nature of conventional accounting.

It is the *system* itself that needs to be changed. Backward-looking symbols of volume for *stewardship reporting* have to be clearly separated from forward-looking measures of value for *performance reporting*. An essential prerequisite is the segregation of funds and value.

137

Part V
The segregation of funds and value

INTRODUCTION

The conventional system of 'venture' accounting has its origins in mediaeval Italy. It has survived fundamentally unchanged for over five hundred years for a very good reason. For recording transactions and for keeping track of resources in the 'physical dimension', the conventional system of accounting has never been surpassed. It has therefore proved to be an excellent instrument for a function that is indispensable for running a business of any appreciable size: stewardship reporting.

Performance reporting, however, is an entirely different matter.

For a short-lived project, like a mediaeval venture, where the final reckoning can be deferred until completion, 'backward-looking symbols of volume' are perfectly adequate for the function of reporting performance. For a modern corporation, however, accounts are required at regular annual intervals during its life. Consequently, the system has been stretched beyond its original design into the 'value dimension' of performance reporting. It has become a *hybrid* system, in which records of the past are inextricably entangled with what are in effect forecasts of the future. It provides a reliable indication of the return on capital only on certain (usually hidden) assumptions which no longer normally apply.

Effective operation of the 'invisible hand' requires (1) disclosure of the rate of return that the managers of business corporations are planning to obtain on the resources under their control and (2) an accounting system capable of monitoring its accuracy. Disclosure of the planned investment rate is an essential precondition for bringing investment in the equity capital of business firms into line with other forms of investment.

The conventional system of accounting is, by its very nature, unsuitable for this purpose. It is a *hybrid* system, in which it is not possible to distinguish between 'backward-looking symbols of volume' (based on past funds flows) and 'forward-looking measures of value' (dependent on future events). 'Truth in accounting' is impossible until they are disentangled.

Chapter 14

Financial performance and the investment rate

The financial performance of an entity is identified by the Accounting Standards Board as 'the return it obtains on the resources it controls' (2005: 27).

Accurate information on 'the return obtained on resources' is vital to any type of economy – from the smallest and least developed to the largest and most complex, from Robinson Crusoe alone on a desert island to a modern, highly advanced, industrial society.

There are two basic essentials. One is an effective channel of communication for transmitting the message; the other is the quality of the message itself.

As long as competition is genuinely free, the market place is a fairly reliable channel of communication. (The proviso is essential: freedom of competition is not the same thing as licence to exploit monopoly.) The message itself, for the major area of economic activity, is contained in the annual accounts of business enterprises. Therein lies the problem. Provided that it is implemented with 'due diligence', the conventional system of accounting is an excellent instrument for record keeping and for *stewardship reporting* on the propriety with which a business handles the resources it controls. In *performance reporting* on its efficiency in obtaining a return 'on the resources it controls', however, conventional accounts can be highly misleading.

INFORMATION AND PUBLIC ACCOUNTABILITY

The holders of a company's equity share capital are residual owners of the company. The holders of its loan stock are long-term creditors. Nevertheless, their economic relationship with the company is very similar. Both are owners of a 'package' containing a stream of future distributions from the company.

The relationship between the initial contribution from investors and the subsequent flow of distributions to investors can be expressed in the form of a discounted rate of return which may be called the investment rate. The investment rate is the *internal rate of return* of the flows across the investment threshold.

An essential feature of the investment rate is that it is not necessarily something to be maximized (see Chapter 7 and Appendix B). It is, however, a crucial piece of information that needs to be disclosed. It is a description of what the investment 'package' contains. Without that information, investors are not in a position to make a rational choice between alternative types of investment.

For almost all forms of investment, the investment rate is disclosed as a matter of routine. Investment in the equity capital of public companies is a glaring exception. Publication of the investment rate on equity capital – disclosure of what the 'package' contains – is necessary simply to bring equity investment into line with the alternatives. Above all, it is a vital step towards bringing managerial capitalism under the control of market forces.

MANAGERIAL CAPITALISM

The entrepreneurs of the nineteenth-century economics textbooks are enterprisers who both own and manage their businesses. They are gamblers with their own money. The overwhelming majority of business is now conducted by limited liability companies run by professional managers who are employed to gamble with other people's money.

The service that they sell is the use of their professional expertise to earn a better return on their investors' capital than the investors can manage for themselves. No less than any other individuals in the market, professional managers can be expected to pursue their own self-interest. To single them out as exceptions who do not need to be subject to market forces is described in Chapter 12 as the 'fatal conceit of managerial capitalism'. If professional managers are to act in the interests of their 'customers', the 'invisible hand' of market forces needs to operate at its full strength.

Their 'customers' in this sense include, not just those who buy the firm's products, but all the so-called 'stakeholders'. Suppliers, employees, and creditors, for example, 'invest' their goods, or services, or capital in exchange for a 'return'. Information about the 'return' is normally disclosed in the form of the terms and conditions of business, the terms and conditions of employment, or the terms and conditions of interest and repayment of capital. Most of the stakeholders are told what their 'package' contains.

The 'invisible hand' cannot operate in respect of equity capital unless the managers of corporations provide similar information about the 'package' they are offering to equity shareholders. Like all other sellers, the managers have an obligation to disclose 'what the package contains'. The problem with an equity investment 'package' is that no one can know for certain exactly what is inside. The stream of distributions between the firm and investors across the *investment threshold* is subject to the vagaries of commercial fortune. As long as a business is a 'going concern', any description of 'what the package contains' is not a matter of record; it is a question of speculation – and the expectation is subject to constant change.

This is not, however, a valid excuse for the failure of management to disclose 'the return it [is planning to] obtain on the resources it controls'. On the contrary, it is a powerful argument for an accounting system capable of monitoring its accuracy.

In the market for loan stock, routine publication of the nominal value and the investment rate (together with the dates of payment of interest and capital) is sufficient to enable investors to make rational decisions. But the stream of distributions is normally fixed by contract.

How can equivalent information be made available for investors in the equity share capital of publicly quoted companies where the stream of distributions is uncertain?

DISCLOSURE OF THE PLANNED INVESTMENT RATE

Short-Term Exploitation Plc and Long-Run Development Plc, which have been used in previous chapters to illustrate the problem, are useful for indicating a possible solution. Figure 14.1 analyses their expected and actual operations in terms of flows across the various thresholds of measurement. The left-hand side of the table reproduces the pictorial representation of the activities of Short-Term Exploitation Plc already shown in Figure 11.4. The right-hand side of the table is a similar representation of the activities of Long-Run Development Plc.

Apart from the greater margin on Hi-Vals, the main difference between the two companies is in the timing of their activity: the upper (Year 1) segment contains three batches for Short-Term Exploitation Plc and only one batch for Long-Run Development Plc. The middle (Year 2) segment contains two batches for each company. The lower (Year 3) segment contains only one batch for Short-Term Exploitation Plc but three batches for Long-Run Development Plc.

Figure 14.1 gives a clear view of the problem of attempting to publish the investment rate before the end of the life of an investment: some of the flows across the invest-ment threshold are still in the future. At the end of the first year in the life of the two firms, for example, the flows across the *project* threshold during the year are a question of historical fact. The investment rate, which depends on flows across the *investment* threshold for as long as investors' capital is committed, is a matter of future conjecture.

Since conventional accounts are perfectly adequate in the role of record keeping and resource accounting for the purpose of stewardship reporting, it is important that they should be retained and that they should not be jeopardized. For absolute safety in this respect, any accounts introduced for disclosure of the planned investment rate should, therefore, be kept quite separate.

The data in Figure 14.1 can be used in order to provide an illustration of the construction of 'value accounts' on the basis of the planned investment rate.

During the next three years, the managers of each firm plan to manufacture and sell six batches of product. The planned investment rate – the internal rate of return (calculated on page 71) – across the investment threshold is 21 per cent per annum over the three years for investors in Short-Term Exploitation Plc and 44 per cent per annum for investors in Long-Run Development Plc.

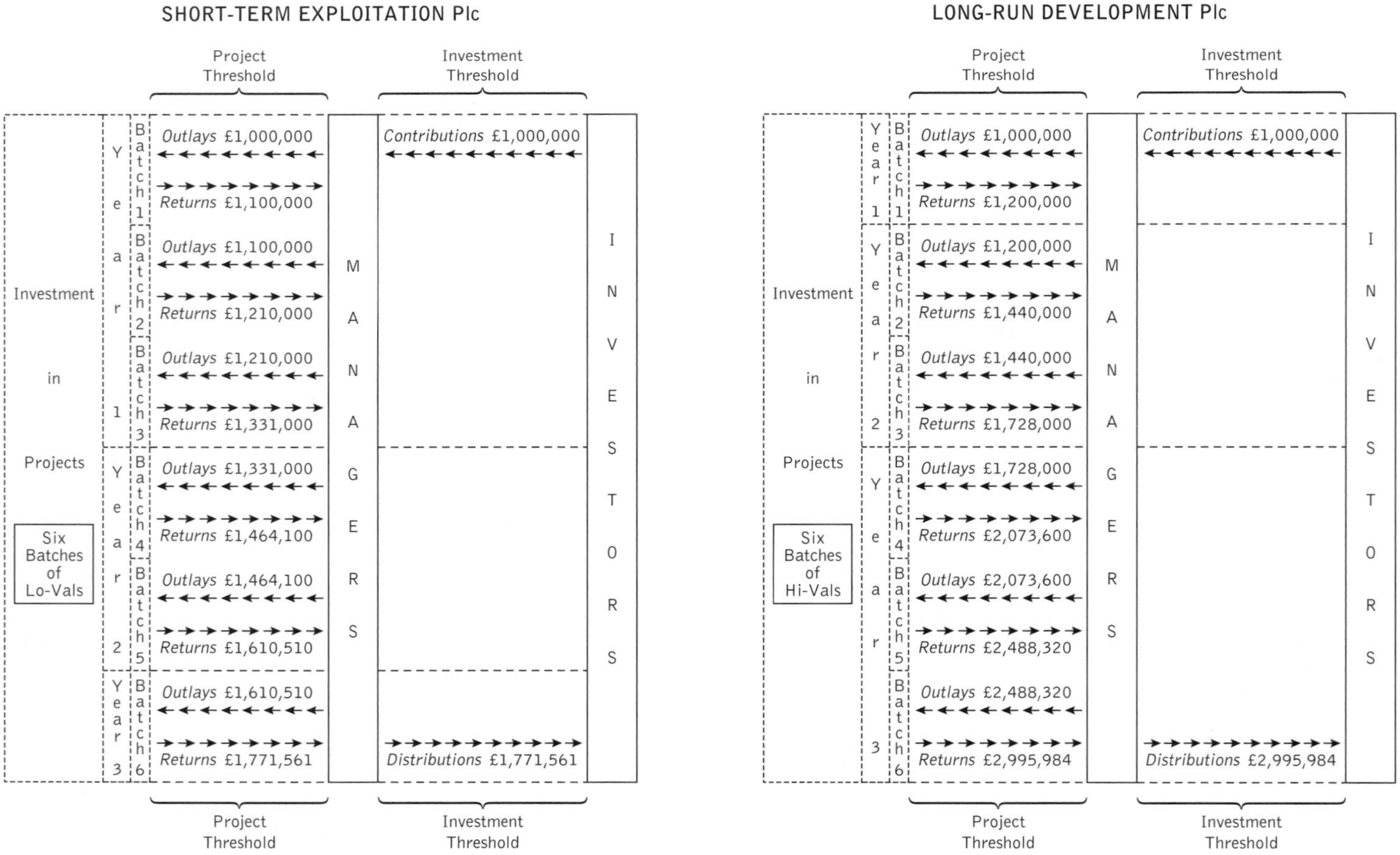

SHORT-TERM EXPLOITATION Plc

Project Threshold — MANAGERS — Investment Threshold — INVESTORS

Contributions £1,000,000

Investment in Projects — Six Batches of Lo-Vals

Year 1
- Batch 1: Outlays £1,000,000 — Returns £1,100,000
- Batch 2: Outlays £1,100,000 — Returns £1,210,000
- Batch 3: Outlays £1,210,000 — Returns £1,331,000

Year 2
- Batch 4: Outlays £1,331,000 — Returns £1,464,100
- Batch 5: Outlays £1,464,100 — Returns £1,610,510

Year 3
- Batch 6: Outlays £1,610,510 — Returns £1,771,561

Distributions £1,771,561

LONG-RUN DEVELOPMENT Plc

Project Threshold — MANAGERS — Investment Threshold — INVESTORS

Contributions £1,000,000

Investment in Projects — Six Batches of Hi-Vals

Year 1
- Batch 1: Outlays £1,000,000 — Returns £1,200,000
- Batch 2: Outlays £1,200,000 — Returns £1,440,000

Year 2
- Batch 3: Outlays £1,440,000 — Returns £1,728,000
- Batch 4: Outlays £1,728,000 — Returns £2,073,600

Year 3
- Batch 5: Outlays £2,073,600 — Returns £2,488,320
- Batch 6: Outlays £2,488,320 — Returns £2,995,984

Distributions £2,995,984

Figure 14.1 Expected and actual operations of Short-Term Exploitation Plc and Long-Run Development Plc

Although there is no way of telling whether the results will turn out according to plan, the *nominal* value of investors' capital can be calculated on the basis of the *planned* investment rate.

The *nominal value* of investors' capital is equal to:
>   *actual* contributions from investors
> **plus:**   *notional* 'earnings' at the planned investment rate
> **less:**   *actual* distributions to investors.

The 'value accounts' over the life of both firms are presented in Table 14.1, on the initial assumption that all expectations are fulfilled.

Because it has been assumed that everything turns out according to plan for both firms, the planned investment rate is actually earned. Consequently, at the end of the life of the investment, the nominal value exactly matches the actual distribution to investors. A zero discrepancy proves the accuracy of the investment rate.

Information about the nominal value, the investment rate, and the timing of the distributions is sufficient to make investment in equity share capital comparable with alternative opportunities. It is exactly the type of information that is made available to the holders of loan stock and practically every other form of investment as a matter of course.

At the end of the first year, for example, the value accounts of Short-Term Exploitation Plc indicate that its equity share capital is equivalent to an investment of £1,210,000 at a rate of 21 per cent per annum for two more years. The equity share capital of Long-Run Development Plc, by comparison, is equivalent to an investment of £1,440,000 at a rate of 44 per cent per annum for two more years.

If the accuracy of the value calculations could be guaranteed, all risk would be removed, and there would be no need for any further information – accounting or otherwise. Investment in the equity share capital of a business enterprise, however, is characterized by risk and uncertainty. The normal expectation is that the planned investment rate will *not* actually be earned.

As events unfold in ever-changing business conditions, the investment rate is open to continuous revision. It is a continuously moving target. The planned investment rate is therefore not always what was initially intended. If new opportunities arise or are created, the planned rate may be improved. If, for whatever reason, conditions deteriorate, managers may lower their sights – like aircrew 'planning' an emergency landing. The planned investment rate may well be neither intended nor desired by the firm's managers; it is simply what they are planning to achieve in the circumstances.

Table 14.1 *Value accounts for both firms (where all expectations are fulfilled)*

Value accounts at the end of Year 1	Short-Term Exploitation Plc	Long-Run Development Plc
	£	£
Contribution (at beginning of year)	1,000,000	1,000,000
plus: 'Earnings' at planned investment rate (during year)	210,000	440,000
Nominal value (at end of year)	1,210,000	1,440,000
Planned investment rate	21.0% p.a.	44.0% p.a.

Value accounts at the end of Year 2	Short-Term Exploitation Plc	Long-Run Development Plc
	£	£
Nominal value (at beginning of year)	1,210,000	1,440,000
plus: 'Earnings' at planned investment rate (during year)	254,100	633,600
Nominal value (at end of year)	1,464,100	2,073,600
Planned investment rate	21.0% p.a.	44.0% p.a.

Value accounts at the end of Year 3	Short-Term Exploitation Plc	Long-Run Development Plc
	£	£
Nominal value (at beginning of year)	1,464,100	2,073,600
plus: 'Earnings' at actual investment rate (during year)	307,461	912,384
Nominal value before distribution (at end of year)	1,771,561	2,985,984
less: Distribution (at end of year)	(1,771,561)	(2,985,984)
Nominal value after distribution (at end of year)	0	0
Actual investment rate	21.0% p.a.	44.0% p.a.

REVISION OF THE INVESTMENT RATE

The planned investment rate depends on the subjective expectations of the firm's managers. Suppose, for the sake of argument, that the managers of both firms in the illustration behave in a conventional 'Keynesian' manner by 'assuming that the existing state of affairs will continue indefinitely, except in so far as [there are] specific reasons to expect a change' (1936: 152). This happens to be consistent with the hidden assumption behind the use of conventional accounts for performance reporting, namely, that the

146

volume of activity in the current accounting period will be repeated in every future period (see Chapter 8). There is, of course, no intention to suggest that the assumption is realistic. It is simply used as an example in order to illustrate the effect of changing expectations on the value accounts.

Suppose that, at the end of the first year, the managers of Short-Term Exploitation Plc base their expectations on the repetition of the first year's activity of three batches during each of the next two years. The expectation, therefore, is that a total of nine batches will be produced and sold – resulting in an expected distribution to shareholders at the end of the third year (shown on the left-hand side of Table 14.2) of £2,357,948. On the basis of those expectations, the planned investment rate is equal to ($\sqrt[3]{2.357948}$ $-1 =$) 0.331 or 33.1 per cent per annum. This 'Year 1 rate' is shown in a box in the row for the ninth batch in Table 14.2.

If Long-Run Development's first year activity of one batch is expected to be repeated in the next two years, a total of three batches will be produced and sold – resulting in an expected distribution to shareholders at the end of the third year (shown on the right-hand side of Table 14.2) of £1,728,000. On the basis of those expectations, the planned investment rate is equal to ($\sqrt[3]{1.728} - 1 =$) 0.2 or 20 per cent per annum. This 'Year 1 rate' is shown in a box in the row for the third batch on the right-hand side of Table 14.2.

The corresponding value accounts for both firms at the end of Year 1 are shown in Table 14.3. They differ from the accounts in Table 14.1 above because the planned investment rates are based on different expectations.

Table 14.2   The effect of changing plans and expectations

Batch	Short-Term Exploitation Plc			Long-Run Development Plc		
	Cash purchase of inputs	Planned investment rate at year-end	Cash sales of Lo-Vals	Cash purchase of inputs	Planned investment rate at year-end	Cash sales of Hi-Vals
	£		£	£		£
First	1,000,000		1,100,000	1,000,000		1,200,000
Second	1,100,000		1,210,000	1,200,000		1,440,000
Third	1,210,000		1,331,000	1,440,000	Year 1: 20.0% p.a.	**1,728,000**
Fourth	1,331,000		1,464,100	1,728,000		2,073,600
Fifth	1,464,100		1,610,510	2,073,600	Year 2: 35.5% p.a.	**2,488,320**
Sixth	1,610,510	Year 3: 21.0% p.a.	**1,771,561**	2,488,320	Year 3: 44.0% p.a.	**2,985,984**
Seventh	1,771,561	Year 2: 24.9% p.a.	**1,948,717**			
Eighth	1,948,717		2,143,589			
Ninth	2,143,589	Year 1: 33.1% p.a.	**2,357,948**			

Table 14.3 *Value accounts for both firms at the end of Year 1*

Value accounts at the end of Year 1	Short-Term Exploitation Plc	Long-Run Development Plc
	£	£
Contribution (at beginning of year)	1,000,000	1,000,000
plus: 'Earnings' at planned investment rate (during year)	331,000	200,000
Nominal value (at end of year)	1,331,000	1,200,000
Planned investment rate (Basis of expectation: not intended for publication)	33.1% p.a. (3 batches a year in future)	20.0% p.a. (1 batch a year in future)

At the end of the second year, however, expectations are revised in the light of experience in the second year. This time the managers of Short-Term Exploitation Plc base their expectations on repetition of the second year's level of activity of two batches during the final year. The expectation, therefore, is that a total of seven batches will be produced and sold – resulting in an expected distribution to shareholders at the end of the third year (shown on the left-hand side of Table 14.2) of £1,948,717. On the basis of these changed expectations, the planned investment rate is revised to $(\sqrt[3]{1948717} - 1 =) 0.249$ or 24.9 per cent per annum. This 'Year 2 rate' is shown in a box in the row for the seventh batch in Table 14.2.

If Long-Run Development's second-year activity of two batches is expected to be repeated in the final year, a total of five batches will be produced and sold – resulting in an expected distribution to shareholders at the end of the third year (shown on the right-hand side of Table 14.2) of £2,488,320. On the basis of those expectations, the planned investment rate is equal to $(\sqrt[3]{2.48832} - 1 =) 0.355$ or 35.5 per cent per annum. This 'Year 2 rate' is shown in a box in the row for the fifth batch on the right-hand side of Table 14.2.

Since the nominal value is based upon the planned investment rate, it is subject to 'correction' every time the investment rate is revised. In the case of Short-Term Exploitation Plc, the revised rate at the end of Year 2 is 24.9 per cent per annum. The nominal value at the beginning of Year 2, recalculated at the revised rate, is equal to $(£1,000,000 \times 1.249 =) £1,249,000$. This is lower than the nominal value of £1,331,000 at the end of Year 1 based on the old rate. Table 14.4 showing the accounts of both firms at the end of Year 2 shows how the 'correction' of $(£1,331,000 - £1,249,000 =) £82,000$ can be presented as a deduction from the nominal value at the beginning of the year.

A similar 'correction' in the accounts of Long-Run Development Plc to reflect the upward revision of the planned investment rate (from 20 per cent per annum to 35.5 per cent per annum) results in an increase in the nominal value at the beginning of the year of $(£1,355,000 - £1,200,000 =) £155,000$.

148

Table 14.4 *Value accounts for both firms at the end of Year 2*

Value accounts at the end of Year 2	Short-Term Exploitation Plc	Long-Run Development Plc
	£	£
Nominal value (at beginning of year)	1,331,000	1,200,000
Capital correction	(82,000)	155,000
Revised value	1,249,000	1,355,000
plus: 'Earnings' at planned investment rate (during year)	311,000	481,000
Nominal value (at end of year)	1,560,000	1,836,000
Planned investment rate	24.9% p.a.	35.5% p.a.
(Basis of expectation: not intended for publication)	(2 batches a year in future)	(2 batches a year in future)

The 'earnings' for the year are calculated, at the revised planned investment rate on the 'corrected' nominal value.

At the end of the third year, which is also the end of the life of both firms, the investment rate can be revised on the basis of the actual results. A total of six batches have actually been produced and sold by both firms – resulting in an actual distribution at the end of the third year of £1,771,561 to the shareholders of Short-Term Exploitation Plc and of £2,985,984 to the shareholders of Long-Run Development Plc. The corresponding investment rates are reduced to 21 per cent per annum for Short-Term Exploitation and increased to 44 per cent per annum for Long-Run Development.

The corresponding value accounts for both firms at the end of Year 3 are shown in Table 14.5.

INTERPRETATION OF THE VALUE ACCOUNTS

The nominal value and the planned investment rate on equity share capital are like the nominal value and the interest rate on loan stock: they constitute an accurate description of the investment 'package' *provided that everything goes exactly according to plan*. Subject to that proviso, the value accounts contain an accurate description of the investment 'package'; and the information is sufficient to enable rational buying or selling in the capital market.

The proviso that everything goes according to plan is, however, essential.

In the case of the two sets of accounts presented in Table 14.1, the proviso is fulfilled: the planned investment rate is actually achieved. For Short-Term Exploitation Plc, 21 per cent per annum is planned and delivered; and, for Long-Run Development Plc, 44 per cent per annum is planned and delivered. The value accounts of Short-Term

149

Table 14.5 *Value accounts for both firms at the end of Year 3*

Value accounts at the end of Year 3	Short-Term Exploitation Plc	Long-Run Development Plc
	£	£
Nominal value (at beginning of year)	1,560,000	1,836,000
Capital correction	(95,900)	237,600
Revised value	1,464,100	2,073,600
plus: 'Earnings' at actual investment rate (during year)	307,461	912,384
Nominal value before distribution (at end of year)	1,771,561	2,985,984
less: Distribution (at end of year)	(1,771,561)	(2,985,984)
Nominal value after distribution (at end of year)	0	0
Actual investment rate	21.0% p.a.	44.0% p.a.

Exploitation Plc, for example, indicate that, at the end of Year 1, its equity capital is equivalent to a two-year investment of £1,210,000 at 21 per cent per annum. The value accounts of Long-Run Development, at the same date, indicate that its equity capital is equivalent to a two-year investment of £1,440,000 at 44 per cent per annum.

The problem is that, in the normal course of events, everything does *not* go according to plan.

In the real world, the planned investment rate may need to be revised in the light of events as they unfold. Although they illustrate just one of the many ways in which expectations can be formed, Tables 14.4 and 14.5 draw attention to economic reality. The value accounts are a description of 'what the package contains' – not in fact, but in the opinion of the firm's managers. The probability that the description of the contents is liable to need correction is simply a reflection of the risk and uncertainty associated with investment in the equity share capital of a business enterprise.

Disclosure of the 'capital correction', in the second-year accounts of both firms in Table 14.4, is an open admission of the extent to which the previous year's figures are considered to be inaccurate. Short-Term Exploitation's first-year accounts in Table 14.3, for example, indicate that, at the end of Year 1, its equity capital is equivalent to a two-year investment of £1,331,000 at 33.1 per cent per annum. In the second-year accounts in Table 14.4, this is reduced to £1,249,000 at 24.9 per cent per annum. Long-Run Development's first-year accounts indicate that, at the end of Year 1, its equity capital is equivalent to a two-year investment of £1,200,000 at 20.0 per cent per annum. In the second-year accounts, this is increased to £1,355,000 at 35.5 per cent per annum.

Provided that the *revised* expectations turn out to be correct, the second-year value accounts constitute an accurate description of what the investment 'package' contains.

The necessity for further corrections in the third-year accounts of both firms, however, indicates that even the second-year corrections are insufficient.

Any correction is an indication of a mistake in forecasting. Although a positive 'correction' is likely to be more welcome than a negative one to those who still hold their shares, the opposite applies to those who have sold them. Inaccurate information – in any direction – is misleading; and it is liable to result in mistaken economic decisions.

Revision of the investment rate is a characteristic difference between a company's equity share capital and its loan stock. In both cases, the investment rate is a description of 'what the package contains'. In the case of loan stock, the contents are fixed by contract; in the case of ordinary shares, they are subject to the vagaries of commercial fortune.

The value accounts present a 'true and fair view' of business and commercial reality. They are a reflection of the impact of changing business plans and expectations on flows to investors across the *investment* threshold. Because they contain no details of flows across the *project* threshold, the value accounts give no operational details away to competitors.

The fact that the description of 'what the investment package contains' is liable to keep changing is no reason for failing to disclose the 'return the managers are planning to obtain on the resources under their control'. Nor is it any reason for failing to admit that, in an uncertain world, mistakes are likely to be the normal experience.

In the illustration used in this chapter, the assumption of a finite three-year life for both firms is an artificial contrivance that allows the accuracy of the *planned* investment rate during the life of each firm to be verified by comparison with the *actual* rate calculated with hindsight after the end of the firm's life.

In the real world, however, as long as a business remains a 'going concern', the actual investment rate cannot be known for certain. That is no reason for failing to disclose the planned rate; but it emphasizes the necessity of an accounting system capable of monitoring its accuracy.

Chapter 15

A segregated system of funds and value accounting

THE CONVENTIONAL 'HYBRID' SYSTEM OF ACCOUNTING

In its traditional role of *stewardship reporting* on the 'safekeeping' of resources, the conventional 'hybrid' accounting system is perfectly adequate. It ain't broke, so there is no need to fix it. The system of recording funds flows as they occur provides a comprehensive record of a firm's external transactions. The use of monetary *symbols of volume* according to the 'accounting code' is ideal for resource accounting. As long as it is implemented in accordance with traditional professional standards, the historical cost system is reliable for the detection of error or fraud.

It is only when it is thrust into the role of *performance* reporting on the *efficiency* of managers and employees that the conventional system of accounting breaks down. Once the monetary *symbols of volume* are treated as *measures of value*, the conventional accounts lose their 'purity' as funds accounts.

> As the value of an asset depends on its future returns, asset valuations are in the nature of estimates, even though there may be no explicit intention on the part of the accountant to make forecasts. For example, the balance sheet value of an asset may be simply a statement of its invoice cost. The fact that the valuation can be confirmed or denied by subsequent events, however, gives it the character of an estimate *de facto*.
>
> (Rayman, 1971: 301)

The mere presence of what are, in effect, asset values 'contaminates' the conventional accounts and turns them into a 'hybrid' mixture of funds and value. 'Accounting information is a strange conglomeration of figures, some based on funds, some on values, and some on an unidentifiable mixture of both' (Rayman, 1969: 68).

Because it is difficult to tell which figures are records of fact and which figures are estimates of value, the 'hybrid' accounts can be seriously misleading.

> To speak of accounting as if it included anticipatory calculations may lead to confusion among its exponents as well as its users. For it may result in the mixing of ascertained

measures with hypothetical magnitudes in such a way that the mixture is deemed, mistakenly, to have the merit of objectivity.

(Chambers, 1966: 98)

As a result of the incorporation of asset valuations into the conventional system of accounting, the validity of published financial information is dependent upon the outcome of future events.

(Rayman, 1971: 301)

It does enormous harm to the reputation of the accountancy profession when audited accounts, published ostensibly as a matter of historical record, are subject to drastic subsequent restatement. Spectacular cases involving dishonesty or negligence do particular damage; but the blame can be placed on individuals. Spectacular cases like the Rolls-Royce collapse in 1969, where dishonesty and negligence are *not* involved, may do even more damage, because they raise fundamental questions about the nature of the accounting system itself.

But this is precisely the type of confusion which has been encouraged by accounting standards bodies all over the world. Instead of maintaining a 'Chinese wall' to keep *stewardship accounting* strictly segregated from *performance reporting*, they have encouraged the trend to mix them even more inextricably together.

The most serious conflict of interest in the area of financial reporting lies within the accounting system itself.

The first essential step towards 'truth in accounting' is to disentangle records of past transactions from forecasts of value.

SEGREGATED FUNDS ACCOUNTING

The segregation of 'funds' requires no interference with conventional accounting procedures. Funds accounting is the basis of the conventional system of *record keeping*. It is also the basis of the conventional system of *resource accounting* used for stewardship reporting.

Provided that professional standards are properly implemented, the conventional accounts provide a reliable record of a firm's transactions and a reliable means of tracing the stock and flow of a firm's resources. The segregation of 'funds' simply means business as usual. The use of monetary *symbols of volume* according to a chosen 'accounting code' – even one based on historical cost – remains an extremely effective method for the preparation of resource accounts. No change is required in their *preparation*.

What *is* required, however, is a radical change in their *presentation*. It is essential to make clear that the conventional profit and loss account and balance sheet are resource accounts. The monetary figures are *symbols of volume* and must not be misinterpreted as *measures of performance or value*. It is simply a question of being as scrupulous as previous generations in acknowledging the truth.

153

It has long been accepted in accounting practice that a balance sheet . . . is an historical record and not a statement of current worth. Stated briefly its function is to show in monetary terms the capital, reserves and liabilities of a business at the date as at which it is prepared and the manner in which the total moneys representing them have been distributed over the several types of assets. Similarly a profit and loss account is an historical record.

(ICAEW, 1952: para. 1)

To draw attention to a fifty-year-old professional recommendation is not, however, enough. Why should this warning not be prominently displayed on the published accounts themselves? All that it needs is a rewording of the auditors' report so that it tells the truth.

In our opinion the accounts give a true and fair view of how the capital invested in the firm has been distributed over the several types of asset as at [date] and of the change in the volume of its resources from operations for the year then ended and have been properly prepared in accordance with the Companies Act 1985.

WARNING:
Under no circumstances should any balance sheet figure be misinterpreted as a measure of the value either of individual items or of the firm as a whole. Similarly, no figure in the profit and loss account should be misinterpreted as a measure of economic performance for the purpose of calculating the return on capital invested in the firm.

The main obstacle to honest acknowledgement of the limitations of the conventional 'hybrid' system of accounting is the widespread belief that the fault lies, not with the system itself, but with its implementation by individuals. 'The principal difficulties in using accounting data are the result, not of fundamental deficiencies in accounting concepts, but in the practical application of these concepts' (Kay and Mayer, 1986: 206). Dropping the pretence that accounting standards can make conventional financial statements 'relevant for making economic decisions' (ASB, 2005: 89; IASB, 2005: 36) would help to reassure those who are 'somewhat suspicious of many current efforts to reform accounting in the direction of making it more "accurate"' (Boulding, 1962: 54).

A known untruth is much better than a lie, and provided that the accounting rituals are well known and understood, accounting may be untrue but it is not lies; it does not deceive because we know that it does not tell the truth.

(Boulding, 1962: 55)

It would also help if the conventional financial statements were given titles which reflected their nature as resource accounts more accurately. The profit and loss account could, perhaps, be renamed 'operational flow of resources during the period', and the balance sheet could be renamed 'volume of resources at the end of the period'. Whatever the exact wording, however, renaming the existing resource accounts to give a better indication of their nature is important. Not only does it serve as a warning of their limitations; it is also likely to encourage pressure for information that is more relevant for assessing performance.

Table 15.1 provides an example of the funds flow statement and the resource accounts for each of the three years in the life of Short-Term Exploitation Plc (illustrated in the previous chapter).

The funds flow statement is a comprehensive record of the firm's 'external' transactions. Normally, it would include the full range of credit transactions. Since all the transactions in this particular illustration are for cash, the funds flow statement in Table 15.1 is almost identical to a conventional cash flow statement.

Apart from some of the labels (intended as a reminder that the figures are symbols of volume, not measures of value), the resource accounts are exactly the same as conventional accounts – provided that the same 'accounting code' is used for choosing the monetary symbols. Normally they would include the full range of revenues and expenses in the (renamed) profit and loss account and the full range of fixed and current assets in the (renamed) balance sheet. Since all the transactions in this particular illustration are for cash, all the operational flows are cash flows, and cash is the only resource.

In short, 'segregated' funds accounting is exactly the same as conventional 'hybrid' accounting without any change in procedure. The only difference is the prominent attachment of a warning to the effect that the profit and loss account and balance sheet are *resource accounts* and should not be misinterpreted as *performance reports*.

To repeat the comment made at the beginning of this chapter.

In its traditional role of *stewardship reporting* on the 'safekeeping' of resources, the conventional 'hybrid' accounting system is perfectly adequate. It ain't broke, so there is no need to fix it.

In the role of *performance* reporting on the *efficiency* of managers and employees, however, the conventional 'hybrid' accounting system is totally out of place. It is very definitely broke, so there is a need to fix it – and the need is urgent.

Explicit recognition and disclosure of the fact that conventional 'hybrid' accounts are *not* appropriate for the measurement of business performance is a vital first step towards the development of accounts that *are*. Attention can then be focused exclusively on the provision of the additional accounting information necessary for the efficient allocation of capital resources in a market economy.

Table 15.1 'Segregated' funds accounts of Short-Term Exploitation Plc

Funds flow statement for Year 1

	£
Flow of funds	
Financing:	
Issue of share capital	1,000,000
Operating activities:	
Funds inflow from sales	3,641,000
Less: Funds outflow on purchases	(3,310,000)
Funds flow from operations	331,000
INCREASE IN FUNDS	1,331,000

Stock of funds	
Opening stock of funds: Cash	0
Closing stock of funds: Cash	1,331,000

Resource accounts at the end of Year 1

Equities in resources	£
Capital	1,000,000
Operational flow of resources:	
Funds inflow from sales *	3,641,000
Less: Goods outflow on sales *	(3,310,000)
Change in volume of resources	331,000
TOTAL VOLUME	1,331,000

Volume of resources	£
Cash	1,331,000
TOTAL VOLUME	1,331,000

Funds flow statement for Year 2

Flow of funds	£
Operating activities:	
Funds inflow from sales	3,074,610
Less: Funds outflow on purchases	(2,795,100)
Funds flow from operations	279,510
INCREASE IN FUNDS	279,510

Resource accounts at the end of Year 2

Equities in resources	£
Capital and retained resources	1,331,000
Operational flow of resources:	
Funds inflow from sales *	3,074,610
Less: Goods outflow on sales *	(2,795,100)
Change in volume of resources	279,510
TOTAL VOLUME	1,610,510

Stock of funds

	£
Opening balance: Cash	1,331,000
Closing balance: Cash	1,610,510

Volume of resources

	£
Cash	1,610,510
TOTAL VOLUME	1,610,510

Funds flow statement for Year 3†

Flow of funds

	£
Operating activities:	
Funds inflow from sales	1,771,561
Less: Funds outflow on purchases	(1,610,510)
Funds flow from operations	161,051
INCREASE IN FUNDS	161,051

Resource accounts at the end of Year 3†

Equities in resources

	£
Capital and retained resources	1,610,510
Operational flow of resources:	
Funds inflow from sales *	1,771,561
Less: Goods outflow on sales *	(1,610,510)
Change in volume of resources	161,051
TOTAL VOLUME	1,771,561

Stock of funds

	£
Opening balance: Cash	1,610,510
Closing balance: Cash	1,771,561

Volume of resources

	£
Cash	1,771,561
TOTAL VOLUME	1,771,561

* These details would normally appear in a separate operational flow of resources account.

† Immediately prior to the final distribution to shareholders.

Note: As a matter of technical detail, the 'funds flow from operations' in the funds flow statement is not generally the same as the 'operational flow of resources' in the resource accounts. The former normally represents the cost of inputs acquired; the latter normally represents the cost of outputs sold. They are the same in this case because no stocks of input or output are held at the end of the period.

SEGREGATED VALUE ACCOUNTING

The segregation of 'funds' and 'value' requires no interference with conventional accounting procedures. Funds accounting remains the basis of the segregated system of record keeping and resource accounting for reporting on *stewardship*. The major innovation is the introduction of separate value accounts for reporting on *performance*.

The performance of a firm's managers in obtaining a return on the resources under their control can be measured by reference to the flows between the firm and investors across the *investment threshold*. The *actual* investment rate, however, cannot be ascertained for certain until the end of the firm's life. In the case of a 'going concern', the closest approximation is the *planned* investment rate. The construction of the value accounts on the basis of the nominal value implied by the planned investment rate has been described in the previous chapter. Since the planned rate is a matter of subjective opinion based on the expectations of the firm's managers, it needs to be monitored by the objective records of fact.

That is precisely how the 'segregated' system is designed to work. The funds accounts can be used to monitor the value accounts.

OPERATION OF THE SYSTEM

In a 'segregated system of funds and value accounting', the *funds* accounts are published together with the *value* accounts. 'Forward-looking measures of value' based on the planned investment rate are available for direct comparison with 'backward-looking symbols of volume' in the conventional resource accounts based on the funds records.

The main problem in using the funds accounts to monitor the planned investment rate is that the relationship between the funds accounts and the value accounts is not at all straightforward.

The nominal values in the value accounts are calculated on the basis of the planned investment rate. Provided that the planned investment rate is accurate, then (as shown in the previous chapter) at the end of the firm's life the nominal value will be exactly matched by funds available for final distribution to the firm's owners.

Even if the planned investment rate turns out to be perfectly accurate over the *whole life* of a firm, however, there is no guarantee that the funds accounts will match the value accounts during any particular *period*. The only case where a match is guaranteed is the unlikely event that the 'hidden assumption' of 'perpetual repetition' is fulfilled.

> Throughout the life of the firm, each accounting period will be an exact replica of every other: with a constant population of assets and the *perpetual repetition* of identical transactions.
>
> (Chapter 8: 80)

Applied to the illustration used in the previous chapter, the conventional assumption is that, in every accounting period, Short-Term Exploitation Plc will repeat its first-year manufacture and sale of three batches of Lo-Vals and the distribution to shareholders of £331,000. Long-Run Development will repeat its first-year manufacture and sale of one batch of Hi-Vals and the distribution to shareholders of £200,000. The consequence of the conventional assumption is shown in Table 15.2. Where the planned investment rate is accurate and every accounting period is an exact replica of Year 1, the funds accounts and value accounts are a perfect match over the whole lifetime of both firms.

'Perpetual repetition' is, however, an extreme assumption which is never likely to be fulfilled. Nevertheless, it is a useful reference point for exploring possibilities that are more realistic.

Once the perpetual repetition assumption is dropped, the funds accounts are unlikely to be 'in step' with the value accounts, *even if the planned investment rate is accurate*.

In Table 15.3, the resource accounts are presented side by side with the value accounts (per Table 14.1) for each year in the life of Short-Term Exploitation Plc and Long-Run Development Plc. Because everything is assumed to turn out exactly according to plan, so that the *planned* investment rate is *actually* earned, then at the end of the life of the investment the nominal value exactly matches the actual distribution to investors.

Nevertheless, during the life of both firms, the funds accounts and the value accounts are clearly 'out of step'. The divergence occurs because neither firm's activity is distributed evenly over time. Short-Term Exploitation's is concentrated in the first year, whereas Long-Run Development's is concentrated in the final year. The discrepancy between funds and value is an indication of this fact.

According to the first-year value accounts in Table 15.3, Short-Term Exploitation Plc is 'on course' for a return on capital of 21 per cent per annum and Long-Run Development Plc is 'on course' for 44 per cent per annum. In both cases, the 'segregated' accounts reveal discrepancies between funds and value. In the case of Short-Term Exploitation, the explanation is that the level of activity in subsequent years is expected to fall. In the case of Long-Run Development, the explanation is that the level of activity in subsequent years is expected to rise.

In the simple illustration presented in Table 15.3, confirmation of the investment rate arrives at the end of the three-year life of both firms. In the normal case of a 'going concern' with an indefinite life, the end of its investment 'voyage' may never be in sight. As long as a firm remains a 'going concern', there can be no ultimate confirmation of the investment rate. It is a question of judging how far the promise implied by the value accounts is consistent with the progress actually revealed in the funds accounts.

The point clearly demonstrated in Table 15.3 is of crucial importance. *The absence of discrepancies between funds and value is not in itself evidence of the accuracy of the planned investment rate.*

On the other hand, an ever-widening divergence between the funds and value accounts lays the published investment rate open to increasing doubt. In the normal

Table 15.2 'Segregated' funds and value accounts

Short-Term Exploitation Plc

Resource accounts at the end of each Year		Value accounts at the end of each Year	
Equities in resources	£		£
Capital	1,000,000	Nominal value (beginning of year)	1,000,000
Funds inflow from sales *	3,641,000		
less: Goods outflow on sales *	(3,310,000)	'Earnings' - at planned	
Operational flow of resources	331,000	investment rate (during year)	331,000
less: Distribution to shareholders	(331,000)	less: Distribution to shareholders	(331,000)
Change in volume of resources	0		0
TOTAL VOLUME	1,000,000	Nominal value (end of year)	1,000,000
Volume of resources	£		
Cash	1,000,000	Planned investment rate	33.1% p.a.
TOTAL VOLUME	1,000,000	(3 batches per year for rest of life)	

Long-Run Development Plc

Resource accounts at the end of each Year		Value accounts at the end of each Year	
Equities in resources	£		£
Capital	1,000,000	Nominal value (beginning of year)	1,000,000
Funds inflow from sales *	1,200,000		
less: Goods outflow on sales *	(1,000,000)	'Earnings' - at planned	
Operational flow of resources	200,000	investment rate (during year)	200,000
less: Distribution to shareholders	(200,000)	less: Distribution to shareholders	(200,000)
Change in volume of resources	0		0
TOTAL VOLUME	1,000,000	Nominal value (end of year)	1,000,000
Volume of resources	£		
Cash	1,000,000	Planned investment rate	20.0% p.a.
TOTAL VOLUME	1,000,000	(1 batch per year for rest of life)	

* These details would normally appear in a separate operational flow of resources account.

course of events, the investment rate is liable to be revised in the light of unforeseen circumstances.

Table 15.4 shows the funds and value accounts where the planned investment rate is revised on the assumption that the level of activity experienced in the most recent period will be repeated in all future periods. The figures are from Tables 14.3, 14.4, and 14.5. The revision of the rate is an acknowledgement of the extent to which plans have not turned out according to expectations.

The first-year accounts in Tables 15.3 and 15.4 illustrate two 'extreme' possibilities. In Table 15.3, the investment rate is accurate, but there is a big divergence between funds and value. In Table 15.4, the investment rate is inaccurate, yet funds and value are in perfect harmony.

This simply confirms that it is not possible to draw conclusions solely from the presence or absence of discrepancies between funds and value. An obvious difficulty is that, at the end of Year 1, it is easier to defend the inaccurate rate in Table 15.4 than to justify the accurate rate in Table 15.3.

The object of publishing 'segregated' funds and value accounts is to expose to public scrutiny, comment, and analysis the presence or absence of any discrepancies. Whether or not the explanations are justified cannot be confirmed, however, until the investment 'voyage' has been completed.

Since a 'going concern' is *by definition* not at the end of its life, the accuracy of the planned investment rate can never be confirmed. Comparison between funds accounts and value accounts, though valuable, needs to be supplemented. Publication of the planned investment rate cannot simply be left to the unfettered discretion of the firm's managers. The obvious difficulty is that the value accounts are based on forecasts of the future. There is no way of verifying them in advance. Nevertheless, there is an equally obvious need for some form of independent report that the value accounts are issued in good faith as a 'true and fair view' that is consistent with a genuine business plan.

This is extremely dangerous territory for the auditor. The boundaries of responsibility between management and the auditor need to be drawn very carefully. A great deal of controversy has arisen because the conventional 'hybrid' system of accounting has caused them to become hopelessly blurred. The segregation of funds and value allows them to be clearly defined.

Table 15.3 'Segregated' funds and value accounts (where the planned investment rate is accurate from the beginning)

Short-Term Exploitation Plc

End of Year 1

Resource accounts at the end of Year 1	£	Value accounts at the end of Year 1	£
Equities in resources			
Capital	1,000,000	Nominal value (beginning of year)	1,000,000
Funds inflow from sales *	3,641,000	'Earnings' – at planned investment rate	
less: Goods outflow on sales *	(3,310,000)		
Operational flow of resources	210,000	(during year)	210,000
TOTAL VOLUME	1,210,000	Nominal value (end of year)	1,210,000
	£		
Volume of resources		Planned investment rate	21% p.a.
Cash	1,210,000		£
TOTAL VOLUME	1,210,000	TOTAL VOLUME	1,210,000

End of Year 2

Resource accounts at the end of Year 2	£	Value accounts at the end of Year 2	£
Equities in resources			
Capital	1,210,000	Nominal value (beginning of year)	1,210,000
Funds inflow from sales *	3,074,610	'Earnings' – at planned investment rate	
less: Goods outflow on sales *	(2,795,100)		
Operational flow of resources	254,100	(during year)	254,100
TOTAL VOLUME	1,464,100	Nominal value (end of year)	1,464,100
	£		
Volume of resources		Planned investment rate	21% p.a.
Cash	1,464,100		£
TOTAL VOLUME	1,464,100	TOTAL VOLUME	1,464,100

Long-Run Development Plc

End of Year 1

Resource accounts at the end of Year 1	£	Value accounts at the end of Year 1	£
Equities in resources			
Capital	1,000,000	Nominal value (beginning of year)	1,000,000
Funds inflow from sales *	1,200,000	'Earnings' – at planned investment rate	
less: Goods outflow on sales *	(1,000,000)		
Operational flow of resources	200,000	(during year)	440,000
TOTAL VOLUME	1,200,000	Nominal value (end of year)	1,440,000
	£		
Volume of resources		Planned investment rate	44% p.a.
Cash	1,200,000		
TOTAL VOLUME	1,200,000		

End of Year 2

Resource accounts at the end of Year 2	£	Value accounts at the end of Year 2	£
Equities in resources			
Capital	1,200,000	Nominal value (beginning of year)	1,440,000
Funds inflow from sales *	3,168,000	'Earnings' – at planned investment rate	
less: Goods outflow on sales *	(2,640,000)		
Operational flow of resources	528,000	(during year)	633,600
TOTAL VOLUME	1,728,000	Nominal value (end of year)	2,073,600
	£		
Volume of resources		Planned investment rate	44% p.a.
Cash	1,728,000		
TOTAL VOLUME	1,728,000		

Resource accounts at the end of Year 3†

Equities in resources	£
Capital	1,610,510
Funds inflow from sales *	1,771,561
less: Goods outflow on sales *	(1,610,510)
Operational flow of resources	161,051
TOTAL VOLUME	1,771,561

Volume of resources	£
Cash	1,771,561
TOTAL VOLUME	1,771,561

Value accounts at the end of Year 3†

	£
Nominal value (beginning of year)	1,464,100
'Earnings' - at planned investment rate (during year)	307,461
Nominal value (end of year)	1,771,561
Actual investment rate	21% p.a.

Resource accounts at the end of Year 3†

Equities in resources	£
Capital	1,728,000
Funds inflow from sales *	7,547,904
less: Goods outflow on sales *	(6,289,920)
Operational flow of resources	1,257,984
TOTAL VOLUME	2,985,984

Volume of resources	£
Cash	2,985,984
TOTAL VOLUME	2,985,984

Value accounts at the end of Year 3†

	£
Nominal value (beginning of year)	2,073,600
'Earnings' - at planned investment rate (during year)	912,384
Nominal value (end of year)	2,985,984
Actual investment rate	44% p.a

* These details would normally appear in a separate operational flow of resources account.
† Immediately prior to the final distribution to shareholders.

Table 15.4 'Segregated' funds and value accounts (where the planned investment rate is revised on the assumption that the most recent volume will continue)

Short-Term Exploitation Plc

Resource accounts at the end of Year 1

Equities in resources	£
Capital	1,000,000
Funds inflow from sales *	3,641,000
less: Goods outflow on sales *	(3,310,000)
Operational flow of resources	331,000
TOTAL VOLUME	1,331,000

Volume of resources	£
Cash	1,331,000
TOTAL VOLUME	1,331,000

Value accounts at the end of Year 1

	£
Nominal value (beginning of year)	1,000,000
'Earnings' - at planned investment rate (during year)	331,000
Nominal value (end of year)	1,331,000
Planned investment rate	33.1% p.a.
(3 batches a year in future)	

Resource accounts at the end of Year 2

Equities in resources	£
Capital	1,331,000
Funds inflow from sales *	3,074,610
less: Goods outflow on sales *	(2,795,100)
Operational flow of resources	279,510
TOTAL VOLUME	1,610,510

Volume of resources	£
Cash	1,610,510
TOTAL VOLUME	1,610,510

Value accounts at the end of Year 2

	£
Nominal value (beginning of year)	1,331,000
Capital correction	(82,000)
Revised value	1,249,000
'Earnings' - at planned investment rate (during year)	311,000
Nominal value (end of year)	1,560,000
Planned investment rate	24.9% p.a.
(2 batches a year in future)	

Long-Run Development Plc

Resource accounts at the end of Year 1

Equities in resources	£
Capital	1,000,000
Funds inflow from sales *	1,200,000
less: Goods outflow on sales *	(1,000,000)
Operational flow of resources	200,000
TOTAL VOLUME	1,200,000

Volume of Resources	£
Cash	1,200,000
TOTAL VOLUME	1,200,000

Value accounts at the end of Year 1

	£
Nominal value (beginning of year)	1,000,000
'Earnings' - at planned investment rate (during year)	200,000
Nominal value (end of year)	1,200,000
Planned investment rate	20.0% p.a.
(1 batch a year in future)	

Resource accounts at the end of Year 2

Equities in Resources	£
Capital	1,200,000
Funds inflow from sales *	3,168,000
less: Goods outflow on sales *	(2,640,000)
Operational flow of resources	528,000
TOTAL VOLUME	1,728,000

Volume of Resources	£
Cash	1,728,000
TOTAL VOLUME	1,728,000

Value accounts at the end of Year 2

	£
Nominal value (beginning of year)	1,200,000
Capital correction	155,000
Revised value	1,355,000
'Earnings' - at planned investment rate (during year)	481,000
Nominal value (end of year)	1,836,000
Planned investment rate	35.5% p.a.
(2 batches a year in future)	

Resource accounts at the end of Year 3† / **Value accounts at the end of Year 3†**

Equities in resources	£	Value accounts	£
Capital	1,610,510	Nominal value (beginning of year)	1,560,000
		Capital correction	(95,900)
Funds inflow from sales *	1,771,561	Revised value	1,464,100
less: Goods outflow on sales *	(1,610,510)	'Earnings' – at planned investment rate (during year)	307,461
Operational flow of resources	161,051		
TOTAL VOLUME	1,771,561	Nominal value (end of year)	1,771,561
Volume of resources	£		
Cash	1,771,561	Actual investment rate	21.0% p.a.
TOTAL VOLUME	1,771,561		

Resource accounts at the end of Year 3† / **Value accounts at the end of Year 3†**

Equities in resources	£	Value accounts	£
Capital	1,728,000	Nominal value (beginning of year)	1,836,000
		Capital correction	237,600
Funds inflow from sales *	7,547,904	Revised value	2,073,600
less: Goods outflow on sales *	(6,289,920)	'Earnings' – at planned investment rate (during year)	912,384
Operational flow of resources	1,257,984		
TOTAL VOLUME	2,985,984	Nominal value (end of year)	2,985,984
Volume of resources	£		
Cash	2,985,984	Actual investment rate	44.0% p.a.
TOTAL VOLUME	2,985,984		

* These details would normally appear in a separate operational flow of resources account.
† Immediately prior to the final distribution to shareholders.

Chapter 16

Management and the auditor: a question of public accountability

Managers and auditors are both subject to the civil and criminal law for dishonesty or negligence in the disclosure of financial information.

> Fraud is proved when it is shown that a false representation has been made (1) knowingly, (2) without belief in its truth, or (3) recklessly, careless whether it be true or false. . . . To prevent a false statement from being fraudulent, there must, I think, always be an honest belief in its truth.
>
> (Lord Herschell in *Derry* v. *Peek*, 1889: 14 A.C.337)

But 'honest belief', though necessary, is not always sufficient. If it is the result of benign neglect, it is no defence against a charge of negligence. Both managers and auditors are responsible for exercising 'due diligence' in the performance of their duties. 'Due diligence' does not mean never making mistakes; it implies taking reasonable steps to act in accordance with professional standards as they evolve.

An auditor accused of negligence cannot simply claim to have been 'misled by management'. The defence is more incriminating than the charge. There is only one question that is relevant: what steps did the auditor take to avoid being misled?

Financial information is of two kinds: matters of fact and questions of opinion about the future. In principle, the division of responsibility between auditors and managers is clear: the responsibility of auditors ought to be limited to the facts, whereas the responsibility of managers should extend to future expectations. In practice, the division of responsibility is compromised by the 'hybrid' nature of the conventional system of accounting which makes it difficult to distinguish between what is fact and what is opinion.

That confusion is the legacy of the failure of successive generations of standard setters to make a clear distinction between the physical and the value dimension.

THE AMBIGUITY OF THE 'HYBRID' SYSTEM OF ACCOUNTING

The conventional 'hybrid' system of accounting has proved to be ideal for tracing the stock and flow of resources in the 'physical dimension'. The balance sheet of a 'going concern', for example, is a description of what Edwards and Bell call its 'box of tools'. 'In its efforts to maximize profit the business firm must determine how large a box of tools to hold, how it is to be financed, and what kinds of tools the box should contain' (1961: 34). In normal circumstances, it is well within the professional competence of an auditor (exercising 'due diligence') to verify that the balance sheet gives a 'true and fair view' of exactly what is in the 'box of tools'.

The standard wording of the auditors' report recommended by the Auditing Practices Board, however, is somewhat ambiguous.

> In our opinion the financial statements give a true and fair view of the state of the company's affairs as at . . . and of its profit [loss] for the year then ended and have been properly prepared in accordance with the Companies Act 1985.
>
> (APB, 2005: 910 and 1851; cf. 2005: 588)

The implication is that a 'box of tools' with a balance sheet value of £200 million is worth twice as much as a box of tools with a balance sheet value of only £100 million. That may or may not be so. The best plumber is not necessarily the one with the most expensive box of tools.

> Even if it were possible to show each individual item at its current value, the balance sheet would still give an imperfect indication of the potential of the firm as a whole, for the same reason that a list of the chemical constituents of the human body is a poor guide to a man's personality.
>
> (Rayman, 1970: 426)

The box's physical contents are a matter of past record; their value to a 'going concern' depends on how efficiently they can be used in combination to produce something that customers can be persuaded to buy – and that is a matter of future speculation. Verifying the contents is the responsibility of the auditor; planning their use is the responsibility of management.

The fatal error lies in transporting the conventional 'hybrid' accounts across the boundary from the physical dimension of resource accounting, where (as symbols of volume) they are perfectly legitimate, into the value dimension of performance reporting, where (as measures of value) they are not. The result is inevitable: the distinction between facts and forecasts is obscured, and the division of responsibility between the auditor and management is blurred.

The auditors may have verified – down to the very last penny – that the whole of the firm's resources have been honestly employed on the firm's business. If, years later, some of the resources turn out to have been so badly or unluckily invested that they have to be written off, the auditors are liable to be wrongly blamed.

The result is lack of proper accountability. Managers may try to shuffle off responsibility for their own bad luck or bad management on to the auditors (Stamp and Marley, 1970: 70, 71). Auditors may try to use the dishonesty of managers as a smokescreen for their own lack of diligence.

THE CLARITY OF THE 'SEGREGATED' SYSTEM OF ACCOUNTING

The guiding principle of the 'segregated' system is strict observance of the boundary between the physical dimension and the value dimension. Records of transactions and symbols of volume are segregated from estimates of value. The division of responsibility between a firm's auditor and its management follows naturally: the auditor's reesponsibility is limited to the facts; management's responsibility extends to the forecasts.

This distinction is maintained in the segregated system by reserving the resource accounts for symbols of volume and the value accounts for measures of value.

For the purpose of *stewardship reporting* on the honesty of managers and employees, auditing under a 'segregated' system is exactly the same as auditing under the conventional 'hybrid' system. It is a question of establishing the accuracy of the records of transactions and ensuring that the monetary symbols of volume used in the conventional resource accounts are adequate for tracing the stock and flow of the firm's resources.

> Simply by verifying the existence of the assets at the balance sheet date and by testing a representative sample of the transactions undertaken during the accounting period, the auditors are able to satisfy themselves whether or not the assets have been properly used on the company's business.
>
> (Chapter 2: 25)

For the purpose of *performance reporting* on the efficiency of managers and employees, by contrast, auditing under a 'segregated' system is fundamentally different from auditing under the conventional 'hybrid' system. In the segregated value accounts, there are no matters of fact. The nominal values are based on the planned investment rate that the firm's managers expect to obtain on the resources they control, provided that everything goes according to their business plan. The value accounts are therefore entirely at the discretion of the firm's management. This imposes upon the auditor an additional, rather difficult, role.

VALUE ACCOUNTS AND THE AUDITOR

Even though the value accounts are based entirely on subjective forecasts which are outside the professional competence of the auditor, there are two important questions of fact upon which the auditor *can* report:

1 Is the planned investment rate consistent with a properly budgeted business plan?
2 How close are the actual results of the current accounting period to what was previously budgeted in the business plan?

There is no need for publication of the actual business plan or the financial budgets and forecasts themselves. It is sufficient to indicate the closeness of the outcome, perhaps by reporting the percentage by which actual costs and revenues have turned out above or below forecast. There is therefore no question of giving away secrets of operational details to competitors.

The role of the auditor can be illustrated in relation to the changing business plans of Short-Term Exploitation Plc (details of which are shown in Table 14.2). During Year 1, Short-Term Exploitation makes and sells three batches of Lo-Vals. At the end of the year, the managers operate on the assumption that they will continue to make and sell three batches of Lo-Vals per year.

Estimates are a matter of subjective opinion and possible controversy. It is unlikely that all members of the management team will be confident in their own forecasts – let alone in agreement with those of their colleagues. In the absence of certainty or even unanimity, the figures are normally accepted as approximations. For example, the planned investment rate in Table 16.1 possibly represents a consensus that the 'most likely' outcome is roughly 33 per cent per annum within a range of, say, between 28 per cent per annum and 38 per cent per annum

The 'segregated' accounts at the end of Year 1 are shown in Table 16.2. The resource accounts are the same as in Table 15.4; but the planned investment rate in the value accounts is presented as an approximation within a range (with figures rounded and the range declared). Many writers have called for a range of values to be provided; but that is difficult in the conventional 'hybrid' accounts since they contain a mixture of records of fact and estimates of value. In the 'segregated' system, however, there is no need to disturb the resource accounts. The value accounts, on the other hand, are openly declared to be based on management forecasts. It would be entirely appropriate for them to be presented in a multi-columnar format with nominal values calculated on the basis of different planned investment rates at various points of the range.

An example of the modified auditors' report is attached to the resource accounts and the value accounts in Table 16.2. The exact wording can be varied; but there are two vitally important warnings to be conveyed:

Table 16.1 The 'business plan' of Short-Term Exploitation Plc at the end of Year 1

	Project flows			Investment flows		
	Planned volume of activity	Cash purchase of inputs	Cash sales of 'Lo-Vals'	Contributions from shareholders	Distributions to shareholders	Planned investment rate
		£	£	£	£	
Year 1 Actual result	Three batches	1,000,000 1,100,000 1,210,000	1,100,000 1,210,000 1,331,000	1,000,000		
		3,310,000	3,641,000			
Year 2 Forecast	Three batches	1,331,000 1,464,100 1,610,510	1,464,100 1,610,510 1,771,561			
		4,405,610	4,846,171			
Year 3 Forecast	Three batches	1,771,561 1,948,717 2,143,589	1,948,717 2,143,589 2,357,948			
		5,863,867	6,450,254		2,357,948	33.1% p.a.

Table 16.2 'Segregated' accounts of Short-Term Exploitation Plc at the end of Year 1

Resource accounts at the end of Year 1		Value accounts at the end of Year 1	
Equities in resources	£		£
Capital	1,000,000	Nominal value (beginning of year)	1,000,000
Funds inflow from sales *	3,641,000		
less: Goods outflow on sales *	(3,310,000)	'Earnings' – at planned investment rate (during year)	330,000
Operational flow of resources	331,000		
Total volume	1,331,000	Nominal value (end of year)	1,330,000
Volume of resources	£		
Cash	1,331,000	Planned investment rate	33% p.a.
Total volume	1,331,000	(between approximately 28% and 38%)	

Report of the Auditors:
In our opinion the resource accounts give a true and fair view of how the capital invested in the firm has been distributed over the several types of asset as at the end of Year 1 and of the change in its resources during that year and have been properly prepared in accordance with the Companies Act 1985.

WARNING:
Under no circumstances should any figure be misinterpreted as a measure of the value either of individual items or of the firm as a whole. Similarly, no figure in the operational flow of resources account should be misinterpreted as a measure of economic performance for the purpose of calculating the return on capital invested in the firm.

Report of the Auditors:
In our opinion the value accounts are a true and fair reflection of the financial budgets and forecasts which have been properly prepared in accordance with the company's business plan.

WARNING:
Under no circumstances should any figure be misinterpreted as a representation of fact. The value accounts are derived solely from forecasts made by the company's managers.
The auditors have ascertained that the value accounts are consistent with such forecasts; but they express no opinion on the accuracy of the forecasts themselves. As the value accounts are dependent on the outcome of future events, it is likely *as a matter of normal routine* that they will require correction in the future.

* These details would normally appear in a separate operational flow of resources account.

1 the resource accounts are symbols of volume and must not be misinterpreted as measures of value or performance; and

2 the value accounts are based on management forecasts and must not be misinterpreted as records of fact.

During Year 2, however, things do not go according to the original plan: only two batches of Lo-Vals are produced and sold; and the business plan is revised on the assumption that only two batches a year will be achieved in future. The new business plan is shown in Table 16.3.

The value accounts at the end of Year 2 are therefore 'corrected' in Table 16.4, which is an 'approximate' version (with figures rounded and the range declared) of the Year 2 accounts in Table 15.4.

In reporting on the value accounts, there are two specific questions for the auditor to address:

1 To what extent has the previous year's forecast been missed?

2 Are the revision of the planned investment rate and the corresponding correction of the value accounts consistent with the current forecasts in the current business plan?

It is not necessary to reveal details of either the previous or the current plans and forecasts. In the case of Short-Term Exploitation Plc, it is sufficient to report:

1 that the level of activity actually achieved in Year 2 was only just over 60 per cent of the level anticipated in the previous year's business plan; and

2 that the downward revision of the planned investment rate (from 33 per cent to 25 per cent per annum) and the corresponding reduction (of £80,000) in the value accounts are consistent with the revised business plan.

Ensuring that the value accounts are consistent with the forecasts is an important part of the auditor's responsibility; but it says nothing whatever about the quality of the underlying forecasts. What is to stop them being pure invention?

This raises an important question in relation to forecasts. Precisely where is the line of demarcation to be drawn between the responsibility of the auditor and the responsibility of management?

THE LINE OF DEMARCATION

When it comes to reporting on the management forecasts underlying the value accounts, it is clear that the apparently neat black-and-white distinction between fact and opinion leaves a serious gap. The auditor can ascertain that the nominal values are consistent

Table 16.3 The revised 'business plan' of Short-Term Exploitation Plc at the end of Year 2

	Project flows			Investment flows		
	Planned volume of activity	Cash purchase of inputs	Cash sales of 'Lo-Vals'	Contributions from shareholders	Distributions to shareholders	Planned investment rate
		£	£	£	£	
Year 1 Actual result	Three batches	1,000,000	1,100,000	1,000,000		
		1,100,000	1,210,000			
		1,210,000	1,331,000			
		3,310,000	3,641,000			
Year 2 Actual result	Two batches	1,331,000	1,464,100			
		1,464,100	1,610,510			
		2,795,100	3,074,610			
Year 3 Forecast	Two batches	1,610,510	1,771,561		1,948,717	24.9% p.a.
		1,771,561	1,948,717			
		3,382,071	3,720,278			

Table 16.4 'Segregated' accounts of Short-Term Exploitation Plc at the end of Year 2

Resource accounts at the end of Year 2		Value accounts at the end of Year 2	
Equities in resources	£		£
Capital	1,331,000	Nominal value (beginning of year)	1,330,000
		Capital correction	(80,000)
Funds inflow from sales *	3,074,610	Revised value	1,250,000
less: Goods outflow on sales *	(2,795,100)	'Earnings' - at Planned Investment Rate (during year)	312,500
Operational flow of resources	279,510		
Total volume	1,610,510	Nominal value (end of year)	1,562,500
Volume of resources	£		
Cash	1,610,510	Planned investment rate	25% p.a.
Total volume	1,610,510	(between approximately 20% and 30%)	

Report of the Auditors:
In our opinion the resource accounts give a true and fair view of how the capital invested in the firm has been distributed over the several types of asset as at the end of Year 2 and of the change in its resources during that year and have been properly prepared in accordance with the Companies Act 1985.

WARNING:
Under no circumstances should any figure be misinterpreted as a measure of the value either of individual items or of the firm as a whole. Similarly, no figure in the operational flow of resources account should be misinterpreted as a measure of economic performance for the purpose of calculating the return on capital invested in the firm.

Report of the Auditors:
In our opinion the value accounts are a true and fair reflection of the financial budgets and forecasts which have been properly prepared in accordance with the company's business plan.

WARNING:
Under no circumstances should any figure be misinterpreted as a representation of fact. The value accounts are derived solely from forecasts made by the company's managers.
  The auditors have ascertained that the value accounts are consistent with such forecasts; but they express no opinion on the accuracy of the forecasts themselves. As the value accounts are dependent on the outcome of future events, it is likely *as a matter of normal routine* that they will require correction in the future.

* These details would normally appear in a separate operational flow of resources account.

with forecasts beforehand and can monitor the forecasts by comparison with the actual results afterwards. But there is no check on the forecasts before the event.

The gap can be filled only by drawing the auditor into the grey area of reporting on the 'reasonableness' of the forecasts. But this is something that needs to be handled with extreme caution. The mistake to be avoided at all costs is the mistake made in the conventional system. The accounts must not be allowed to give the false impression that forecasts have been 'verified' as 'accurate' by the auditors.

A logical 'line of demarcation' therefore suggests itself: the auditor should take responsibility for reporting on the *procedures* for forecasting and budgeting, but *not* for the actual forecasts and budgets themselves.

Extracts from the *Statements of Auditing Standards* (quoted in Chapter 13) issued by the Auditing Practices Board (2005) make clear that auditing involves far more than merely checking the books. Investigation of a firm's system of *financial* control requires forensic skills in order to verify that the resources entrusted to management have been *honestly* employed on the firm's business. In the United States, this responsibility is made explicit by section 404 of the Sarbanes-Oxley Act 2002. However, the application of the Act to the conventional 'hybrid' system may widen the 'expectation gap' discussed in the next chapter.

'Segregation' implies an extension of the scope of the auditor's responsibility. In order to verify how *efficiently* the firm's managers believe they are employing the resources entrusted to them, the auditor needs to apply similar skills to the system of *management* control.

Because procedures for budgeting and forecasting vary with the nature of the business, it is more difficult to establish standards. For some firms, budgeting might be a well-established routine involving the collation of advance orders and the calculation of costs based on relevant experience; for others it could range from educated guesswork about the effect of contracts already negotiated to speculation about the chances of an untried product. A lot depends on whether the firm's activities are concentrated on old and well-established lines of business or on completely new ventures. The standards expected of auditors in reporting on the procedures adopted for calculating the planned investment rate would be a matter for the Auditing Practices Board.

Whatever the exact details, 'segregation' imposes an extra general requirement: the auditors' report has to contain an opinion on whether or not the value accounts are consistent with budgeting procedures that are reasonable having regard to the nature of the firm's business.

TOWARDS TRUTH IN ACCOUNTING?

The segregation of funds and value implies a clear division of responsibility between the auditor and management. The consequent increase in public accountability promises to make a significant contribution to corporate governance through 'truth in accounting' by providing the information necessary for the operation of an efficient market.

Part VI

Truth in accounting

INTRODUCTION

By comparison with the conventional 'hybrid' system of accounting, the 'segregated' system outlined in Part V has a number of advantages.

It promises to close the 'expectation gap' between what accounts actually mean and what the general public has been led to believe that they mean. By avoiding the theoretical blind alley in which modern accounting has become trapped, it provides an opportunity for fulfilling the objectives of the conceptual framework project launched by the FASB in 1976.

Truth in accounting is not something to be pursued simply for its own sake. In the interests of economic democracy, a significant improvement in corporate governance is urgently needed. The segregated system is based on the belief that the most effective way of making the managers of public companies accountable for their economic performance is not by regulation, but by bringing them under the control of market forces. For that purpose, an essential requirement is public disclosure, by those described by Adam Smith as 'the managers of other people's money', of the rate of return they are planning to achieve. Without that information, rational allocation of resources in a market economy is not possible.

The neo-Soviet approach to accounting and management needs finally to be abandoned.

Chapter 17

Elimination of the expectation gap

In January 1970, after a spate of 'financial scandals', an Accounting Standards Steering Committee was set up by the Council of The Institute of Chartered Accountants in England and Wales 'with the object of developing definitive standards for financial reporting' (ASB, 2005: 3). Subsequently renamed the Accounting Standards Committee, it was replaced in August 1990 by the present Accounting Standards Board. Similar bodies were established in other countries with a similar object. The International Accounting Standards Committee was founded in June 1973 by accountancy bodies in Australia, Canada, France, Germany, Japan, Mexico, the Netherlands, the United Kingdom and Ireland, and the United States of America. In April 2001, it was reconstituted as the International Accounting Standards Board which has assumed responsibility for setting accounting standards.

The results of thirty years of standard setting are not, however, encouraging.

> There is . . . an expectation gap between the breadth and depth of assurance the public commonly considers the auditors' report to represent and what it in fact provides.
>
> (Company Law Review Steering Group, 1999: 121)

WHAT THE PUBLIC HAS BEEN LED TO EXPECT

The two financial statements most familiar to the general public are the balance sheet and the profit and loss account. Their meaning is laid down by statute.

> The balance sheet shall give a true and fair view of the state of affairs of the company as at the end of the financial year; and the profit and loss account shall give a true and fair view of the profit or loss of the company for the financial year.
>
> (Companies Act 1985: section 228(2))

The message is repeated in the auditors' report attached to the published accounts (APB, 2005: 588 and 910).

In its *Statement of Principles for Financial Reporting*, the Accounting Standards Board reinforces the belief that a company's financial statements should contain 'the information

179

required by investors . . . [about] the return it obtains on the resources it controls' (2005: 27). 'Put simply, accounting profit is the return the reporting entity has earned on its capital. . . . Any surplus of gains over losses during a period represents a return *on* capital for that period' (2005: 66).

Almost from birth, the standard-setting bodies have claimed to be pursuing accounting values of ever-increasing 'relevance'. Their crowning achievement is the movement towards 'fair value accounting'. It is hardly surprising that audited accounts are expected to present a 'true and fair view' of:

1 the value of a company's net assets, and
2 its financial performance – including 'the return it obtains on the resources it controls'.

That is what the public has been led to expect.

WHAT THE PUBLIC ACTUALLY GETS

It is a sad but undeniable fact of commercial life that, for one reason or another, businesses occasionally fail. Not even the largest and most powerful corporations are immune from financial collapse. That is something which is widely understood. It is a risk, nevertheless, that many are prepared to accept. What they find difficult to stomach is the spectacle of enormous sums being wiped off accounting values that the auditors have only recently reported as 'true and fair'.

In the public outcry that follows almost inevitably, intense anger may be directed against the managers responsible for the collapse. But particular fury is often reserved for the auditors. This is not so much a case of 'shooting the messenger' because the news is bad; it is more a case of justifiable disgust with a watchdog whose reassurances have proved worthless. Auditors are perceived as being well paid for the express purpose of making sure that the financial 'view' is 'true and fair'. If it turns out to be totally false, there can be no surprise that those who have relied on it feel an acute sense of betrayal.

Once the auditors have reported that the financial statements present a 'true and fair view', in the public mind at least, the accounts acquire the status of 'facts'. If the 'facts' turn out to be wrong, it is automatically assumed that the auditors have failed to do their job.

It makes no difference if a company's collapse is entirely due to bad luck, bad management, or even deliberate fraud, on the part of its directors. The auditors are held responsible because they are the ones whose opinion that the accounts present a 'true and fair view' has turned out to be utterly worthless.

To repeat the conclusion of the Company Law Review Steering Group: 'There is . . . an expectation gap between the breadth and depth of assurance the public commonly considers the auditors' report to represent and what it in fact provides' (1999: 121). One of the most serious threats to the reputation of the accountancy profession is the mistaken but growing belief that the auditors are 'toothless watchdogs' who do not provide what they are paid for.

THE NATURE OF THE EXPECTATION GAP

The public expectation is, however, based on a misunderstanding – the misinterpretation of accounting symbols of volume as economic measures of value.

After almost every high-profile 'financial scandal', representatives of the profession are wheeled out into the media spotlight in an effort to defend accounting standards. On these occasions, they are strangely reticent about the 'relevance' of financial statements 'for making economic decisions' (ASB, 2005: 89). They tend, instead, to return to the old-fashioned tradition of explaining that balance sheet figures are not intended to be values and that the profit and loss account does not measure the return on capital in the sense that is normally understood by investors.

> The assessment of profit of a going concern for so short a period as 12 months is usually not a simple matter of objective recording and calculation; it calls largely for commercial judgment in evaluating the outcome of transactions not yet completed.
>
> (R.G. Leach, *The Times*, 22 September 1969)

> The nature of accounting, the nature of reporting is that it is full of subjective judgments.
>
> (John Collier, *BBC: File on Four*, 9 October 2001)

That, so to speak, is the 'small print'. The principal objection, however, is not to the smallness of the print, but to the fact that it is not drawn to the attention of the general public until it is too late. Why wait until *after* a financial collapse before alerting the general public to the fact that the accounts do not mean what they appear to mean? What possible excuse can there be for erecting a warning sign at the bottom of a dangerous cliff instead of at the top?

ELIMINATION OF THE EXPECTATION GAP

The segregated system is designed to eliminate the expectation gap by giving explicit warning (1) that the resource accounts are symbols of volume not measures of value and (2) that the value accounts are based, not on fact, but on forecasts made by the company's managers. In the reworded auditors' report (along the lines suggested in the previous chapter), those warnings are prominently displayed *when the accounts are published*. It is made absolutely clear that the figures are liable to be revised 'as a matter of normal

181

routine' – even where the audit has been carried out to the highest standards of competence and integrity.

Prior to the launch of a new product, for example, a company may have spent £x million on research and development, £y million on plant and equipment, and £z million on inventories. At the date of publication of the accounts, the product may not be due to come to market for months or even years. Nobody can tell whether or not it will turn out be a commercial success. All that any auditor can do is to verify that every last penny has been spent in the way shown in the accounts. Balance sheet figures of £x million, £y million, and £z million give a 'true and fair view' of what has been spent on research and development, plant and equipment, and inventories. If the product turns out to be a failure, those costs will have been wasted, and millions of pounds may have to be written off. That is a sign of failure, not of the auditor, but of the product. It is something that no accounting standard can possibly prevent.

With their constant claims that conventional financial statements are 'relevant for making economic decisions', however, the standard-setting bodies have created a false climate. The auditor is looked upon as the 'insurer of last resort', the audit fee is regarded as a premium against business risk, and, if anything goes wrong, anyone who suffers damage feels entitled to compensation from the auditor.

What the auditor is competent to provide (and what investors are perfectly entitled to expect) is reasonable protection against the risk of fraud and error. What investors are not entitled to expect is protection against *business* risk. This is something the auditor does not provide, cannot provide, and, above all, *should* not provide. It is, after all, the acceptance of business risk that makes the economic world go round. To revert to the lottery analogy used in Chapter 1, it is the auditor's duty to verify the purchase of the tickets, not to give a guarantee that they will be winners.

If there is an expectation gap and the general public is misled, it is not because the auditors have failed to do their job properly; it is because the standard-setting bodies have failed to do theirs.

Dropping the pretence that conventional accounts are relevant for performance reporting is vital for two reasons, (1) to heighten public awareness that resource accounts are simply symbols of volume for *stewardship reporting* on the 'safekeeping of resources'; and (2) to stimulate public demand for information that is relevant for *performance reporting* on their 'efficient use'.

The expectation gap can then be filled by segregated value accounts openly based on the planned investment rate. The general public is left in no doubt that the return on investment in a going concern is a matter, not of past record, but of future speculation. Disclosure of the planned investment rate should not be regarded as something strange and unfamiliar; it happens to be the type of information normally provided as a matter of routine for alternative forms of investment.

Rational investment choice is impossible unless the market is provided with information on what the investment 'package' contains. It is then up to the individual participants to work out for themselves the value of any investment 'package' in the light of their own particular opportunities, their own personal preferences, and their own subjective attitude to risk; *no one else can do it for them*. The main obstacle is the vested intellectual interest of the standard setters who, because they remain obstinately dug into the theoretical blind alley described in Part III, insist that they can.

The only way that this obstacle can be removed is by the construction of an alternative conceptual framework.

Chapter 18

Reconstruction of the conceptual framework

THE MISSED OPPORTUNITY

In his letter introducing the 'conceptual framework project', the chairman of the Financial Accounting Standards Board sounds an optimistic note. 'The framework should lead to increased public confidence in financial statements' (FASB, 1976). That hope is repeated in the body of the document itself.

> To add credence to financial reporting – to minimize skepticism about financial statements – is a major purpose of a conceptual framework and, indeed, can be said to be an important aspect of the mission of the Financial Accounting Standards Board.
>
> (FASB, 1976: 8, 9)

Chapter 2 of *International GAAP 2005* contains a thorough examination of the origins and development of the conceptual framework project. It includes a quotation from an evaluation made by Professor David Solomons in 1986.

> Under a rigorous grading system I would give Concepts Statement No 5 [*Recognition and Measurement in Financial Statements of Business Enterprises* (1984)] an F and require the board to take the course over again. . . . My judgment of the project as a whole must be that it has failed.
>
> (quoted in Ernst & Young, 2004: 84)

After an equally thorough examination of the IASB's *Framework for the Preparation and Presentation of Financial Statements*, the authors of *International GAAP 2005* deliver a similar verdict.

> There is no really fundamental difference between the IASB and FASB conceptual frameworks. . . . In truth the IASB's Framework is little more than a synopsis of the FASB conceptual statements. It is perhaps unfortunate, and certainly was a lost opportunity at the time, that the IASB did not take the chance presented by the

publication of a conceptual framework document to explore more fundamentally the questions posed by such an endeavour.

(Ernst & Young, 2004: 99)

It is a matter of regret that some distinguished standard setters seem to have employed their considerable scholarship precisely in order to dodge such questions – with the result that their findings sometimes give the impression of having been 'spin-doctored'. The contrast between the directness of the Sandilands Report (1975) and the evasiveness of the ASB's *Statement of Principles for Financial Reporting* (2005: 13–99) is instructive.

Yet the approach outlined in the early stages of the conceptual framework project is highly promising. 'This Statement contains no conclusions about matters such as the identity, number, or form of financial statements. . . . Thus . . . the Statement should not be interpreted as implying a particular set of financial statements' (FASB, 1978: 2). References to 'the financial statements now most frequently provided' which include a 'balance sheet or statement of financial position' and an 'income or earnings statement' come with a warning of the ever-present danger of prejudgement. 'To list those examples from existing practice implies no conclusions about the identity, number, or form of financial statements because those matters are yet to be considered in the conceptual framework project' (1978: 4).

The FASB is therefore clearly on record that any conceptual framework must start with a clean sheet. The question to be considered is 'what type of financial statements will fulfil the objectives of financial reporting?' The subsequent development of the standard-setting process, however, is an object lesson of how awareness of a danger is no guarantee that it will be avoided. For the question that seems to have preoccupied the standard setters is 'how can the objectives of financial reporting be fulfilled by the *existing* type of financial statements?' The clear failure to abide by the FASB assurances has attracted well-aimed criticism. 'A conceptual framework should be more than an *ex post facto* justification of an already chosen approach' (Ernst & Young, 2004: 99).

A NEW OPPORTUNITY

The argument presented in this book represents an attempt to meet the aspirations expressed by the FASB at the outset of the conceptual framework project by following Canning's advice and 'going back to fundamentals for a fresh start' (1929: 9). The segregated system outlined in Part V follows the FASB's view of accountability in business. 'Management of an enterprise is periodically accountable to the owners not only for the custody and safekeeping of enterprise resources but also for their efficient and profitable use' (FASB, 1978: 25). This is reflected in the emphasis throughout this book on the two major functions of financial reporting:

1 *stewardship reporting* on the safekeeping of resources, and
2 *performance reporting* on their efficient use.

185

The segregated system is the result of starting with a clean sheet and considering (without preconceptions) what set of financial statements is appropriate for these two functions.

STEWARDSHIP REPORTING AND THE CONCEPTUAL FRAMEWORK PROJECT

Stewardship reporting requires a reliable system of recording transactions that satisfies the requirement stated by the Accounting Standards Board in *FRS 5*. 'A reporting entity's financial statements should report the substance of the transactions into which it has entered' (2005: 405).

To return to the simple example used in Chapter 2, suppose a firm purchases four widgets for £10,000 cash. The transaction has two elements: (1) an outflow of £10,000 cash; and (2) an inflow of four widgets. For recording both elements – and therefore the *substance* – of the transaction, Pacioli's double-entry bookkeeping system has proved its worth for over five centuries. As it is unlikely to be bettered, it remains the ideal choice; and it is adopted for the stewardship function in the segregated system.

Given that the title of *FRS 5* is 'Reporting the substance of transactions', the Accounting Standards Board is open to criticism for confusing the issue by introducing the question of valuation. 'The future economic benefits inherent in an asset are never completely certain in amount; there is always some risk that the benefits will turn out to be greater or less than expected' (2005: 401). That is perfectly true; but future benefits, though they may be a reflection on the wisdom of a transaction, do not affect its substance. If the *substance* of the transaction is the purchase of four widgets for £10,000, the *value* of the widgets (important though it may be for other reasons) has no bearing on this. To move out of the physical dimension is a step too far; it is liable to distract attention from the real issue: an accurate record of the substance of the transaction.

It is not just for recording transactions that Pacioli's five-hundred-year-old system is the first choice; it is also the clear favourite for keeping track of resources. The tables in Chapter 2 illustrate that historical cost is an excellent basis for providing monetary *symbols of volume*. As a result, conventional historical accounts are highly effective in symbolizing the operational flow of resources during the period (in the profit and loss account) and the stock of resources at the end of the period (in the balance sheet).

For stewardship reporting on the safekeeping of resources, conventional historical cost accounting is therefore a logical choice for a conceptual framework project that starts with a clean sheet. It clearly meets the FASB's major requirement for resource accounting in the 'physical dimension'. 'Financial reporting should provide information about the economic resources of an enterprise, the claims to those resources . . . , and the effects of transactions, events, and circumstances that change resources and claims to those resources' (1978: 19, 20). The conventional historical cost system is therefore adopted unchanged for the segregated system outlined in Chapter 15.

186

Without the distraction of asset valuation, there is a much greater likelihood of meeting the requirements of standards like *FRS 5*.

> Transactions requiring particularly careful analysis will often include features such as –
> (i)   the party that gains the principal benefits generated by an item is not the legal owner of the item,
> (ii) a transaction is linked with others in such a way that the commercial effect can be understood only by considering the series as a whole, or
> (iii) an option is included on terms that make its exercise highly likely.
>
> (ASB, 2005: 401)

To dismiss stewardship reporting on the safekeeping of resources as mere 'bean counting' betrays ignorance of its complexity. It is a dangerous undervaluation of a function that is vitally important to the operation of a modern economy. Some of the most serious financial scandals have been characterized by failure to perform this function adequately. 'Regulators, as is from time to time unhappily illustrated when businesses fail, are far more interested in the proper stewardship of assets that currently exist than in predicting future cash flows' (Ernst & Young, 2004: 100).

Segregated resource accounts, prepared without the distraction of value measurement, permit a return to the old-fashioned professional tradition with its emphasis on the necessity of an effective system of internal control. For reasons to be explained in the next chapter, it is a tradition liable to achieve more than the Sarbanes-Oxley Act passed into United States law in 2002.

In moving beyond the 'physical dimension' of stewardship reporting on the safekeeping of resources and into the 'value dimension' of performance reporting on their efficient use, however, the choice of an appropriate financial statement is less obvious.

PERFORMANCE REPORTING AND THE CONCEPTUAL FRAMEWORK PROJECT

'The principal role of financial reporting' is, in the opinion of the FASB, 'to furnish the investor and lender with information useful to assess the prospective risks and returns associated with an investment' (1976: 3, 4).

> Financial reporting should provide information to help present and potential investors and creditors and other users in assessing the amounts, timing, and uncertainty of prospective cash receipts from dividends or interest and the proceeds from the sale, redemption, or maturity of securities or loans.
>
> (1978: 17)

187

Since the segregated value accounts are based explicitly on these flows, they fulfil the FASB requirement almost to the letter. The 'prospective cash receipts' are flows to investors across the *investment* threshold discussed in Chapter 11. The provision of information to help investors to make their own assessment is consistent with Kaldor's view that this is something 'which they alone are ultimately capable of deciding' (1955: 68). It is also consistent with Fisher's theory of income. This suggests that the conventional conceptual framework based on the approach adopted by Hicks (1939) should be abandoned in favour of the alternative, discussed in Chapters 4 and 9, based on the approach adopted by Fisher (1906).

> The implication of Fisher's approach is that different incomes need to be calculated for different investors in the same company, depending on the actual stream of consumption derived from their investment.
>
> (Chapter 4: 42)

The Fair Value Company (illustrated in Tables 9.1 and 9.2) is an extreme case where an 'event' makes some investors better off and others worse off. Income measurement applicable to all investors is not merely difficult; it is impossible. Segregated value accounts do not make the attempt. Instead, they provide information that enables individual investors to do so for themselves. Disclosure of the planned investment rate brings investment in the equity capital of business enterprises into line with other forms of investment.

Conventional financial statements are based on *past* flows across the *project* threshold. It is difficult to see how these statements could have been chosen 'to help present and potential investors and creditors and other users in assessing the amounts, timing, and uncertainty of prospective cash receipts' if the conceptual framework project had been started with a clean sheet.

Fair value accounting is not the answer. It has already been shown (in Part III) to be the dead end of a theoretical blind alley. If the accounts of Short-Term Exploitation Plc and Long-Run Development Plc are drawn up in accordance with the IASB's standards on fair value, they produce exactly the same figures as the resource accounts in Table 15.3. There is no way of 'predicting the ability of the entity to generate cash and cash equivalents in the future' (IASB, 2005: 36) from the first-year accounts. On the contrary, they demonstrate just how misleading past cash flows from projects across the *project* threshold can be as a guide to the future cash flows to investors across the *investment* threshold. Even though all the assets are cash (*ipso facto* at fair value), the fair value (resource) accounts are of little use to 'present and potential investors and creditors . . . [who] rank comparability among the most important qualities of useful financial information . . . in making rational investment and lending decisions' (FASB, 1976: 8, 10).

Given the stated purpose of providing information on 'prospective cash receipts' to investors, the only explanation for choosing the conventional financial statements is not that they fit into the conceptual framework, but that they conform to existing practice.

If the IASB were subjected to a Solomons-type evaluation, could it expect the award of a grade as high as an F?

REGULATION OR MARKET FORCES?

It is in performance reporting that the segregated system is clearly superior to the conventional system for meeting the objectives of the FASB's conceptual framework project. According to the FASB, 'the principal role of financial reporting [is] to furnish the investor and lender with information useful to assess the prospective risks and returns associated with an investment' (1976: 3, 4) including 'the amounts, timing, and uncertainty of prospective cash receipts' (1978: 17). By contrast with conventional 'hybrid' accounts based on past flows across the project threshold, segregated value accounts (of the type illustrated in Table 15.3) are based on future flows planned across the investment threshold. They are almost tailor-made to FASB specifications.

> Financial accounting is not designed to measure directly the value of a business enterprise, but the information it provides may be helpful to those who wish to estimate its value. . . . Although financial reporting should provide basic information to aid them, they do their own evaluating, estimating, predicting, assessing, confirming, changing or rejecting.
>
> (FASB, 1978: ix)

The segregated accounts provide an indication of what the investment 'package' *contains*. The misleading impression given by the standard-setting bodies is that conventional accounts, particularly when based on concepts like fair value, can provide an indication of what the 'package' is *worth*.

It is difficult to resist the conclusion that the greatest obstacle to 'truth in accounting' may be the standard-setting process itself. The current neo-Soviet approach seems to represent an attempt to secure corporate governance by regulation. Perhaps the job can be done more effectively by market forces?

Chapter 19

Accounting truth and economic reality

Sixty-five years have elapsed since the publication of MacNeal's *Truth in Accounting*. Little seems to have changed.

> Financial statements are undoubtedly the principal means by which investors are informed. They are undoubtedly relied upon by millions of investors. But they can never become the key to the solution of the basic problem of protecting the small investor until the faulty accounting principles underlying their preparation are changed to permit a presentation of simple truth as it is instinctively understood by laymen everywhere. . . . Financial statements today are composed of a bewildering mixture of accounting conventions, historical data, and present facts, wherein even accountants are often unable to distinguish between truth and fiction.
>
> (1939: 57 and vii)

'Truth in accounting' is not some sort of Holy Grail; nor is it a variety of Philosopher's Stone. There is no great mystery to be unravelled – no new discovery to be made. It is simply a question of being honest about the well-known characteristics of the existing accounting system.

Pacioli's mediaeval system of 'venture accounting', based on historical records of past transactions, is still an excellent instrument for stewardship reporting on the *safekeeping* of resources. But it is no longer reliable for performance reporting on their *efficient use* in a modern going concern – except on the false assumption that each accounting period is an exact replica of every other.

The solution proposed in this book is 'segregation': keep Pacioli's mediaeval system for reporting on stewardship – and develop something different for reporting on performance.

TRUTH IN STEWARDSHIP REPORTING

Probably the least contentious aspect of the segregated system is the retention of Pacioli's transactions-based system of historical-cost resource accounts. The main departure is the

190

renaming of the profit and loss account and balance sheet in order to indicate that they symbolize the volume of operations during the accounting period and the volume of resources – the contents of the firm's 'box of tools' – at the balance sheet date. The auditors' report (illustrated in Tables 16.2 and 16.4) is designed to give explicit warning that nothing in these resource accounts should be misinterpreted either 'as a measure of value' or 'as a measure of economic performance'.

This is an unashamed reversion to the traditional view that properly audited accounts should offer protection, not against the risk of doing business, but against the risk of fraud and error. For this essential but limited role, historical cost is a perfectly reasonable choice. There can be very few high-profile accounting scandals that have been caused by the use of historical costs rather than current values. There can be very few that would have been prevented by the use of current values rather than historical costs.

The retention of a transactions-based historical cost system of accounting for stewardship does not mean that there is no place for current market values. On the contrary, whatever current values (entry or exit) are considered 'relevant' for an item or group of items *should* be shown prominently in the balance sheet – but in a note alongside the historical figures (and that includes the disclosure of liabilities incurred without any corresponding transaction). They would then appear under their true colours as estimates. They would not (as they are in the conventional system) be allowed to masquerade as facts.

This meets MacNeal's call for 'the truthful balance sheet' (1939: 189–194) which discloses the 'economic values' of *all* balance sheet items (not just of financial instruments). If Chambers is the father of fair value accounting (see page 89), then MacNeal is its grandfather – and, for items not traded in an active market, nothing in his argument precludes the choice of a more accurate term, 'for instance "calculated value"' (Ernst & Young, 2004: 125). The disclosure of such values is a useful and important indication of potential at the balance sheet date.

On the other hand, the very fact of an item's appearance in the balance sheet is conclusive evidence that the opportunity for exchanging it at its market value has been rejected. It would, indeed, be more accurate and less misleading if 'fair value accounting' were renamed 'rejected opportunity accounting'. The segregated system therefore parts company with MacNeal's proposal for 'the truthful profit and loss statement' (1939: 194–199) made up of changes in economic value during the accounting period. It is because they represent differences between rejected opportunities that value *changes* are not recognized in the segregated system for the purpose of reporting performance.

TRUTH IN PERFORMANCE REPORTING

Although the use of segregated value accounts for performance reporting is a radical departure from the conventional approach, it is based on an inescapable fact of economic and business life. 'It has been said that we should call no man happy until he is dead;

likewise perhaps we should call no firm profitable until it has been finally liquidated' (Boulding, 1962: 53).

Any report on the performance of an ongoing business must include any impact its past may have on its future. The value accounts are openly based on the subjective expectations of the firm's managers expressed in the form of their 'planned investment rate'. In the debate over what should replace historical cost, one of the most frequently quoted justifications is the famous observation attributed to Keynes, that 'it is better to be vaguely right than precisely wrong'. But the essential prerequisite for truth in performance reporting is not so much to be vaguely right as to be rightly vague. That is why the auditors' report (illustrated in Tables 16.2 and 16.4) draws attention to the fact that the value accounts are based upon management forecasts and gives an explicit warning that 'it is likely *as a matter of normal routine* that they will require correction in the future'. This is simply stating a fact of business and economic life and repeats the warning given by one of the ICAEW's most distinguished presidents (quoted, without apology, for the third time).

> The assessment of profit of a going concern for so short a period as 12 months is usually not a simple matter of objective recording and calculation; it calls largely for commercial judgment in evaluating the outcome of transactions not yet completed.
>
> (R.G. Leach, *The Times*, 22 September 1969)

That may be highly inconvenient; but it is the truth. In the segregated system, this warning is clearly signposted at the top of the cliff (prominently displayed in the accounts when they are published) rather than at the bottom of the cliff (grudgingly admitted in the media after a collapse has occurred).

Segregated value accounts drive home the essential economic reality. Truth in performance reporting is dependent on the constant revision of expectations in the light of continually changing circumstances.

Insofar as it leaves the traditional system of stewardship accounting completely undisturbed, the segregated system has a stronger claim than many other proposals to be 'evolutionary rather than revolutionary'. On the other hand, segregated performance reporting based on the planned investment rate does mark a clean break with tradition – a break that could be regarded as shocking.

'THE INVESTOR WHO . . .'

During the 1920s and 1930s, H.M. Bateman became famous for a series of cartoons entitled 'The Man Who . . .'. In each case, a perfectly innocent remark provoked such shock and horror that onlookers fell off their chairs, monocles shot out of the eyes of apoplectic colonels, ladies swooned, parrots fell off their perches, and even the cats and dogs were in a state of collapse.

192

It is possible to imagine that 'The Investors Who Wanted to Know the Planned Rate of Return on their Investment' might provoke similar outrage. Yet is such a reaction justified? Before spending money on home improvements, for example, it is quite normal to ask the contractor two questions: (1) 'What are you proposing to do?' and (2) 'How much are you intending to charge?' It is not normal to say: 'Do whatever you think and charge whatever you like.' Yet those are the instructions, in effect, to those entrusted with the management of a public company. As long as they operate within the company's constitution and obey the law of the land, their remit is: 'Do whatever you want and take whatever remuneration you like.'

Effective corporate governance is an urgent necessity; but is it more likely to be achieved by further additions to the existing mountain of regulations or by exposure to market forces?

CORPORATE GOVERNANCE: A NEO-SOVIET APPROACH?

In the 1960s, members of the Institute of Chartered Accountants in England and Wales had to make do with less than two hundred pages of 'recommendations on accounting principles'. The 2005/2006 issue of *Accounting Standards* published by the Accounting Standards Board has 3,086 pages, the 2005/2006 issue of *Auditing & Reporting* published by the Auditing Practices Board has 2,796 pages, and *International Financial Reporting Standards (IFRSs™) 2005* published by the International Accounting Standards Board has 2,305 pages. The only thing that seems to be growing faster than the financial scandals themselves is the sheer volume of standards designed to prevent them.

The Sarbanes-Oxley Act passed in the United States in 2002 simply adds to the burden. Section 302 on 'corporate responsibility for financial reports' requires a company's principal executive and financial officers to sign a declaration that 'the financial statements, and other financial information included in the report, fairly present in all material respects the financial condition and results of operations'. Section 404 requires 'each annual report . . . to contain an assessment . . . of the effectiveness of the internal control structure and procedures . . . for financial reporting [to which] each registered public accounting firm that prepares or issues the audit report for the issuer shall attest'.

Is this likely to achieve anything that could not have been achieved by tightening up the enforcement of existing regulations? It would probably be more effective, and certainly much cheaper, to return to the principles set out in Chapter 1 of Spicer and Pegler's *Practical Auditing* (1911).

Although the Sarbanes-Oxley Act has been criticized as a very expensive sledge-hammer to crack a nut, the real objection is that it may actually make matters worse by widening the expectation gap. The conventional accounting return can be dramatically influenced by the volume of activity. Short-Term Exploitation Plc and Long-Run Development Plc have been used throughout this book to illustrate the powerful incentive built into the conventional system to keep activity high – by fair means (like short-termist decisions) or foul (like premature recognition of revenue).

Insofar as the Sarbanes-Oxley Act succeeds in deterring illegal manipulation, it creates an even more powerful incentive to achieve 'better' performance by the perfectly legal means of 'short-termism'. The first-year accounts of Short-Term Exploitation Plc are drawn up strictly in accordance with accounting standards (including those on fair value accounting) that apply all over the world. Compliance with the Sarbanes-Oxley Act requires the company's auditors and principal officers to sign a declaration that accounts showing a return on capital employed of 33.1 per cent are 'fairly presented'. And that is so, even if they believe that the company is on course for a return of only 20 per cent per annum.

> An honest management may be prevented from telling the truth, or may perhaps even be prevented from knowing it, while a dishonest management may find itself in a position to take full advantage of the distortion of facts.
>
> (MacNeal, 1939: ix)

English law is quite clear on the subject of 'false accounting'.

> Where a person dishonestly, with a view to gain for himself or another . . ., in furnishing information for any purpose produces . . . any account . . . which to his knowledge is or may be misleading, false or deceptive in a material particular; he shall, on conviction on indictment, be liable to imprisonment for a term not exceeding seven years.
>
> (Theft Act 1968: section 17)

The case of Short-Term Exploitation Plc raises an interesting question: by seeking to enforce current accounting standards, does the Sarbanes-Oxley Act prevent false accounting or does it make it compulsory?

By contrast, the segregated system reduces the incentive to short-termism and false accounting by shifting the focus of performance reporting from the resource accounts to the value accounts; and, by limiting the resource accounts to strictly audited historical transactions, it reduces the opportunity.

For performance reporting, the contrast between the two systems could hardly be more striking. In the conventional system, the view published as 'true and fair' is based on *undisclosed* assumptions normally known to be false; in the segregated system it is based on *openly disclosed* assumptions believed to be true.

If accounts are prevented from reflecting the truth, however, the fault lies not with the law but with the accounting standards that the law seeks to enforce.

WHAT'S WRONG WITH THE STANDARD-SETTING PROCESS?

There is a well-established method for testing accounting standards.

> It is . . . by reconstructing the most perfect conditions under which accounting could be practiced, and by determining what the ideal aim of accounting should be under such conditions. After this has been done, it can be determined how far present conditions vary from perfect conditions and what compromises this variance necessitates in the practical accomplishment of the ideal aim.
>
> (MacNeal, 1939: 174, 175)

That is the approach that has been followed in this book. Simple sets of accounts (like those of Short-Term Exploitation Plc, Long-Run Development Plc, and the Fair Value Company) have been subjected to the acid test of the 'Kaldor criterion'. Any flaws in the system are immediately exposed. It is easy to see that, whether it is adjusted for inflation or presented in terms of fair values, the conventional system is liable to give an indication of 'the return an entity obtains on the resources it controls' that may be seriously misleading.

The conspicuous failure of the accounting standards bodies to conduct such simple tests justifies MacNeal's criticism of those who 'start from a basis of expediency and . . . work toward the ideal only as expediency might dictate'. 'The tendency is to change the ideals themselves by inventing theories which justify the practices necessitated by expediency' (MacNeal, 1939: 175). That is a pretty accurate description of the history of accounting standards from the inflation accounting controversy of the 1970s to the advent of fair value accounting.

Complaints from politicians, investment analysts, the banking community, and within the accountancy profession itself have drawn attention to the meaningless and misleading fluctuations that can be produced by fair value accounting. Too often, when confronted with these difficulties, however, standard-setting bodies have taken the decision to 'look them squarely in the eye and pass on'. This has given rise to what Keynes might have described as 'mingled rage and perplexity in face of the standard-setting bodies, because they are denying what is obvious'. 'One recurs to the analogy between the sway of the fair value school of accounting theory and that of certain religions' (1936: 350, 351 *mutatis mutandis*).

ECONOMIC DEMOCRACY

'Financial scandals' which involve wrongdoing on a massive scale are always guaranteed to hit the headlines. But more harm is probably done to the economy by the routine distortion imparted by the system itself, so that, by acting in strict conformity with IASB

195

standards, 'the sincere and honest accountant of today is all too likely to be an unconscious purveyor of misinformation' (MacNeal, 1939: ix).

> The main damage from the present system does not stem from the few companies . . . where things go spectacularly wrong. The real worry concerns the many companies where, unspectacularly, things merely go less than right.
>
> (*The Economist*, 29 August 1970: 9)

It is a question of effective corporate governance. Those who are appointed for their professional expertise in the management of business enterprises should be accountable 'not only for the custody and safekeeping of enterprise resources but also for their efficient and profitable use' (FASB, 1978: 25). Is there any reason why they should not disclose the rate of return they are planning to obtain on the resources with which they have been entrusted? What better way can there be of stimulating competition at the managerial level than exposure to the invisible hand of market forces? Not only is it likely to impose a far more effective form of corporate governance than any number of regulations; it is also consistent with the view taken by the FASB.

> Financial reporting is not an end in itself but is intended to provide information that is useful in making business and economic decisions – for making reasoned choices among alternative uses of scarce resources in the conduct of business and economic activities.
>
> (FASB, 1978: 5)

Conventional accounts, however, cannot give a reliable indication of the return on investment in a going concern except on the 'perpetual repetition' assumption that each accounting period is an exact replica of every other. But this is something that the standard-setting bodies seem unable to admit. Accounts published as 'true and fair' in accordance with modern accounting standards are therefore normally an indication, not of the return that *is* being earned, but of the return that is *not* being earned. Thousands of pages of accounting standards have been issued ostensibly for the purpose of keeping investors informed. Yet millions of savers and pensioners with investments in the equity share capital of public companies have no realistic idea of the return on their pensions and savings.

Fortunately, there is a simple remedy for bringing the standard-setting bodies themselves to account – and it might just work. It is to follow the example of the Lords Justices assembled in Privy Council on 12 July 1720, and to declare illegal the promotion of any enterprise '*for earning a rate of return of great advantage, but nobody to know what it is*'.

Appendix A

'Economic income': the fatal flaw

The notion of 'economic income' – commonly held up in the literature of accounting as the 'theoretical ideal' – is normally based on the argument presented by Hicks in Chapter 14 of *Value and Capital*.

This appendix considers the question, raised in Chapter 4, whether there is a flaw in the argument.

The starting point is what Hicks calls the 'central criterion'. 'A person's income is what he can consume during the week and still expect to be as well off at the end of the week as he was at the beginning' (1939: 176).

'Well-offness' is identified with the ability to consume. At the beginning of any period, an individual has the opportunity of consuming at various different levels according to various different time patterns. 'Income' for the period is what can be consumed during the period without altering the *hypothetical* consumption prospect. What is 'maintained intact' is the ability to look forward to the same *hypothetical* consumption prospect at the end of the period as at the beginning. Consequently, any number of 'hypothetical consumption concepts' of income can be developed, depending on which particular hypothetical consumption prospect is chosen as the standard to be maintained.

ILLUSTRATION

The return expected from an investment is a single cash receipt of £13,200 in two years' time. The expected annual rates of interest (chosen for ease of calculation) are as follows: during Year 1 – 10 per cent; during Year 2 – 20 per cent; thereafter 10 per cent. In other words, the annual rate of interest is 10 per cent throughout, except for Year 2 when it is 20 per cent.

In order to give Hicks's argument every possible assistance, it is assumed that all markets are perfect, all prices are stable, all tastes remain unchanged, and all expectations are fulfilled.

Table A.1 shows a few of the opportunities (or *hypothetical* consumption prospects) made possible by the £13,200 return expected from the investment. They include the following alternatives: (1) the immediate consumption of £10,000, (2) the consumption of £4,245.61 at the end of each of the next three years (the three-year annuity), (3) the consumption of £2,816.39 at the end of each of the next five years (the five-year annuity), and (4) the consumption of £1,081.97 at the end of each year indefinitely (the perpetual annuity). The table indicates how these opportunities can be financed (from the expected return of £13,200 at the end of Year 2) by borrowing or lending at the market rates of interest.

If 'well-offness' is identified with the opportunity for immediate consumption, then immediate consumption of £10,000 is the 'standard consumption prospect' to be maintained intact. Table A.2 shows that £1,000 can be consumed at the end of Year 1, if the opportunity of consuming £10,000 immediately is to be preserved. In Hicksian terminology, the potential consumption of £1,000 is 'Income No.1'.

If 'well-offness' is identified with the opportunity for constant annual consumption, then the perpetual annuity of £1,081.97 is the 'standard consumption prospect' to be maintained intact. Table A.2 shows that £1,081.97 can be consumed at the end of Year 1, if the opportunity of consuming £1,081.97 at the end of every subsequent year is to be preserved. In Hicksian terminology, the potential consumption of £1,081.97 is 'Income No.2'.

Table A.1 *Four hypothetical consumption prospects*

End of:		Immediate consumption	Three-year annuity	Five-year annuity	Perpetual annuity
		£	£	£	£
Year 0	Standard consumption	−10,000.00			
Year 0	Balance	−10,000.00			
Year 1	Interest at 10%	−1,000.00			
Year 1	Standard consumption		−4,245.61	−2,816.39	−1,081.97
Year 1	Balance	−11,000.00	−4,245.61	−2,816.39	−1,081.97
Year 2	Interest at 20%	−2,200.00	−849.12	−563.27	−216.39
Year 2	Standard consumption		−4,245.61	−2,816.39	−1,081.97
Year 2	Investment Returns	+13,200.00	+13,200.00	+13,200.00	+13,200.00
Year 2	Balance	0.00	3,859.65	7,003.95	10,819.67
Year 3	Interest at 10%		+385.96	+700.39	+1,081.97
Year 3	Standard consumption		−4,245.61	−2,816.39	−1,081.97
Year 3	Balance		0.00	4,887.95	10,819.67
Year 4	Interest at 10%			+488.79	+1,081.97
Year 4	Standard consumption			−2,816.39	−1,081.97
Year 4	Balance			2,560.35	10,819.67
Year 5	Interest at 10%			+256.04	+1,081.97
Year 5	Standard consumption			−2,816.39	−1,081.97
Year 5	Balance			0.00	10,819.67

Table A.2 *Four hypothetical consumption concepts of Income*

End of:		Immediate consumption Income No.1	Three-year annuity Income No.1.3	Five-year annuity Income No.1.5	Perpetual annuity Income No.2
		£	£	£	£
Year 1	Potential consumption	−1,000.00	−1,321.64	−1,213.36	−1,081.97
Year 1	**Standard consumption**	**−10,000.00**			
Year 1	Balance	−11,000.00	−1,321.64	−1,213.36	−1,081.97
Year 2	Interest at 20%	−2,200.00	−264.33	−242.67	−216.39
Year 2	**Standard consumption**		**−4,245.61**	**−2,816.39**	**−1,081.97**
Year 2	Investment Returns	+13,200.00	+13,200.00	+13,200.00	+13,200.00
Year 2	Balance	0.00	7,368.42	8,927.58	10,819.67
Year 3	Interest at 10%		+736.84	+892.76	+1,081.97
Year 3	**Standard consumption**		**−4,245.61**	**−2,816.39**	**−1,081.97**
Year 3	Balance		3,859.65	7,003.95	10,819.67
Year 4	Interest at 10%		+385.96	+700.39	+1,081.97
Year 4	**Standard consumption**		**−4,245.61**	**−2,816.39**	**−1,081.97**
Year 4	Balance		0.00	4,887.95	10,819.67
Year 5	Interest at 10%			+488.79	+1,081.97
Year 5	**Standard consumption**			**−2,816.39**	**−1,081.97**
Year 5	Balance			2,560.35	10,819.67
Year 6	Interest at 10%			+256.04	+1,081.97
Year 6	**Standard consumption**			**−2,816.39**	**−1,081.97**
Year 6	Balance			0.00	10,819.67

If 'well-offness' is identified with the opportunity for consuming in three equal annual instalments, then a three-year annuity of £4,245.61 is the 'standard consumption prospect' to be maintained intact. Table A.2 shows that £1,321.64 can be consumed at the end of Year 1, if the opportunity of consuming £4,245.61 at the end of each of the next three years is to be preserved. If Hicksian terminology is suitably modified, the potential consumption of £1,321.64 can be called 'Income No.1.3'.

If 'well-offness' is identified with the opportunity for consuming in five equal annual instalments, then a five-year annuity of £2,816.39 is the 'standard consumption prospect' to be maintained intact. Table A.2 shows that £1,213.36 can be consumed at the end of Year 1, if the opportunity of consuming £2,816.39 at the end of each of the next five years is to be preserved. If Hicksian terminology is suitably modified, the potential consumption of £1,213.36 can be called 'Income No.1.5'.

An infinite number of patterns, both regular and irregular, can be chosen as the 'standard consumption prospect' to be maintained intact. Even if the choice of standard is confined to regular patterns, a whole series of income concepts can be developed based on annuities of different lengths. Income No.1.1 measures 'well-offness' in terms of a one-year annuity; Income No.1.2 measures 'well-offness' in terms of a two-year annuity; and so on, right up to the perpetual annuity of Income No.2. Since any pattern, regular or irregular, can be chosen as the 'standard', the number of possible hypothetical consumption concepts of income is infinite.

The 'income concepts' illustrated in Table A.2 are all consistent with the view of income as what remains after 'maintaining capital intact'. Since capital is the source of the consumption prospect, 'maintaining capital intact' means maintaining intact the consumption prospect. The differences between the various income concepts illustrated in Table A.2 are attributable to the variety of consumption patterns chosen as the standard to be maintained.

THE FLAW IN THE ARGUMENT?

The argument used by Hicks to prove the superiority of Income No.2 over Income No.1 is summarized in Chapter 4. A similar argument can, however, be used to prove the superiority of *any* of the hypothetical consumption concepts over any other.

Income No.1.3, for example, can be 'proved' to be superior to Income No.1. According to Income No.1, the owner of the two-year investment in the illustration can spend no more than £1,000 at the end of the first year, if he is to expect to have £10,000 again at his disposal at the end of the year. But there is a problem caused by the expected change in the rate of interest.

> The same sum (£10,000) available at the beginning of the first [year] makes possible a [three-year] stream of expenditures
>
> £4,245.61, £4,245.61, £4,245.61,
>
> while if it is available at the beginning of the second [year] it makes possible a stream
>
> £4,386.71, £4,386.71, £4,386.71.
>
> It will ordinarily be reasonable to say that a person with the latter prospect is better off than one with the former. [Each of the three payments is increased by (£4,386.71 − £4,245.61 =) £141.10, the present value of which at the end of Year 1 is equal to £321.64.] This leads us to the definition of Income No.1.3 (£1,000 + £321.64 = £1,321.64), which is then a closer approximation to the central concept than Income No.1 is.
>
> (Hicks, 1939: 174, *mutatis mutandis*)

The superiority of Income No.1.3 over Income No.2 can be proved in a similar fashion. According to Income No.2, no more than £1,081.97 can be spent at the end of the first year, if the expectation is to be maintained of being able to spend the same amount at the end of each ensuing year. But there is a problem caused by the expected change in the rate of interest.

The same perpetual annuity (£1,081.97) available at the beginning of the first [year] makes possible a [three-year] stream of expenditures

£4,245.61, £4,245.61, £4,245.61,

while if it is available at the beginning of the second [year] it makes possible a stream

£4,350.75, £4,350.75, £4,350.75.

It will ordinarily be reasonable to say that a person with the latter prospect is better off than one with the former. [Each of the three payments is increased by (£4,350.75 − £4,245.61 =) £105.14, the present value of which at the end of Year 1 is equal to £239.67.] This leads us to the definition of Income No.1.3 (£1,081.97 + £239.67 = £1,321.64), which is then a closer approximation to the central concept than Income No.2 is.

(Hicks, 1939: 174, *mutatis mutandis*)

The flaw in the argument lies in treating a hypothetical possibility as if it were the consumption prospect actually chosen. It is *not* 'ordinarily reasonable to assume' that, because an individual *can* become better off by choosing one course of action, he *actually does* become better off even if he chooses another. The non sequitur is clearly exposed in cases where none of the standard patterns are, in fact, chosen. Conversely, the reason why the argument appears able to prove the superiority of *any* hypothetical concept over all the rest is the implicit assumption that the hypothetical pattern (peculiar to the particular concept in question) is the one actually chosen.

Ironically what Hicks's argument really proves is the validity of Fisher's criticism that the only flow of consumption that is relevant in determining 'well-offness' is the one actually chosen.

Suppose that the plan in the illustration is to consume £13,200 at the end of Year 2 and that the intention is actually carried out. It is by no means clear why Income No.2 should be regarded as 'a closer approximation to the central concept than Income No.1 is'. Nor is it clear that any of the hypothetical consumption concepts are relevant in determining how much better off the investor has become during Year 1. All of them are vulnerable to Fisher's objection that what matters to an individual is the actual stream of consumption – not some hypothetical alternative that can be consumed but isn't.

201

The weakness of the hypothetical consumption concepts of income in the measurement of economic performance is that the amount of consumption potentially available is not determined solely by the returns produced by the investment; it is also dependent on the rates of interest at which consumption in one period can be 'exchanged' for consumption in another period by the process of borrowing or lending. The hypothetical consumption stream may be affected, not by a change in the actual consumption stream itself, but simply by a change in the rate of interest at which the actual stream is discounted or accumulated. But, if individuals choose not to avail themselves of the opportunity of borrowing or lending, the interest rates at which they could do so have no effect on their 'well-offness'. The *opportunity* to obtain a larger consumption stream makes no one better off, unless it is *actually* obtained.

It is true that, if the rate of interest never varies, all the hypothetical consumption concepts give the same result. For example, if the rate of interest remains at 14.89 per cent per annum throughout, the income for Year 1 is £1,489.13 according to every concept from Income No.1, through Incomes No1.1, No.1.2, No.1.3, . . . and so on, right up to Income No.2. Nevertheless, the problems that arise when the rate of interest is subject to change are an indication of an inherent weakness.

Table A.2 concerns a 'textbook' world from which all real-life complications have been abstracted. The hypothetical consumption concepts of income can be seen in proper perspective. They simply measure the consequences of deferring a standard consumption prospect for the duration of the period in question. Where such a prospect is neither adopted nor even contemplated in the first place, it is difficult to see its relevance as a measure of economic performance.

What, then, is the relevance of 'income'?

THE RELEVANCE OF INCOME

If 'income' is to serve in the role suggested by Hicks 'as a guide for prudent conduct' (1939: 172), then it is as a guide to the *consumption* decision ('to give people an indication of the amount which they can consume without impoverishing themselves'). But it is of doubtful relevance in the measurement (either *ex ante* or *ex post*) of the performance promised or achieved by a productive economic activity. As a guide to the *production* decision, it has little to offer.

For that purpose, the income concept contains a fatal internal contradiction. Economic performance cannot be measured without reference to the sole end and object of all economic activity, namely, consumption. Fisher's actual consumption concept of income is vulnerable to the criticism that it 'may fluctuate in any manner whatsoever'.

The calculation of income consists in finding some sort of *standard* stream of values whose present capitalized value equals the present value of the stream of receipts which is actually in prospect. It is a standard stream in that it maintains some sort of constancy, as against the actual expected stream of receipts, which may fluctuate in any manner whatsoever. . . . We are replacing the actual expected stream of receipts by a standard stream, whose distribution over time has some definite standard shape. We ask, not how much a person actually does receive in the current week, but how much he would be receiving if he were getting a standard stream of the same present value as his actual expected receipts. That amount is his income.

(Hicks, 1939: 184)

The implication that this concept is less arbitrary than Fisher's is, however, groundless. Although the standard shape is definite *once it has been chosen*, the *choice* of the standard stream is just as arbitrary as the actual stream. Under both concepts, the income from an investment can rise or fall for reasons wholly unconnected with its performance.

This fatal weakness in the income concept is particularly serious, since the adoption of 'fair value' in the measurement of financial performance is justified on the basis of its closeness to 'economic income'.

The economic concept of income is founded on the maintenance of an enterprise's capital. Specifically, income is defined as the amount that can be distributed to equity owners of an enterprise while maintaining its capital, after adjustment for owners' contributions and withdrawals. Accounting conceptual frameworks generally accept that this should be the objective for income determination. . . . From a capital market perspective, an increase in the fair value of a financial asset is income in the important sense that it represents the amount that can be distributed to owners while maintaining the value of the capital invested in the financial asset to earn the current market rate of return. In other words, on a fair value basis capital is maintained in terms of the present value of the market's expectation of future cash flows to be generated by the asset discounted at the current available market rate of return adjusted for commensurate risk.

(Joint Working Group of Standard Setters, 2000: 233)

Appendix B

The 'accountant's rate of profit' (ARP) and the 'internal rate of return' (IRR)

THE INTERNAL RATE OF RETURN (IRR)

The 'internal rate of return' is 'an accurate *description* of the average rate of return per period over the life of the investment' (Chapter 7: 71). Nevertheless, the IRR is *not* a magnitude which a rational investor should seek to maximize: bigger is not necessarily better.

The apparent paradox is easily resolved.

The internal rate return of the investment is the rate at which the net present value of the investment is exactly equal to zero. It is equal to r in the equation:

$$\sum_{t=0}^{n} \frac{x_t}{\left(1+r\right)^t} = 0$$

where $x_0, {}_1, {}_2, {}_3, \cdots, {}_n$, is the net revenue series or equity cash flow. The possibility of multiple solutions does not exist in the case of financial investments where contributions from investors are followed by distributions to investors. Three investments of this type are described in Table B.1.

If the contributions and distributions are paid and received at the stated dates, the internal rate of return is an accurate description of the average annual return over the life of the investment. The IRR represents the rate of interest that the contribution would have to earn in a bank account in order to produce the same distributions at the same dates.

Although the IRR is an accurate description of the average annual rate of return earned by the three investments, it is not possible to make a rational choice between the investments on the basis of the *size* of the IRR alone.

Suppose the investor does not intend to spend the proceeds of any investment until the end of Year 2. Since Investment C is the only one where the whole capital is invested

Table B.1 *The equity cash flow from three alternative investments*

		Beginning of Year 1	End of Year 1	End of Year 2	Internal rate of return
Investment A	$\begin{bmatrix} \text{Contributions} - \\ \text{Distributions} + \end{bmatrix}$	– £1,000	+ £1,240		24% p.a.
Investment B	$\begin{bmatrix} \text{Contributions} - \\ \text{Distributions} + \end{bmatrix}$	– £1,000	+ £600	+ £720	20% p.a.
Investment C	$\begin{bmatrix} \text{Contributions} - \\ \text{Distributions} + \end{bmatrix}$	– £1,000	+ £0	+ £1,369	17% p.a.

until the end of Year 2, the choice is dependent on the rate of return which the investor would earn *outside* the other two investments.

Table B.2 shows the balance accumulated at the end of Year 2 by each of the investments with three different 'external rates'. It is evident that a rational choice between the three investments cannot be made on the basis of the internal rate alone, where the outcome may affected by the external rate.

What this demonstrates is *not* that the IRR is a misleading indicator of the return on an investment, but that it needs to be accurately expressed. 'Accurate expression' of the internal rate of return requires, not just correct calculation of the rate, but also the specification of *both* 'dimensions' of the investment on which the rate is earned. '[The IRR] is meaningless, . . . unless Jevons' two dimensions of capital investment – the amount of the investment and the duration of the investment – are specified' (Rayman, 1972: 18; cf. Jevons, 1871: 229–233).

Table B.3 demonstrates that Investment A's 24 per cent IRR is on an investment of £1,000 for the duration of one year, whereas Investment B's IRR of 20 per cent is on an investment of £500 for the duration of one year *plus* an investment of £500 for the duration of two years, and Investment C's IRR of 17 per cent is on an investment of £1,000 for the duration of two years.

Not only is the IRR of each of the three alternatives an accurate description of the return on the investment, but specification of the 'two dimensions' makes clear the extent to which the IRRs are or are not comparable. For an investor who intends to wait for two years before spending any of the proceeds (and whose 'outside' investment opportunities earn less than 10 per cent per annum), there is no paradox in deciding that Investment C's 17 per cent per annum for two years is preferable to Investment A's 24 per cent per annum for one year. In the special case, where the external rate is the *same* as the internal rate (for example, because the opportunity for investment at the internal rate is available at any time), then the investment with the highest IRR will produce the greatest returns.

Table B.2 The balance accumulated by the three investments

'External rate' = 5%

	Investment A	£	Investment B	£	Investment C	£
End of Year 1	Distribution	1,240	Distribution	600	Distribution	0
	Return @ 5%	62	Return @ 5%	30	Return @ 5%	0
End of Year 2	Distribution	0	Distribution	720	Distribution	1,369
	Balance	1,302	Balance	1,350	Balance	1,369
	Ranking	3rd	Ranking	2nd	Ranking	1st

'External rate' = 10%

	Investment A	£	Investment B	£	Investment C	£
End of Year 1	Distribution	1,240	Distribution	600	Distribution	0
	Return @ 10%	124	Return @ 10%	60	Return @ 10%	0
End of Year 2	Distribution	0	Distribution	720	Distribution	1,369
	Balance	1,364	Balance	1,380	Balance	1,369
	Ranking	3rd	Ranking	1st	Ranking	2nd

'External rate' = 15%

	Investment A	£	Investment B	£	Investment C	£
End of Year 1	Distribution	1,240	Distribution	600	Distribution	0
	Return @ 15%	186	Return @ 15%	90	Return @ 15%	0
End of Year 2	Distribution	0	Distribution	720	Distribution	1,369
	Balance	1,426	Balance	1,410	Balance	1,369
	Ranking	1st	Ranking	2nd	Ranking	3rd

Table B.3 Specification of the 'two dimensions' of each investment

	Investment A		Investment B			Investment C	
	Duration:	ONE year	Duration:	ONE year	TWO years	Duration:	TWO years
		£		£	£		£
Initially	Amount	1,000	Amount	500	500	Amount	1,000
After one year	Return @ 24%	+240	Return @ 20%	+100	+100	Return @ 17%	+170
	Distribution	1,240	Distribtn./Balance	600	600	Balance	1,170
After two years			Return @ 20%		+120	Return @ 17%	+199
			Distribution		720	Distribution	1,369

The IRR is, by far, the most commonly used method of describing the returns to investors from various types of financial investment. An indication of the distribution pattern is a convenient and readily understandable method of indicating the 'two dimensions'. For most types of financial investment, this is close to becoming the norm. These investments include bank and building society deposits, company debentures and loan stock, government securities, life assurance policies, and national savings. In Britain, the IRR is commonly quoted in financial advertisements in the form of an 'APR' or 'annual(ized) percentage rate' together with an indication of the likely pattern of distributions.

It is not without significance that almost the sole exception is investment in the equity share capital of limited companies.

THE ACCOUNTANT'S RATE OF PROFIT (ARP)

The relationship between the accountant's rate of profit (ARP) and the internal rate of return (IRR) is an area of longstanding controversy. The outcome of this controversy is crucially important for the setting of accounting standards. The criterion for judging the validity of the ARP (which seems to be accepted by critics and supporters alike) is its closeness to the IRR (see, for example, Harcourt (1965), Solomon (1971), Kay (1976), and Wright (1978)). The implication is that in an economic utopia (free from the accounting problems normally encountered in the real world) the ARP would be an accurate measure of the IRR.

A useful test case is provided by the activities of the two firms (whose accounts are presented in Table 7.3). None of Harcourt's 'irrelevant factors' are present: there are no price changes, no expectations are disappointed, and (since the only balance sheet asset is cash) there are no arbitrary valuations.

Because there are no distributions to shareholders until the end of the life of both firms, a simple discounted average of the annual ARPs is equal to the lifetime IRR.

For Short-Term Exploitation Plc, the IRR is equal to:

$$\sqrt[3]{(1.331 \times 1.21 \times 1.1)} - 1 = \sqrt[3]{1.771561} - 1 = 0.21; \text{ or } 21 \text{ per cent.}$$

For Long-Run Development Plc, the IRR is equal to:

$$\sqrt[3]{(1.2 \times 1.44 \times 1.728)} - 1 = \sqrt[3]{2.985984} - 1 = 0.44; \text{ or } 44 \text{ per cent.}$$

It is important to emphasize that *this method of calculation is not appropriate in all cases*. A simple discounted average works in this instance only because all profits are reinvested. Each ARP therefore carries equal weight. If there are distributions, however, the later ARPs are earned on a smaller balance and are deprived of some of their influence. Consequently, the ARPs need to be suitably weighted. (In the special case where the ARP remains constant from period to period, differences in weightings are of no consequence and the constant ARP is equal to the lifetime IRR.)

A weighting formula which applies generally is given by Edwards *et al.*

The IRR is equal to the average ARP of an activity weighted by the book value of capital employed discounted at the IRR, thus enabling the IRR of an activity to be derived iteratively from the ARPs and book values of capital employed over the activity's lifetime.

(1987: 25)

It involves picking a value for *r* and continuing to do so until a value for *r* is found which satisfies the equation (1987: 26):

$$r = \frac{\displaystyle\sum_{t=1}^{T} \frac{a_t V_{t-1}}{(1+r)^t}}{\displaystyle\sum_{t=1}^{T} \frac{V_{t-1}}{(1+r)^t}}$$

where a_t is the ARP in period t and V_{t-1} is the book value of capital employed at the end of the previous period.

In the case of Short-Term Exploitation Plc, the choice of 21 per cent for *r* satisfies the equation by giving the following value for the right-hand side:

$$\frac{(0.331 \times 1,000,000)}{1.21} + \frac{(0.21 \times 1,331,000)}{1.21^2} + \frac{(0.1 \times 1,610,510)}{1.21^3}$$

$$\frac{1,000,000}{1.21} \qquad \frac{1,331,000}{1.21^2} \qquad \frac{1,610,510}{1.21^3}$$

$$= \frac{273,553.72 + 190,909.09 + 90,909.09}{826,446.28 + 909,090.91 + 909,090.91} = \frac{555,371.90}{2,644,628.10} = 0.21$$

The essential point, which is clearly brought out by Edwards *et al.*, is that a suitably weighted average of the ARPs is always equal to the lifetime IRR *whatever method of accounting is used*. The one important proviso is that no value changes are allowed to bypass the ARPs.

> It requires *all* changes in the book value of capital employed to flow through the profit and loss account: the balance sheet and the profit and loss account are thus fully articulated.
>
> (1987: 24)

In the case of Short-Term Exploitation Plc, there is a lifetime change in book value from £1,000,000 to £1,771,561. As long as the change of £771,561 goes through the profit and loss account during the firm's lifetime, the average ARP is always equal to the lifetime IRR of 21 per cent. The same applies to the lifetime change of £1,985,984 in Long-Run Development Plc's book value.

Table B.4 is just one example which indicates that accounting conventions, however arbitrary or peculiar, have no bearing whatsoever on the identity between the lifetime weighted average of the ARPs and the lifetime IRR.

In the case of both companies, opening book values for the beginning of Year 2 and Year 3 have been arbitrarily assumed (and any other figures could have been assumed instead). The one thing that Table B.4 does have in common with Table 7.3 is that both companies have the same opening contribution of capital at the beginning of Year 1 and the same closing distribution at the end of Year 3. This proves the long-term identity between the ARP and the IRR.

> It is . . . true (as Kay has shown) that, over the entire life of an investment, the accounting *rates of profit* must average out (with suitable weights) to the internal rate of return.
>
> (Wright, 1978: 466)

It also emphasizes how seriously misleading the ARPs of individual periods can be as a guide to the return on capital.

Table B.4 The irrelevance of the choice of accounting method

	Short-Term Exploitation Plc			Long-Run Development Plc		
	Opening book value	Accounting profit or loss	ARP	Opening book value	Accounting profit or loss	ARP
Year 1	£1,000,000	+£400,000	+40.00%	£1,000,000	−£200,000	−20.00%
Year 2	£1,400,000	+£420,000	+30.00%	£800,000	+£400,000	+50.00%
Year 3	£1,820,000	−£48,439	−2.66%	£1,200,000	+£1,785,984	+148.83%
Three-year total/average		+£771,561	+21.00%*		+£1,985,984	+44.00%*

* *Note:* As there are no distributions, a simple (unweighted) discounted average of the ARPs is equal to the IRR:
Short-Term Exploitation Plc: $\sqrt[3]{(1.4 \times 1.3 \times 0.9734)} - 1 = 0.21$; Long-Run Development Plc: $\sqrt[3]{(0.8 \times 1.5 \times 2.4883)} - 1 = 0.44$.

The present value fallacy: a graphical representation

The fallacy discussed in the text of Chapter 9 can be illustrated in terms of the 'Fisher diagrams' commonly encountered in textbooks on investment theory (see Fisher, 1907, 1930; cf. Hirshleifer, 1958).

INVESTMENT STRATEGY IN AN ECONOMIC UTOPIA

Figure C.1 is the standard textbook representation of a two-period economic utopia in terms of Fisher diagrams. Present consumption is measured along the horizontal axis; future consumption is measured up the vertical axis. All individuals are assumed to have the same initial endowment, OW_P. They have identical productive opportunities for converting present consumption into future consumption along the 'investment opportunity boundary', $W_P W_F$, which is concave to the origin in conformity with the assumption of diminishing marginal returns as present consumption is sacrificed in return for future consumption. They can also exchange present consumption for future consumption by borrowing or lending in a perfect capital market. The slope of the 'market opportunity line', $M_P M_F$, represents the market rate of interest at which every individual can borrow or lend without restriction.

The differing subjective preferences of each individual are represented by a family of 'willingness lines' (indifference curves) showing the amount of present consumption each individual is willing to give up in return for future consumption. The willingness lines are convex to the origin in conformity with the assumption of an increasing marginal rate of time preference as present consumption is sacrificed in return for future consumption.

$B_I B_I$ is just one of the family of willingness lines of an individual whose 'time preference' for present consumption over future consumption is relatively strong; $L_I L_I$ is one of the family of willingness lines of an individual whose time preference is relatively weak. For the sake of simplicity, it is assumed that $B_I B_I$ is representative of all individuals with a relatively *strong* time preference, and that $L_I L_I$ is representative of all individuals with a relatively *weak* time preference.

To reach the highest possible level of satisfaction, each individual has to make two decisions: an investment decision and a financing decision.

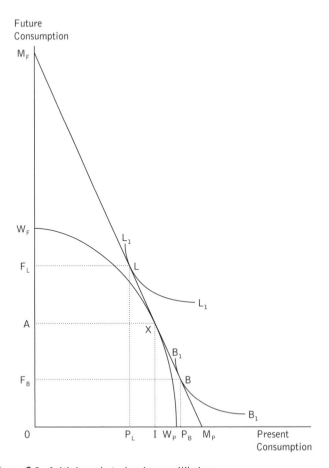

Figure C.1 Initial market-clearing equilibrium

The 'optimal' investment decision is not affected by the individual's subjective preferences: it is to move along the investment opportunity boundary until its slope (the marginal rate of return on investment) is equal to the market rate of interest. All individuals move from W_P to point X in Figure C.1 by investing IW_P.

The 'optimal' financing decision, by contrast, is dependent on the individual's subjective preferences. Individuals with a relatively strong time preference reach their highest level of satisfaction, B_1B_1, by *borrowing* until their subjective marginal rate of time preference is equal to the market rate of interest (moving from point X to point B by borrowing IP_B). Individuals with a relatively weak time preference reach their highest level of satisfaction, L_1L_1, by *lending* until their subjective marginal rate of time preference is equal to the market rate of interest (moving from point X to point L by lending IP_L).

Market-clearing equilibrium is achieved when the rate of interest (the slope of M_PM_F) is such that the aggregate amounts which individuals with a relatively strong time preference wish to borrow at the market rate of interest are exactly equal to the aggregate

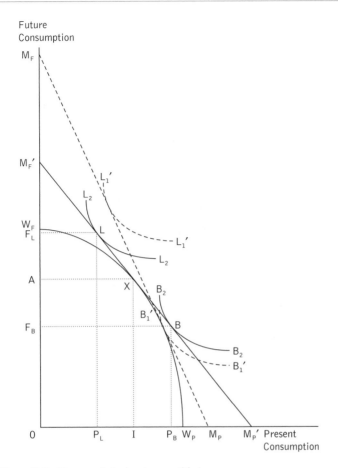

Figure C.2 New market-clearing equilibrium

amounts which individuals with a relatively weak time preference wish to lend. If the B_1B_1 curves and the L_1L_1 curves in Figure C.1 are assumed respectively to be representative of these two groups, the market clears when IP_B is equal to IP_L.

In an economy of millions of individuals, each with a different family of subjective willingness curves, millions of tangency points are likely to occur over the whole length of the market line. Highly profligate individuals (with a strong preference for present consumption) reach their optimum towards the lower right extreme at M_p; very thrifty individuals (with a strong preference for future consumption) reach their optimum towards the upper left extreme at M_F. As long as the aggregate amount offered by lenders is exactly equal to the aggregate amount demanded by borrowers, the slope of M_pM_F represents the market-clearing equilibrium rate of interest.

The significance of a perfect capital market is that the optimal investment strategy (at point X) is the same for all individuals *irrespective of their subjective consumption preferences.* M_p represents the maximum present value of each individual's investment opportunities

213

(and M_F represents the maximum future value). Given unrestricted access to a perfect capital market, a higher present (or future) value is preferable to a lower present (or future) value irrespective of subjective time preferences. A higher present (or future) value can be converted into a greater consumption stream *of any time shape* than can a lower present (or future) value.

The effect of a change in tastes in favour of greater thrift is shown in Figure C.2. Technology, represented by the investment opportunity boundary, $W_P W_F$, remains unchanged. The initial market opportunity line, $M_P M_F$, from Figure C.1 is reproduced as a dashed line in Figure C.2. The increased preference for future consumption over present consumption is indicated by the willingness lines shifting upwards to the left (from $L_1 L_1$ and $B_1 B_1$ in Figure C.1 to the dashed curves, $L_1' L_1'$ and $B_1' B_1'$, in Figure C.2). Since the points of tangency between the willingness lines and the initial 'dashed' market opportunity line have shifted upwards to the left, the (reduced) amount that individuals with a relatively strong time preference wish to borrow falls below the (increased) amount that individuals with a relatively weak time preference wish to lend. The result is disequilibrium. At the initial rate of interest, markets no longer clear. In an economic utopia of perfectly competitive markets, the rate of interest (represented by the slope of the market opportunity line) must fall.

The new equilibrium is shown in Figure C.2. With the flatter market opportunity line, $M_P' M_F'$, the tangency points, L and B, necessary to restore equality between desired borrowing and lending (IP_B and IP_L) are with new willingness lines, $L_2 L_2$ and $B_2 B_2$. Whereas $B_2 B_2$ represents a *higher* level of satisfaction than before for borrowers with a relatively strong time preference, $L_2 L_2$ represents a *lower* level of satisfaction than before for lenders with a relatively weak time preference.

Both figures reproduce the standard textbook argument which confirms the validity of Fisher's 'nineteenth-century version' of the net present value decision rule, discussed in Chapter 10.

> Since any time-shape may be transformed into any other no one need be deterred from selecting an income because of its time-shape, but may choose it exclusively on the basis of maximum present value. . . . It will then happen that his income as finally transformed will be larger than it could have been if he had chosen some other use which afforded that same time-shape.
>
> (1907: 144; cf. 1930: 138, 139)

Given unrestricted access to a perfect capital market, an investment opportunity with a greater present value affords the investor a bigger consumption stream, *whatever the chosen time pattern*. The maximization of NPV at point X in Figure C.1 (and at the shifted point X in Figure C.2) is the optimal investment strategy for all individuals *irrespective of their subjective individual time preferences*.

It is the inference drawn by the International Accounting Standards Board in *IAS 39* that is false. 'A gain or loss on a financial asset or financial liability classified as at fair value through profit or loss shall be recognised in profit or loss' (2005: 1684). It is a classic example of the present value fallacy.

Because an investor is better off with a bigger present value than with a smaller present value *at any given moment*, it does not *necessarily* follow that the investor becomes better off as a result of an increase in present value *over a period of time*.

A comparison between Figure C.1 and Figure C.2 exposes this argument as a non sequitur.

Although the present value has increased from M_p in Figure C.1 to M_p' in Figure C.2, the future value has fallen from M_F to M_F'. Individuals with a relatively strong time preference (represented by the *BB* curves) are better off with the new optimum than with the old optimum; individuals with a relatively weak time preference (represented by the *LL* curves) are worse off. Even in the perfect market-clearing equilibrium of an economic utopia, therefore, *change* in present value does *not* provide an unambiguous measure of *change* in 'well-offness' irrespective of individual subjective preferences.

There are, of course, many cases where an increase in present value makes *all* individuals better off. An expansion of the investment opportunity boundary which resulted in a parallel shift of the market opportunity line M_pM_F to the right would benefit *all* individuals whatever their consumption preferences. An increase in present value caused, not by an improvement in investment opportunities, but by a change in the interest rate at which they are discounted, may make some individuals better off and others worse off if their consumption preferences are different.

The case of the Fair Value Company discussed in Chapter 9 provides a numerical illustration of this possibility.

'Fair value accounting' is therefore based upon a dangerous fallacy. Its implementation carries a serious risk of 'false accounting'.

The vital distinction between funds and value

The distinction between 'funds' and 'value' corresponds to the distinction between the basic economic activities of the firm – production and exchange.

> Production is the process of transforming input into output and involves operations within the firm. Exchange is the process of buying input and selling output, which results in transactions with outsiders. External transactions are reflected in the flow of funds or purchase potential between the firm and outsiders. Internal operations are reflected in the flow of value or service potential within the firm.
>
> (Rayman, 1969: 53)

The definitions used for this purpose are based on the notion of property rights as claims that become operative when they are acknowledged according to the rules of society (which may be governed by law, custom, or other usage). These claims are classified in two ways: first, according to whether or not they are restricted to specific resources; second, according to whether or not they are current, in the sense of being operational *now* rather than at some time in the *future*. The four types of claim are represented in Figure D.1.

Funds

'Funds' are defined, from the point of view of a given entity like the firm, as current non-specific claims between the firm and all other entities. Since specific resources are not involved, the term describes a relationship between the firm and the 'outside world'. The relationship can, perhaps, be best described as one of 'current indebtedness'. This relationship may manifest itself in many different forms, as cash or trade debts for example, but these are the appearance rather than the substance.

> What it is desired to emphasize here and what appears to be often overlooked is the dynamic character of 'funds.' If funds are regarded as cash or working capital or current assets, a pool available in some quantity at any given point of time is strongly and perhaps inevitably suggested.
>
> (Goldberg, 1951: 489)

	Current	Non-current
Non-specific	FUNDS [positive, if in favour; negative, if against]	NON-FUNDS ASSETS [if in favour] or EQUITIES [if against]
Specific	NON-FUNDS ASSETS [positive, if in favour; negative, if against]	NON-FUNDS ASSETS [positive, if in favour; negative, if against]

Figure D.1 The four types of claim

Just as it is not possible to point at 'value' (or 'service potential') in the abstract apart from its manifestation in useful objects, so it is not possible to point at 'funds' (or 'purchase potential') in the abstract but only to items representing a stock of claims. Nevertheless, the concepts of funds and value are independent of their outward manifestations.

According to the definition of 'funds' as 'current non-specific claims', 'funds' *flow* between the firm and outsiders as current non-specific claims are created and cancelled. Where the inflow is greater than the outflow, 'funds' accumulate in the form of a *stock* of claims. The stock of claims or 'funds stock' may consist of various items, some positive and others negative. For a typical firm, positive items include cash, bank deposits, trade debtors, accrued income, accrued loan interest (receivable), matured capital repayments (receivable), unpaid dividends (receivable), etc. Negative items include overdrawn bank accounts, trade creditors, accrued expenses, accrued loan interest (payable), matured capital repayments (payable), unpaid dividends (payable), etc. The amount of the funds stock is equal to the excess of claims in the firm's favour over those against it. It may therefore be either positive or negative. The stock of funds at any given time represents the extent of the firm's 'purchase potential'.

Although they are not restricted to specific *resources*, most current non-specific claims are restricted to specific *entities* in the outside world. The main exception is cash. Cash is a current non-specific claim not restricted to any specific *entity* but which applies to the outside world in general. In the definition of funds as current non-specific claims, therefore, no distinction is made between cash and any other current non-specific claim.

The distinctive feature of this definition of funds is that (unlike definitions of funds as working capital or net current assets) it is not couched in terms of items constituting the stock of funds. Funds are not synonymous with funds stock. What constitutes the stock of funds can be deduced from the definition; it does not depend on knowledge of a list of items drawn up on some arbitrary basis.

217

Non-funds assets

It is consistent with the normal definition of an asset as a store of value or 'service potential' that any positive claim in the firm's favour is an asset. Since current non-specific claims have already been classed as 'funds', however, a special category of 'non-funds assets' needs to be created.

Non-funds assets include claims of the other three types:

1   *Current specific claims* (positive and negative)
    Current claims that are restricted to specific resources include all the asset services to which the firm is currently entitled. In most cases, the current claim to the services of an asset is established by legal ownership and physical possession; but that is not absolutely necessary. A firm's claims to specific resources are part of its non-funds assets, even if the resources themselves are not in the firm's possession or legal ownership (for example, after a payment in advance of delivery or a rental payment in advance of occupation). (A rental agreement transfers a claim to the use of a specific resource from the legal owner of the property to the payer of the rent, without affecting the owner's legal title to the property.) Conversely, outsiders' current claims to specific resources are not part of the firm's assets, even if the resources are held or legally owned by the firm (for example, after the receipt of a rental payment or income in advance). Current specific claims in favour of the firm are therefore included as positive non-funds assets; and current specific claims against the firm are deducted as negative non-funds assets.

2   *Non-current specific claims* (positive and negative)
    Non-funds assets include *non-current specific* claims in the firm's favour. This type of claim is relatively unusual. It does not become current until some date in the future, and, when it does, it attaches to a specific asset. Examples include assets for future delivery or long-term construction contracts. On delivery or completion, the non-current claims become current. Since all positive *specific* claims are non-funds assets, the distinction between *current* specific claims and *non-current* specific claims is not significant in this context. As in the case of current specific claims, outsiders' *non-current* claims to specific resources are not part of the firm's assets, even if the resources are held or legally owned by the firm. Non-current specific claims in favour of the firm are therefore included as positive non-funds assets; and non-current specific claims against the firm are deducted as negative non-funds assets.

3   *Non-current non-specific claims* (if positive)
    Non-funds assets also include *non-current non-specific* claims in the firm's favour. Examples of this type of claim are investments in securities or loans by the firm, where claims do not become current (in the form of dividends, interest, or capital repayment) until some future date that may or may not be initially specified. A ten-year loan made by the firm, for example, is a *non-current* non-specific claim in

favour of the firm, representing a non-funds asset. As it accrues, the interest becomes a *current* non-specific claim in the firm's favour and represents an inflow of funds. The same applies to the repayment of capital when it falls due.

Equities

Non-current non-specific claims of outsiders *against* the firm are 'equities'. Because the firm is regarded as an entity separate from its owners, the owners (or shareholders in the case of limited companies) are included among outsiders. Equities, therefore, include the non-current claims of owners as well as those of long-term creditors. A ten-year loan received by the firm, for example, is a *non-current* non-specific claim against the firm, representing an equity belonging to an outside creditor. As the interest accrues, it becomes a *current* non-specific claim against the firm and represents an outflow of funds. Similarly, a company's share capital is a *non-current* non-specific claim against the firm, representing an equity belonging to its shareholders. Whenever dividends are declared they become *current* non-specific claims against the firm and represent an outflow of funds.

The accounting identity, EQUITIES ≡ ASSETS, becomes:

EQUITIES ≡ NON-FUNDS ASSETS + FUNDS STOCK

For practical convenience, however, it is easy to accommodate the main conventional categories. Non-funds assets can be split between fixed assets, on the one hand, and current assets, on the other. Similarly, equities can be divided between claims belonging to owners (owners' equity) and claims belonging to outside creditors (long-term liabilities):

OWNERS' EQUITY + LONG-TERM LIABILITIES	≡	FIXED ASSETS + CURRENT ASSETS + FUNDS STOCK

The conventional distinctions can therefore be maintained more or less intact. The main departure caused by the definition of funds as current non-specific claims is that the current asset category is thereby restricted to those 'conventional current assets' that are not included in the funds stock.

THE FLOW OF FUNDS

Flows of funds normally occur at the date of delivery of goods or services. Purely as a matter of convenience, no record of the underlying transaction is normally made until the arrival of the relevant documentary evidence. In the majority of cases, this takes the form of a purchase or sales invoice relating to purchases or sales of goods or services. At the end of any accounting period, however, there are typically some transactions for which the documentary evidence has not yet appeared. Part of the routine process of recording *external* transactions is therefore to adjust the accounting records so that all transactions are included in the period in which they occur.

In the case of services like gas, water, and electricity, for example, there is a continuous flow of funds (from the consumer to the provider) as the services are used. The generation of an invoice at the end of the month, quarter, or other period does not itself constitute the flow of funds: it simply acts as confirmation of the consumption that caused the flow of funds to occur. The conventional accounting procedure is to record the cost of what has been consumed but not invoiced as an 'accrued expense'. Sometimes the amount is ascertained accurately by reading the relevant meter; but where the amount is not material a reasonable approximation (perhaps a proportion based on past experience) is often used instead. These approximations are sometimes referred to as *estimates*; but they are measures of *actual* transactions that have taken place *in the past*. They need to be carefully distinguished from *forecasts* of *expected* transactions that may or may not happen *in the future*.

In general, the transactions of most firms during their normal course of operations result in a flow of funds. The flow of funds is the basis of the accounting records in the conventional 'hybrid' system of accounting. At the end of each accounting period, however, the 'purity' of the funds accounts is 'contaminated' by the introduction of monetary symbols in order to distinguish between resources 'used up' during the period (charged in the profit and loss account as expenses) and resources 'left over' (carried forward in the balance sheet as assets).

In the segregated system, the figures in the profit and loss account and the balance sheet are useful as symbols of volume to represent the flow and stock of resources in the 'physical dimension' for stewardship reporting on the 'safekeeping' of resources. In the 'value dimension' of performance reporting on the 'efficient use' of resources, however, the conventional statements can be seriously misleading. For they depend on the assumption of hypothetical transactions that are often not expected to occur. The segregated system requires a separate set of 'value accounts' based on transactions that are actually planned.

References

Accounting Standards Board (ASB) (2005) *Accounting Standards 2005/2006,* London: CCH.

Accounting Standards Committee (1976) *Current Cost Accounting (Exposure Draft ED18),* London: ASC.

Alexander, S.S. (1948) 'Income measurement in a dynamic economy', revised by D. Solomons and reprinted in W.T. Baxter and S. Davidson (eds) (1962) *Studies in Accounting Theory,* London: Sweet & Maxwell.

Auditing Practices Board (APB) (2005) *Auditing & Reporting 2005/2006,* London: CCH.

Baumol, W.J. (1961; 2nd edn 1965) *Economic Theory and Operations Analysis,* Englewood Cliffs, NJ: Prentice-Hall.

Baxter, W.T. (1955) 'The accountant's contribution to the trade cycle', reprinted in R.H. Parker and G.C. Harcourt (eds) (1969) *Readings in the Concept and Measurement of Income,* Cambridge: Cambridge University Press.

—— (1971) *Depreciation,* London: Sweet & Maxwell.

—— (1975) *Accounting Values and Inflation,* Maidenhead: McGraw-Hill.

Böhm-Bawerk, E. von (1888) *The Positive Theory of Capital,* trans. W. Smart (1891), reprinted (1930), New York: Stechert.

Bonbright, J.C. (1937) *The Valuation of Property,* New York: McGraw-Hill.

Boulding, K.E. (1935) 'The theory of a single investment', *Quarterly Journal of Economics,* 49, May: 475–494.

—— (1962) 'Economics and accounting: the uncongenial twins', in W.T. Baxter and S. Davidson (eds) *Studies in Accounting Theory,* London: Sweet & Maxwell.

Bromwich, M. (1992) *Financial Reporting, Information and Capital Markets,* London: Pitman.

Canning, J.B. (1929) *The Economics of Accountancy: A Critical Analysis of Accounting Theory,* New York: Ronald Press.

Chambers, R.J. (1966) *Accounting, Evaluation and Economic Behavior,* reprinted (1974), Houston, TX: Scholars Book Co.

Company Law Review Steering Group (1999) *Modern Company Law for a Competitive Economy: The Strategic Framework,* London: Department of Trade and Industry.

Edwards, E.O. and Bell, P.W. (1961) *The Theory and Measurement of Business Income,* Berkeley and Los Angeles, CA: University of California Press.

Edwards, J.S.S., Kay, J.A. and Mayer, C.P. (1987) *The Economic Analysis of Accounting Profitability,* Oxford: Oxford University Press.

Edwards, R.S. (1938) 'The nature and measurement of income', reprinted in W.T. Baxter and S. Davidson (eds) (1962) *Studies in Accounting Theory,* London: Sweet & Maxwell.

Ernst & Young (2004) *International GAAP® 2005: Generally Accepted Accounting Practice under International Financial Reporting Standards,* London: LexisNexis.

Financial Accounting Standards Board (FASB) (1976) *Scope and Implications of the Conceptual Framework Project,* Stamford, CT: Financial Accounting Standards Board.

—— (1978) *Statement of Financial Accounting Concepts No.1: Objectives of Financial Reporting by Business Enterprises,* Stamford, CT: Financial Accounting Standards Board.

Fisher, I. (1896) *Appreciation and Interest,* reprinted (1991), Fairfield, NJ: Kelley.

—— (1906) *The Nature of Capital and Income,* New York: Macmillan.

—— (1907) *The Rate of Interest,* New York: Macmillan.

—— (1912) *Elementary Principles of Economics,* New York: Macmillan.

—— (1930) *The Theory of Interest,* New York: Macmillan.

Friedman, M. (1974) *Monetary Correction,* London: Institute of Economic Affairs.

Goldberg, L. (1951) 'The funds statement reconsidered', *Accounting Review,* 26, October: 485–491.

—— (1965) *An Inquiry into the Nature of Accounting,* Iowa: American Accounting Association.

Harcourt, G.C. (1965) 'The accountant in a golden age', reprinted in R.H. Parker and G.C. Harcourt (eds) (1969) *Readings in the Concept and Measurement of Income,* Cambridge: Cambridge University Press.

Hayek, F.A. (1988) *The Fatal Conceit: The Errors of Socialism,* London: Routledge.

Hicks, J.R. (1939; 2nd edn 1946) *Value and Capital,* London: Oxford University Press.

—— (1973) *Capital and Time,* London: Oxford University Press.

Hirshleifer, J. (1958) 'On the theory of optimal investment decision', *Journal of Political Economy,* 66, August: 329–352.

Hotelling, H. (1925) 'A general mathematical theory of depreciation', reprinted in R.H. Parker and G.C. Harcourt (eds) (1969) *Readings in the Concept and Measurement of Income,* Cambridge: Cambridge University Press.

Institute of Chartered Accountants in England and Wales (ICAEW) (1952) *Recommendations on Accounting Principles* (N.15 'Accounting in relation to the purchasing power of money'), London: ICAEW.

International Accounting Standards Board (IASB) (2005) *International Financial Reporting Standards (IFRSs™) 2005,* London: International Accounting Standards Committee Foundation.

Jevons, W.S. (1871; 5th edn H.S. Jevons (ed.) 1957) *The Theory of Political Economy,* reprinted (1965), New York: Kelley.

Johnson, L.T. and Lennard, A. (1998) *Reporting Financial Performance: Current Developments and Future Directions,* Norwalk, CT: Financial Accounting Standards Board.

Joint Working Group (JWG) of Standard Setters (2000) *Draft Standard and Basis for Conclusions: Financial Instruments and Similar Items,* London: International Accounting Standards Committee.

Kaldor, N. (1955) *An Expenditure Tax,* London: George Allen & Unwin.

Kay, J.A. (1976) 'Accountants, too, could be happy in a golden age: the accountant's rate of profit and the internal rate of return', *Oxford Economic Papers,* 28, November: 447–460.

—— (1977) 'Inflation accounting – a review article', *Economic Journal,* 87, June: 300–311.

Kay, J.A. and Mayer, C.P. (1986) 'On the application of accounting rates of return', *Economic Journal*, 96, March: 199–207.

Keynes, J.M. (1923) *A Tract on Monetary Reform*, London: Macmillan.

— (1930) *A Treatise on Money*, London: Macmillan.

— (1936) *The General Theory of Employment, Interest and Money*, London: Macmillan.

Lenin, N. (1917) *The State and Revolution*, reprinted in *The Essential Left* (1960), London: George Allen & Unwin.

Littleton, A.C. and Yamey, B.S. (1956) *Studies in the History of Accounting*, London: Sweet & Maxwell.

Lutz, F.A. and Lutz, V.C. (1951) *The Theory of Investment of the Firm*, Princeton, NJ: Princeton University Press.

Mackay, C. (1841; 2nd edn 1852) *Memoirs of Extraordinary Popular Delusions and the Madness of Crowds*, reprinted (1995), Ware: Wordsworth Editions.

MacNeal, K. (1939) *Truth in Accounting*, reprinted (1970), Lawrence, KS: Scholars Book Co.

Menger, C. (1871) *Principles of Economics*, trans. J. Dingwall and B.F. Hoselitz (1981), New York: New York University Press.

Merrett, A.J. and Sykes, A. (1963) *The Finance and Analysis of Capital Projects*, London: Longmans.

Pacioli, L. (1494) *Summa de Arithmetica, Geometria, Proportioni et Proportionalita*, trans, R.G. Brown and K.S. Johnston in *Paciolo on Accounting* (1963), New York: McGraw-Hill.

Paish, F.W. (1977) 'Capital value and income', in W.T. Baxter and S. Davidson (eds) *Studies in Accounting*, London: ICAEW.

Parker, R.H. and Harcourt, G.C. (1969) *Readings in the Concept and Measurement of Income*, Cambridge: Cambridge University Press.

Paterson, R. (1998) 'The ASB's *Statement of Principles* – blueprint or blind alley?', Sir Julian Hodge Lecture, Aberystwyth: University of Wales.

Preinreich, G.A.D. (1938) 'Annual survey of economic theory: the theory of depreciation', *Econometrica*, July: 219–241.

Rayman, R.A. (1969) 'An extension of the system of accounts: the segregation of funds and value', *Journal of Accounting Research*, 7, Spring: 53–89.

— (1970) 'Is conventional accounting obsolete?', *Accountancy*, June: 422–429.

— (1971) 'Accounting reform: standardisation, stabilisation, or segregation?', *Accounting and Business Research*, 4, Autumn: 300–308.

— (1972) 'Investment criteria, accounting information and resource allocation', *Journal of Business Finance*, 4, Summer: 15–26.

— (2004) 'Fair value or false accounting?', Accountancy, October: 82–83.

Roover, R. de (1956) 'The development of accounting prior to Luca Pacioli according to the account-books of medieval merchants', in A.C. Littleton and B.S. Yamey (eds) *Studies in the History of Accounting*, London: Sweet & Maxwell.

Samuelson, P.A. (1937) 'Some aspects of the pure theory of capital', *Quarterly Journal of Economics*, 51, May: 469–496.

(Sandilands) Committee of Enquiry into Inflation Accounting (1975) *Inflation Accounting: Report of the Inflation Accounting Committee* (Cmnd 6225), London: Her Majesty's Stationery Office.

Smith, A. (1759) *The Theory of Moral Sentiments*, reprinted (1880), London: George Bell & Sons.

—— (1776; 5th edn 1789) *An Inquiry into the Nature and Causes of the Wealth of Nations*, E. Cannan (ed.) (1904), 4th edn 1925, London: Methuen.

Solomon, E. (1971) 'Return on investment: the continuing confusion among disparate measures', in R.R. Sterling and W.F. Bentz (eds) *Accounting in Perspective*, Cincinnati, OH: South-Western Publishing.

Solomons, D. (1961) 'Economic and accounting concepts of income', *Accounting Review*, July: 374–383.

—— (1966) 'Economic and accounting concepts of cost and value', in M. Backer (ed.) *Modern Accounting Theory*, Englewood Cliffs, NJ: Prentice-Hall.

Sombart, W. (1902) *Modern Capitalism*, as quoted in Littleton and Yamey (1956).

Spicer, E.E. and Pegler, E.C. (1911) *Practical Auditing*, 13th edn by W.W. Bigg (1961), London: HFL.

Stamp, E. (1971) 'Income and value determination and changing price-levels: an essay towards a theory', *Accountant's Magazine*, June: 277–292.

Stamp, E. and Marley, C. (1970) *Accounting Principles and the City Code*, London: Butterworths.

Sterling, R.R. (1970) *Theory of the Measurement of Enterprise Income*, Lawrence, KS: University Press of Kansas.

Tweedie, D. and Whittington, G. (1984) *The Debate on Inflation Accounting*, Cambridge: Cambridge University Press.

Whittington, G. (1979) 'On the use of the accounting rate of return in empirical research', *Accounting and Business Research*, Summer: 201–208.

—— (1983) *Inflation Accounting: An Introduction to the Debate*, Cambridge: Cambridge University Press.

Wieser, F. von (1889) *Natural Value*, trans. C.A. Malloch (1893), reprinted (1971), New York: Kelley.

Wright, F.K. (1964) 'Towards a general theory of depreciation', *Journal of Accounting Research*, 2, Spring: 80–90.

—— (1978) 'Accounting rate of profit and internal rate of return' *Oxford Economic Papers*, 30, November: 464–468.

Index